No Nonsense Spanish Workbook

Jam-packed with grammar teaching and activities
from beginner to advanced-intermediate levels

By Caitlin H. Cuneo
Spanish for Real People LLC

Copyright © 2020 by Caitlin H. Cuneo
All rights reserved. No part of this publication may be reproduced, distributed, or transmitted in any form or by any means, including photocopying, recording, or other electronic or mechanical methods, without the prior written permission of Caitlin Cuneo or Spanish for Real People LLC.

Website:
www.spanishforrealpeople.com

Editors:
Luisa BenAmi
Kathleen Donohue
Daniel Kelley

Regional Spanish Language Consultants:
Luisa BenAmi (Mexico)
Victoria Asi (Nicaragua)
Lic. Sabrina Pomies (Uruguay/Río de la Plata)
Lic. Pilar Naveira (Uruguay/Río de la Plata)

Design & Formatting:
Jack Cuneo

Flag art:
Caitlin Cuneo

Love this book?
Please leave us a positive review on amazon!

Have comments/questions or need help?
Please contact us at hola@spanishforrealpeople.com. We're here to help!

Table of Contents

INTRODUCTION 6
   The No Nonsense Method 6
   How to Use this Book 9
   Resources on the Web 11

SECTION I: BEGINNING LESSONS 12
   PART 1: THE ALPHABET, MONTHS, DAYS & NUMBERS 13
      Lesson 1: The alphabet (El alfabeto) 14
      Lesson 2: Months of the year (Los meses del año) 15
      Lesson 3: Numbers (Los números) 16
      Lesson 4: When is...? (¿Cuándo es...?) 17
      Lesson 5: Days of the week (Los días de la semana) 19
      Lesson 6: Dates (Las fechas) 20
      Part 1 Quiz 22
      Part 1 Writing Activity 23
   PART 2: TELLING TIME, NOUNS/VERBS/ADJECTIVES & COLORS 24
      Lesson 7: What time is it? (¿Qué hora es?) 25
      Lesson 8: Nouns & Verbs (Los sustantivos y los verbos) 27
      Lesson 9: Noun-adjective agreement 29
      Lesson 10: Colors (Los colores) 30
      Part 2 Quiz 32
      Part 2 Writing Activity 33
   PART 3: QUESTION WORDS, FAMILY & WEATHER 34
      Lesson 11: Questions (Las preguntas) 35
      Lesson 12: Family (La familia) 37
      Lesson 13: What's the weather today? (¿Cómo está el tiempo hoy?) 39
      Lesson 14: Capital Cities of Latin America (Las Ciudades Capitales de América Latina) ... 41
      Part 3 Quiz 42
      Part 3 Writing Activity 43
   PART 4: THE VERB *GUSTAR* 44
      Lesson 15: What do you like to do? (¿Qué te gusta hacer?) 45
      Lesson 16: Questions with Gustar (Me/Te/Nos) 49
      Lesson 17: Questions with Gustar (Le/Les) 51
      Lesson 18: More Practice with "What do you like to do?" 54
      Part 4 Quiz 55
      Part 4 Writing Activity 57
   PART 5: THE SIMPLE FUTURE & POSSESSIVE ADJECTIVES/PRONOUNS 58
      Lesson 19: Simple Future: ir + a + infinitive 59
      Lesson 20: When do you...? (¿Cuándo...?) 61
      Lesson 21: Practice with Simple Future questions 64
      Lesson 22: Possessive Adjectives (Los adjetivos posesivos) 65
      Lesson 23: Possessive Pronouns (Los pronombres posesivos) 67
      Part 5 Quiz 69
      Part 5 Writing Activity 70

SECTION II: THE PRESENT TENSE 71
   PART 6: THE PRESENT TENSE (1ST HALF) 72
      Lesson 24: The Verb Ser in the Present Tense 73

Lesson 25: The Verb Estar in the Present Tense 75
Lesson 26: Estar and Location 77
Lesson 27: What are these people like? (¿Cómo son estas personas?) 79
Lesson 28: Conjugating –ar Verbs in Present Tense 81
Lesson 29: What do these people do? (¿Qué hacen estas personas?) 85
Part 6 Quiz 87
Part 6 Writing Activity 88

PART 7: THE PRESENT TENSE (2ND HALF) 89

Lesson 30: Conjugating –er/–ir Verbs in the Present Tense 90
Lesson 31: Practice with the Present Tense 94
Lesson 32: More Practice with the Present Tense 97
Lesson 33: Stem-changing Verbs in the Present Tense 101
Lesson 34: Practice with Regular & Irregular Verbs in the Present Tense 104
Part 7 Quiz 105
Part 7 Writing Activity 106

PART 8: PRACTICE THE PRESENT TENSE WITH VOCABULARY THEMES 107

Lesson 35: Classes in School (Las clases en la escuela/el colegio) 108
Lesson 36: Things at school (Las cosas en la escuela) 110
Lesson 37: Hobbies (Los pasatiempos) 113
Lesson 38: Colors and Clothing (Los colores y la ropa) 116
Lesson 39: Weather (El Tiempo) 118
Lesson 40: Food & Utensils (La comida y los cubiertos) 119
Lesson 41: Food & Health (La comida y la salud) 121
Lesson 42: Your Room (Tu dormitorio) 123
Lesson 43: At Home (En casa) 126
Part 8 Quiz 129
Part 8 Writing Activities 131

SECTION III: BEYOND THE PRESENT TENSE 134

PART 9: THE PRETERITE TENSE 135

Lesson 44: Conjugating Regular Verbs in Preterite Tense 136
Lesson 45: Practice with the Preterite Tense 140
Lesson 46: More Practice with the Preterite Tense 142
Part 9 Quiz 144
Part 9 Take-it-Apart Grammar (for Reading Comprehension) 145
Part 9 Writing Activities 150

PART 10: DIRECT/INDIRECT OBJECT PRONOUNS & REFLEXIVE VERBS 153

Lesson 47: Direct Object Pronouns 154
Lesson 48: Indirect Object Pronouns 157
Lesson 49: Reflexive Verbs 160
Lesson 50: Direct/Indirect Object & Reflexive Pronouns Together 163
Lesson 51: Practice with Direct/Indirect Object Pronouns 170
Lesson 52: More Practice with Direct/Indirect Object Pronouns 172
Part 10 Quiz 175
Part 10 Take-it-Apart Grammar (for Reading Comprehension) 176
Part 10 Writing Activities 181

PART 11: COMMANDS, DEMONSTRATIVES & COMPARATIVES/SUPERLATIVES 183

Lesson 53: Affirmative Tú Commands (Imperative Mood) 184
Lesson 54: When to Write Accents for Affirmative Tú Commands 187
Lesson 55: Usted, Ustedes & Negative Commands (Imperative Mood) 190

Lesson 56: Demonstratives 194
Lesson 57: Comparatives and Superlatives 197
Part 11 Quiz 200
Part 11 Take-it-Apart Grammar (for Reading Comprehension) 201
Part 11 Writing Activities 206
PART 12: IMPERFECT, PROGRESSIVE, PERFECT & FUTURE TENSES 208
Lesson 58: Imperfect Tense 209
Lesson 59: Present Progressive Tense 212
Lesson 60: Practice with Present Progressive 214
Lesson 61: Past Progressive Tense 216
Lesson 62: Present Perfect Tense 218
Lesson 63: Past Perfect Tense 221
Lesson 64: Future Tense 223
Part 12 Quiz 225
Part 12 Take-it-Apart Grammar (for Reading Comprehension) 226
Part 12 Writing Activities 230
Going out to Eat Skit 231
PART 13: WHY AM I SO CONFUSED? – CONFUSING LITTLE WORDS 232
Lesson 65: Por & Para 233
Lesson 66: Confusing Words that start with "LL" 234
Lesson 67: Confusing words that start with "P" 235
Lesson 68: Confusing Words that start with "D" 236
Lesson 69: The word que 237
Part 13 Quiz 240
Part 13 Take-it-Apart Grammar (for Reading Comprehension) 241
Part 13 Writing Activities 245

SECTION IV: THE SUBJUNCTIVE MOOD **248**
PART 14: THE SUBJUNCTIVE MOOD – LONG LIVE THE KING & QUEEN! 249
Lesson 70: Present Tense in the Subjunctive Mood 250
Lesson 71: Practice with Subjunctive v. Indicative (Present) 256
Lesson 72: Imperfect Tense in the Subjunctive Mood 259
Lesson 73: Past Perfect Subjunctive 262
Lesson 74: Conditional Tense 264
Part 14 Quiz 266
Part 14 Take-it-Apart Grammar (for Reading Comprehension) 267
Part 14 Writing Activities 272

SECTION V: BONUS HOLIDAY ACTIVITIES & MOST COMMON SPANISH VERBS CHART **274**
Halloween: Spooky Spanish! 275
Thanksgiving: del Día de Acción de Dar Gracias 276
Christmas: Navidad 277
World Cup: la Copa Mundial 279
MOST COMMON SPANISH VERBS QUICK REFERENCE CHART 280

SECTION VI: APPENDIX **282**
TIPS FOR SUCCESSFUL USE OF THE 283
NO NONSENSE SPANISH WORKBOOK 283
ANSWER KEY 285

Introduction

The No Nonsense Method

¡Felicitaciones! Congratulations! You have just purchased the No Nonsense Spanish Workbook from Spanish for Real People.

Why No Nonsense?

As the title of the book suggests, this is not your traditional Spanish textbook. You will see things you have not seen before, including innovations in design, organization and structure, font variation and a new way of teaching vocabulary. Do not let this throw you off! Let go of preconceived notions of how Spanish *should* be taught, or biases you may have inherited from other books. This book is written by a formally trained linguist. The activities have been designed with students in mind, and then tried and tested on real students over the years.

You are invited to open your mind, hold on and enjoy the ride! If you find something frustrating at first, that is a sign you are being challenged, and that is a *good* thing. If you can stick with it, you will be more successful in your learning. This book is designed to teach you to think in new ways, in order to optimize your language learning engagement and memory. Try not to be dismissive of new ideas, concepts or activities that you may find difficult; instead, let these serve as lessons to guide you into new and unexplored parts of your brain. Embrace the unknown, and get ready to learn something new!

This workbook is appropriate for students of Spanish as a second (or third!) language, as well as heritage speakers (those who grew up speaking Spanish at home but never received a formal education in Spanish). It covers the basics from beginning Spanish, all the way through AP high school Spanish and intermediate-level college Spanish courses.

No Nonsense Philosophy on Vocabulary

There are a few problems with the way vocabulary is traditionally taught and presented in foreign language courses and textbooks.

- Long, generic lists of words are very hard to memorize and people seldom remember them.
- There are often many different words for the same thing in Spanish, and vocabulary varies drastically by country, region and dialect.

Why does this matter?

Did you know that the Spanish language has over 10 different words for "bus"? In Spain, you might hear it being called an *autobús*. It's a *bus* in Colombia, El Salvador and Costa Rica, and a *ruta* in Nicaragua. In Mexico, it depends where you are, but you'll hear everything from *pesero* to *microbús* (*micro* for short), to *camión*. In Argentina, it's a *colectivo*, or *cole* for short (but watch out, because *cole* could also be short for *colegio*, which means "school"), and just across the river in the neighboring county of Uruguay, it's an *ómnibus*. If you go to Puerto Rico, you'll want to ask where to catch the *guagua*, not to be confused with *guau guau*, which is the sound a dog makes in Spanish.

While this richness of vocabulary can provide a constant source of entertainment for Spanish speakers from all over, it can also be frustrating for students. Are you going to memorize multiple Spanish terms for every word you know in English? That is neither practical nor necessary. But it does bring up an interesting predicament for how to teach vocab to Spanish students.

If you have been using tools like Duolingo or Rosetta Stone to learn vocabulary, you have been studying lists of words that are put together by a person who is essentially picking and choosing words from certain countries without telling you. There's nothing wrong with that approach, but it is inherently biased and can be misleading. And there's a better way!

Learn the Secret Technique Used by Linguists Worldwide

Professional translators, interpreters and language experts have a secret technique that no Spanish textbook will share with you. This method allows linguists to memorize large quantities of terminology quickly and accurately.

This approach will empower you to be proactive in your own learning and give you the tools you need to learn the vocabulary that is most important to you.

Rather than spending hours trying to memorize word lists curated by a stranger, you will learn to create your own glossaries. **Glossaries are lists of words that you put together yourself in a way that makes sense to you.**

In this book, you will be provided with some lists of all-purpose vocabulary to help guide you through specific exercises. These lists will be entitled **Active Vocabulary Learning**. The lists will require you to match the English word to the Spanish word. This may seem difficult at first, but it will force you to engage your brain and make it much more likely that you will actually remember the words because you played an active role in figuring them out.

As you progress through the book, you will see fewer Active Vocabulary Learning sections. This does not mean that you are done learning vocabulary, but rather that you should be looking up new words on your own and maintaining your No Nonsense Glossary.

Why Trust the No Nonsense Method?

This book was created by a trained linguist, with years of language teaching experience. The methods have been developed in response to the author's interactions with real students like you.

This workbook intentionally uses a variety of simple vocabulary to encourage students to practice their grammar without compartmentalizing it into chapters. This is different from what you generally see in traditional Spanish textbooks. Traditional textbooks tend to present themed vocabulary lists with specific grammar on a chapter-by-chapter basis. The danger of this method is that many students develop a "cram" style study technique. They attempt to memorize the vocab list along with the grammar from that chapter for the chapter test or exam, and then proceed to forget it all when they move on to the next chapter. This method does not work when studying a language. The most successful students will remember the vocab and the grammar from previous lessons, and be able to apply it in future chapters. Language learning needs to be cumulative!

This book is meant to be accessible to students of all levels of Spanish proficiency, and more advanced grammar does not correlate with more obscure vocabulary. So don't worry: you shouldn't need to look up every other word in order to do these exercises.

Why font variation?

You will notice a variety of fonts throughout this book. This variation is intentional. It has been shown to help students focus and to aid in memorization. Students are more likely to be able to recall a page where they learned a specific skill, since the pages do not all look the same. The design and font variation are also meant to assist students with certain learning disabilities and ADHD.

How to Use this Book

Instructions for Active Vocabulary Learning Sections

- Scan the list for words you may already know, and match these first.

- Scan the list for cognates. **Cognates** are words that resemble each other in the two languages. For example, October and *octubre*. Match these words. There are also false cognates, where two words appear to be related but are not. Don't worry about this, because you are going to check yourself with a dictionary later.

- Use your intuition to match any other words you think might go together. Often, we have a dormant awareness about words that could come from prior knowledge, the way the word looks or sounds, or the relationship of a new word to a word you already know. For example, if you know the word *amigo* means "friend," you may be able to deduce that *amistad* could mean "friendship."

- Use a Spanish-English dictionary to double-check any of the words you have matched and to match any remaining words.

- Use the No Nonsense Glossary space provided at the beginning of each chapter (or your own No Nonsense Glossary notebook if you need more room) to make note of any new vocabulary from this Active Vocabulary Learning section. It's perfectly fine if all of the words are new to you. What a great opportunity to expand your Spanish vocabulary!

Personalizing Your No Nonsense Glossary

At the beginning of each chapter, you will find a space called "No Nonsense Glossary." This is where you can write down any new words you come across in the lessons, either in the vocabulary lists provided to you, or words you have looked up on your own. Please use this space to jot down new words or words you simply want to remember. If you find you need more space, it is recommended that you purchase a notebook or journal specifically for vocabulary.

The process of learning vocabulary in a foreign language is a very personal experience, and will be different for everyone. Here are some things to consider:

- Which words do you actually want/need to learn? Don't waste your time going over lists of words you already know, or words you'll never use! Use your glossary for new words or words that you find challenging and need extra help remembering.

- Consider the best way to organize your glossary. Would it help you to put the words in alphabetical order, or to put the easy words up front and the hard words at the end, or vice versa? It can also be useful to make multiple glossaries and organize them by category, such as food, transportation, clothing, etc.

- Do you have a connection to a specific Spanish-speaking country? Are you going to be traveling, or do you have family or ancestors from somewhere in particular? If you do, I highly recommend you purchase a Spanish-English dictionary from that country. As your Spanish progresses, you can begin to read newspapers and watch movies or TV shows from your country of choice to familiarize yourself with the vocabulary and accent.

- Do you have any interests or hobbies that you would like to be able to speak about in Spanish? When I taught an Olympic skier, he made a glossary of ski terminology to increase his passion for the material. When I tutored a geologist and a lawyer, they likewise made glossaries about their subjects of expertise. Making glossaries that you find interesting will dramatically increase your likelihood of remembering the terms, and prevent you from becoming bored by lists of words that may seem irrelevant to you.

- Do you love flashcards? Use your glossaries to create flashcards to study. These can be traditional index cards or digital flashcards that you can carry with you on your phone.

How to Use the Answer Key

You will find the Answer Key at the back of this book. Many other traditional textbooks and workbooks intentionally create practice exercises with true/false and multiple-choice questions. They do this because it keeps their answer keys short, and there is always a correct answer.

Unfortunately, true/false and multiple-choice questions are terrible for language learning. Languages are not black and white, and there are always multiple ways to say things. In fact, according to renowned linguist Noam Chomsky, it is the infinite possibility of creative utterances that makes language uniquely human. If we try to limit answers in order to simplify answer keys, we reduce human language to something robotic.

The No Nonsense Spanish workbook encourages students to be creative and to work hard. Many questions will have a correct answer, but many others will have multiple possible correct answers. For these questions, there will be example answers provided in the Answer Key. You are encouraged to look up new words in order to make the exercises more interesting and relevant to you. This also gives you the freedom to focus on vocabulary specific to a country that you may be traveling to or have ancestors from.

Basically, the more you put in, the more you will get out. The more time and energy you put into the practice lessons, the more you will learn. The more active you are in discovering and learning new vocabulary, the more you will retain. Your learning is up to you!

What's the deal with *Vosotros* and *Vos*?

Vosotros is a form of "you plural" (in other words, "y'all" or "you guys") that is used primarily in Spain. Spanish speakers from Latin America use *Ustedes* for "you all." Because of the prevalence of *Ustedes* in Latin America and the United States, many teachers choose not to teach *Vosotros*. This workbook does include *Vosotros* in all verb charts, for those who wish to practice it. It does not appear in any of the exercises, although you can always replace *Ustedes* with *Vosotros* if you prefer to practice European Spanish. This book is meant to accommodate all forms of Spanish as much as possible, so if you prefer to study European Spanish, you can make those adjustments as you practice. For students of European Spanish, it is also recommended that you purchase or subscribe to a dictionary from Spain, so that you can tailor your glossary appropriately to include vocabulary from Spain.

Because there is no official "you plural" in modern American English, we have chosen to use the regional "y'all" in this workbook. This is simply for ease and consistency, and has nothing to do with a preference for a particular dialect of American English. Whenever you see "y'all," just know that it means "you plural."

There is also a *vos* form that is used in some Central and South American dialects of Spanish, such as Argentina, Uruguay, Colombia and Guatemala. This is a second person singular form, which can be used instead of *tú*, or in some cases, it may be used as a less formal option than *tú*. It is not represented in this book, because in all countries that use *vos*, *tú* is also widely used and understood. If you would like to learn the *vos* form, it is recommended that you look up full verb conjugations on www.wordreference.com or take some time to travel to a country where this form is common, and you will pick it up!

¡Disfruta y buena suerte! Enjoy, and best of luck to you in your studies of the Spanish language!

Resources on the Web

Facebook
Take advantage of a variety of media resources in Spanish for free!
www.facebook.com/No-Nonsense-Spanish-Workbook-101569754839122

Website
www.SpanishForRealPeople.com

Section I:
Beginning Lessons

Part 1: The Alphabet, Months, Days & Numbers

No Nonsense Glossary*

Apple	La manzana
first	primer
cousin	prima/primo
when	cuándo
date	fecha
Christmas Eve	La Nochebuena
Christmas	La Navidad
what	cuál
Yesterday	ayer
Always	siempre
sometimes	a veces
we/us	nosotros
we are	somos
we are not	no somos
never	nunca
they are	son
town/people	pueblo
player	jugador
letters	cartas
businesses	negocios
they	Ellos/Ellas
some	unos
wears	usa
last	último
help	ayudar
our	nuestra
tall	alto
shoes	zapatos
behind	detrás de
there is	hay

*For instructions on building your No Nonsense Glossary, see pages 9-10.

Lesson 1: The alphabet (*El alfabeto*)

A (sp<u>a</u>)	B	C* (<u>c</u>at, ni<u>c</u>e, <u>qu</u>een, Te<u>x</u>as, <u>ch</u>at)	D
E (hoor<u>ay</u>)	F	G** (<u>g</u>ame, <u>h</u>ey)	H (silent!)
I (ch<u>ee</u>se)	J (<u>h</u>am)	K	L*** (LL = <u>y</u>o-<u>y</u>o)
M	N	Ñ (o<u>n</u>ion)	O
P	Q (<u>k</u>ey)	R**** (RR = rolled!)	S
T	U (bl<u>ue</u>)	V	W
X (<u>h</u>am)	Y	Z	

*C is hard like "<u>c</u>at" when followed by a, o, sometimes u
*C is soft like "ni<u>c</u>e" when followed by e, i
*C is like "<u>qu</u>een" when followed by u (most of the time)
*C is like "Te<u>x</u>as" when followed by another c
*C is like "<u>ch</u>eese" when followed by h

**G is hard like "<u>g</u>ame" when followed by a, o, u
**G is soft like "<u>h</u>ey" when followed by e, i
***Double L (ll) sounds like "<u>y</u>o-<u>y</u>o" in many countries. Pronunciation of the double L varies by country/dialect.
****Double R (rr) indicates a rolled r in most Spanish-speaking dialects.

Note: Letter names and pronunciation vary somewhat by country. To hear letter names and pronunciation, we recommend searching for YouTube videos of "el alfabeto" or "el abecedario" (the abc's) plus the name of the country you are interested in.
For U.S. Spanish pronunciation, try "El abecedario en español" by "Mi Jardín Infantil".

Lesson 2: Months of the year (*Los meses del año*)

Active Vocabulary Learning

Match the months in English and Spanish. For detailed instructions on Active Vocabulary Learning, see page 9. Don't forget to copy new words over to your Glossary!

Note: Months are written in lower case in Spanish, although they are capitalized in English.

January | enero

February | febrero

March | marzo

April | abril

May | mayo

June | junio

July | julio

August | agosto

September | Septiembre

October | octubre

November | noviembre

December | diciembre

marzo | March

octubre | October

julio | July

enero | January

mayo | May

septiembre | September

diciembre | December

febrero | February

abril | April

junio | June

agosto | August

noviembre | November

Lesson 3: Numbers (*Los números*)

1 – *Uno**
2 – *Dos*
3 – *Tres*
4 – *Cuatro*
5 – *Cinco*
6 – *Seis*
7 – *Siete*
8 – *Ocho*
9 – *Nueve*
10 – *Diez*

11 – *Once*
12 – *Doce*
13 – *Trece*
14 – *Catorce*
15 – *Quince*
16 – *Dieciséis*
17 – *Diecisiete*
18 – *Dieciocho*
19 – *Diecinueve*

20 – *Veinte*
21 – *Veintiuno*
22 – *Veintidós*
23 – *Veintitrés*
24 – *Veinticuatro*
25 – *Veinticinco*
26 – *Veintiséis*
27 – *Veintisiete*
28 – *Veintiocho*
29 – *Veintinueve*

30 – *Treinta*
31 – *Treinta y uno*
32 – *Treinta y dos*
40 – *Cuarenta*
50 – *Cincuenta*
60 – *Sesenta*
70 – *Setenta*
80 – *Ochenta*
90 – *Noventa*
100 – *Cien*

101… – *Ciento uno…*
200 – *Doscientos*
300 – *Trescientos*
400 – *Cuatrocientos*
500 – *Quinientos*
600 – *Seiscientos*
700 – *Setecientos*
800 – *Ochocientos*
900 – *Novecientos*

1,000 – *Mil*
1,000,000 – *Millón*
1,000,000,000 – *Mil millones*

*Before a masculine noun, *uno* becomes *un* (*un coche* – one car). Before a feminine noun, *uno* becomes *una* (*una noche* – one night).

Lesson 4: When is...? (¿Cuándo es...?)

Active Vocabulary Learning

Match the following words in English and Spanish. For detailed instructions on Active Vocabulary Learning, see page 9. Don't forget to copy new words over to your Glossary!

Christmas | La Navidad

What is the date today? | ¿Cuál es la fecha hoy?

The first day of school | El primer día de escuela

New Year's Day | El Día de Año Nuevo

Birthday | El cumpleaños

When | Cuándo

Mother/father | La madre/el padre

My/your | Mi/tu

The Day of the Dead | El Día de los Muertos

Christmas Eve | La Nochebuena

El cumpleaños | Birthday

Cuándo | When

¿Cuál es la fecha de hoy? | What is the date today?

El primer día de escuela | The first day of school

Mi/tu | My/your

La madre/el padre | Mother/father

La Navidad | Christmas

El Día de Año Nuevo | New Year's Day

El Día de los Muertos | Day of the Dead

La Nochebuena | Christmas Eve

Lesson 4 Practice: When is…? *(¿Cuándo es…?)*

Answer the following questions in Spanish. If you don't know when something is, look it up or choose a different holiday with which you are more familiar.

Note: For the first of each month, you would say *el primero de* + [the month].

1) *¿Cuál es la fecha de hoy?*

   Hoy es el __cinco__ de __julio__.

2) *¿Cuándo es tu cumpleaños?*

   Mi cumpleaños es el __cinco__ de __julio__.
   (la fecha)   (el mes)

3) *¿Cuándo es el cumpleaños de tu madre?*

   El cumpleaños de tu madre es el primero de julio

4) *¿Cuándo es Navidad?*

   Navidad es el veinticinco de diciembre

5) *¿Cuándo es el Día de Año Nuevo?*

   El día de Año Nuevo es el primero de enero

6) *¿Cuándo es el Día de los Muertos?*

   El día de Día de los Muertos es el primero/dos de noviembre

7) *¿Cuándo es el primer día de escuela?*

   El primer día de escuela es veinticuatro de agosto

8) *¿Cuándo es el cumpleaños de tu padre?*

   El cumpleaños de mi padre es seis de abril

Lesson 5: Days of the week (*Los días de la semana*)

Active Vocabulary Learning

Match the days of the week in English and Spanish. For detailed instructions on Active Vocabulary Learning, see page 9. Don't forget to copy new words over to your Glossary!

Note: Days of the week are written in lower case in Spanish, although they are capitalized in English.

Monday | el lunes

Tuesday | el martes

Wednesday | el miércoles

Thursday | el jueves

Friday | el viernes

Saturday | el sábado

Sunday | el domingo

el miércoles | wednesday

el lunes | monday

el sábado | saturday

el jueves | thursday

el domingo | sunday

el martes | tuesday

el viernes | friday

Bonus Vocabulary

Today – *hoy*
Tomorrow – *mañana*
Yesterday – *ayer*
The weekend – *el fin de semana*

Year – *el año*
2000 – *dos mil*
1900 – *mil novecientos*

What day is today? – *¿Qué día es hoy?*

What is today's date? - *¿Cuál es la fecha de hoy?*

Lesson 6: Dates (*Las fechas*)

Answer the following questions in Spanish. If you don't know when something is, look it up or choose a different holiday with which you are more familiar.

Note: For the first of each month, you would say *el primero de* + [the month].

1) Hoy es __martes__, __siete__ de __julio__.
   (el día)   (#)   (el mes)

2) Mañana es __miercoles__, __ocho__ de __julio__.

3) Ayer fue __lunes__, __cinco__ de __julio__.

4) Mi cumpleaños es el __cinco__ de __julio__ de __dos mil uno__.
   (#)   (el mes)   (el año)

5) El cumpleaños de mi papá es
   __sies de abril de mil novecientos setenta y cinco__.

6) El último día de escuela es
   __El vientiuno de mayo__.

7) La Nochebuena es
   __el vienticuatro de diciembre__.

8) Halloween es
   __el treinta y uno de octubre__.

9) El Día de Año Nuevo es
   __el primero de enero__.

Lesson 6 More Practice: Dates (*Las fechas*)

Write the following dates in Spanish.

1) May 18th

   el dieciocho de mayo

2) June 6th

   el sies de junio

3) Thursday, April 17th

   jueves, diecisiete de abril

4) Saturday, February 28th

   sábado, veintiocho de febrero

5) Monday, November 24th

   lunes, veinticuatro de noviembre

6) Wednesday, August 8th

   miércoles, ocho de agosto

7) Thursday, September 1st

   jueves, el primero de septiembre

8) Sunday, March 15th

   domingo, quince de marzo

9) Tuesday, July 12th

   martes, doce de julio

Part 1 Quiz

Write the following dates in Spanish.

1) April 4th

   cuatro de abril

2) October 17th

   diecisiete de octubre

3) Monday, January 28th

   lunes, veitiocho de enero

4) Saturday, July 1st

   sábado, primero de julio

5) Wednesday, March 7th, 1987

   miércoles, siete de marzo mil novecientos ochenta y siete

6) Friday, May 30th, 2015

   viernes, tritrenta mayo dos mil quince

Respond to the following questions in Spanish.

1) ¿Cuándo es Navidad?

   el veinticinco de diciembre

2) ¿Cuándo es tu cumpleaños?

   el cinco de julio dos mil y uno

3) ¿Cuándo es el primer día de escuela?

   el veinticuatro de agosto

4) ¿Cuál es la fecha de hoy?

   el seise de julio

Part 1 Writing Activity

How much do things cost?

Use a catalog (print or online) to ask and answer questions about the prices of items.

¿Cuánto cuesta? – How much does it cost?
¿Cuánto cuestan? – How much do they cost?
Dólares – dollars
Centavos – cents
Ganga – bargain

$6.95 – *seis dólares con noventa y cinco centavos*

1) *¿Cuánto cuesta(n)* _____ ?

   Cuesta _____ .

2) *¿Cuánto cuesta(n)* _____ ?

   Cuesta _____ .

3) *¿Cuánto cuesta(n)* _____ ?

   Cuesta _____ .

4) *¿Cuánto cuesta(n)* _____ ?

   Cuesta _____ .

5) *¿Cuánto cuesta(n)* _____ ?

   Cuesta _____ .

6) *¿Cuánto cuesta(n)* _____ ?

   Cuesta _____ .

Part 2: Telling Time, Nouns/Verbs/Adjectives & Colors

No Nonsense Glossary*

Apple	La manzana
Noon	Mediodía
Midnight	Medianoche
Half past	Media
Quarter past	Cuatro
pets	mascotas
bored	aburrida/aburrido
door	puerta
bedroom	dormitorio
I think that	Creo que
near	cerca
park	parque
Open	abrir
nice	simpático

*For instructions on building your No Nonsense Glossary, see pages 9-10.

Lesson 7: What time is it? (¿Qué hora es?)

Active Vocabulary Learning

Match the following words in English and Spanish. For detailed instructions on Active Vocabulary Learning, see page 9. Don't forget to copy new words over to your Glossary!

In the morning (a.m.) | *De la mañana*
Half past (4:**30**) | *Media*
At night (p.m.) | *De la noche*
In the afternoon (p.m.) | *De la tarde*
Quarter past (6:**15**) | *Cuatro*
Noon | *Mediodía*
Midnight | *Medianoche*

Media | Half past
De la mañana | In the morning
De la tarde | In the afternoon
De la noche | At night
Cuarto | Quarter past
Medianoche | Midnight
Mediodía | Noon

How to Tell Time in Spanish

¿Qué hora es? – What time is it?

Son las <u>once y media de la mañana.</u> – It is <u>11:30 a.m.</u>

- For 1:00, you would say *es la una*, instead of <u>son las</u> *uno*.
- If it's past the half hour, you can also say [the coming hour] *menos* [minutes]. *Son las diez menos cuatro.* – It's 9:56.

Write the times in Spanish.

1) 9:00 p.m.

Son las ___nueve de la noche___.

2) 4:15 p.m.

Son las ___cuatro y cuatro de la tarde___.

3) 1:00 a.m.

   Es la __una de la mañana__.

4) 2:30 p.m.

   Son las __dos y media de la tarde__.

5) 7:48 a.m.

   Son las __ocho menos doce de la mañana__.

6) 6:24 a.m.

   Son las __seis y (veinticuatro) de la mañana__.

7) 8:15 p.m.

   Son las __ocho y cuatro de la noche__.

8) 3:08 a.m.

   Son las __tres y ocho de la mañana__.

9) 11:59 p.m.

   Son las __doce menos una de la noche__.

10) 1:30 p.m.

    Es la __una y media de la tarde__.

11) 12:00 p.m.

    Son las __doce de la tarde /__.
    __es mediodía__

Lesson 8: Nouns & Verbs (Los sustantivos y los verbos)

Masculine Nouns

generally end in "o"	
libro	
singular definite article (the): *el* *el libro*	singular indefinite article (a): *un* *un libro*
plural definite article (the): *los* *los libros*	plural indefinite article (some): *unos* *unos libros*

Feminine Nouns

generally end in "a"	
mesa	
singular definite article (the): *la* *la mesa*	singular indefinite article (a): *una* *una mesa*
plural definite article (the): *las* *las mesas*	plural indefinite article (some): *unas* *unas mesas*

Verbs

- Verbs that are not conjugated are called **infinitives**
    - In English, the **infinitive** is the verb with "to" before it (to walk, to eat)

- There are 3 types of verbs in Spanish
    - –ar verbs: ***bailar*** (to dance)
    - –er verbs: ***comer*** (to eat)
    - –ir verbs: ***vivir*** (to live)

Lesson 8 Practice:
Nouns & verbs (*Los sustantivos y los verbos*)

Determine whether the following words are nouns or verbs. If it is a noun, specify whether it is masculine or feminine, and singular or plural.

See how many words you already know and look up the rest to add to your Glossary.

1) *el gato* — cat _____
2) *la mariposa* — butterfly _____
3) *hablar* — to talk _____
4) *los niños* — the boys _____
5) *estar* _____
6) *el plátano* — plantan _____
7) *poner* _____
8) *sentir* _____
9) *las frutas* — the fruts _____
10) *tener* _____
11) *saber* _____
12) *la comida* _____
13) *las casas* _____
14) *el perro* — the dog _____
15) *la mujer* — the woman _____
16) *el hombre* — the man _____
17) *las ensaladas* — the salads _____
18) *cantar* _____

Lesson 9: Noun-adjective agreement

In Spanish, adjectives need to match the nouns they modify in both gender (masculine or feminine) and quantity (singular or plural).

If a noun or adjective ends in "e" it stays the same for both masculine and feminine. For example, *un estudiante inteligente* or *una estudiante inteligente*.

Choose the adjective that correctly modifies the following nouns. Then, see how many of these words you already know and look up the rest to add to your Glossary.

1) *El chico* __alto__ (**alto**/alta/altos/altas)

2) *La fresa* __roja__ (rojo/**roja**/rojos/rojas)

3) *Las mesas* __pequeñas__ (pequeño/pequeña/pequeños/**pequeñas**)

4) *Una mariposa* __bonita__ (bonito/**bonita**/bonitos/bonitas)

5) *Los libros* __caros__ (caro/cara/**caros**/caras)

6) *Una cama* __grande__ (**grande**/grandes)

Fill in the blank with the correct form of the adjective to modify the following nouns.

1) *El camino* __largo__ (largo)   camino; trail, path, way

2) *La camiseta* __blanca__ (blanco)

3) *Los perros* __perezosos__ (perezoso)

4) *Una manzana* __verde__ (verde)

5) *Unas hamburguesas* __deliciosas__ (delicioso)

6) *Un gato* __gordo__ (gordo)

7) *La montaña* __famosa__ (famoso)

8) *Una mujer* __vieja__ (viejo)

9) *Una clase* __interesante__ (interesante)

10) *El coche* __rosado__ (rosado)

Lesson 10: Colors (*Los colores*)

Active Vocabulary Learning

Color in with the appropriate color. For detailed instructions on Active Vocabulary Learning, see page 9. Don't forget to copy new words over to your Glossary!

English: yellow, green, red, blue, black, white, pink, gold, gray/grey, brown, orange, purple

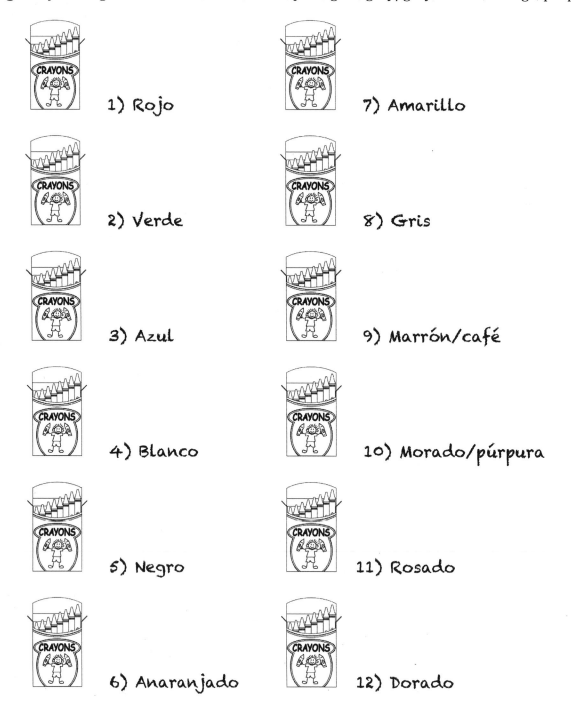

1) Rojo
2) Verde
3) Azul
4) Blanco
5) Negro
6) Anaranjado
7) Amarillo
8) Gris
9) Marrón/café
10) Morado/púrpura
11) Rosado
12) Dorado

Lesson 10 Practice: Colors (*Los colores*)

Answer the following questions using complete sentences in Spanish. If you don't know a word, look it up and be sure to copy over any new words to your Glossary!

Example: *¿De qué color es tu auto?* – What color is your car?
 Mi auto es blanco. – My car is white.

1) *¿De qué color es el sol?*
 El color del sol es amarillo o dorado

2) *¿De qué color es tu gato/perro?*
 Los colores de mis perros son blancos y grises

3) *¿De qué color es tu casa?*
 Mi casa es el color marrón

4) *¿De qué color es tu camiseta?*
 Mi camiseta es negra

5) *¿De qué color es el café?*
 El café es marrón.

6) *¿De qué color es el brócoli?*
 El brócoli es verde

7) *¿De qué color es el limón?*
 El limón es amarillo

8) *¿De qué color es el tomate?*
 El tomate es rojo

9) *¿De qué color es el cielo?*
 El cielo es azul.

10) *¿Cuál es tu color favorito?*
 Mi color preferido es el color púrpura

Part 2 Quiz

Write the following times in Spanish.

1) 4:30 p.m.
Son las cuatro y media en la tarde

2) 8:15 a.m.
Son las ocho y cuarto en la mañana

3) 12:20 p.m.
Son las doce y veinte en la tarde

4) 11:04 a.m.
Son las once y cuatro en la mañana

5) 1:45 p.m.
Son las uno y cuarenta y cinco en la tarde

Respond to the following questions in Spanish.

6) ¿Qué hora es?
Son las nueve y treinta y nueve en la noche.

7) ¿De qué color es tu casa?
Mi casa es marrón

8) ¿De qué color es la nieve (snow)?
La nieve es blanca.

9) ¿Cuál es tu color favorito?
Mi color favorito es púrpura

10) ¿De qué color es el pingüino?
El pingüino es blanco y negro.

Part 2 Writing Activity

Infinitives (*Los Infinitivos*)

Go through the bilingual literature (manuals for household appliances or other electronic devices, the box that your TV or microwave came in, paperwork sent by your local government, health insurance, etc.) you have around your house and find 10 infinitives.

Be sure to look for all three types (–ar, –er, –ir). They do not need to be cognates, so you may have to look up the meaning (*el significado*) if you are unsure.

El infinitivo	*El significado*

Part 3: Question Words, Family & Weather

No Nonsense Glossary*

Apple	La manzana
Casados	married
tormenta	storm

*For instructions on building your No Nonsense Glossary, see pages 9-10.

Lesson 11: Questions (*Las preguntas*)

Note: In Spanish, an upside-down question mark (¿) goes at the beginning of all questions and a regular question mark (?) goes at the end.

¿Quién? – Who?
¿Quién es tu profesor favorito? – Who is your favorite teacher?

¿Qué? – What?
¿Qué te gusta hacer? – What do you like to do?

¿Cuándo? – When?
¿Cuándo es tu cumpleaños? – When is your birthday?

¿Dónde? – Where?
¿Dónde vives? – Where do you live?
¿De dónde eres? – Where are you from?
¿De dónde es tu familia? – Where is your family from?

¿Por qué? – Why?
¿Por qué estudias español? – Why are you studying Spanish?

¿Cómo? – How?
¿Cómo estás? – How are you?
¿Cómo te llamas? – How do you call yourself? (What's your name?) (Informal)
¿Cómo se llama? – How do you call yourself? (What's your name?) (Formal)

¿Cuántos/cuántas? – How many?
¿Cuántos años tienes? – How many years do you have? (How old are you?)
¿Cuántas hermanas tienes? – How many sisters do you have?
Note: Must match the noun it refers to according to gender.

¿Cuánto? – How much?
¿Cuánto cuesta la manzana? – How much does the apple cost?

¿Cuál? – Which?
¿Cuál es tu color favorito? – Which is your favorite color?
¿Cuál es tu número de teléfono? – Which is your phone number?
Note: Although "what" is used in English to inquire about someone's favorite color or phone number, in Spanish *cuál* is used because theoretically there are a limited number of options from which to choose.

Lesson 11 Practice: An Interview (*Una Entrevista*)

Write a question for each question word. Then interview a friend, family member or study partner, or answer the questions yourself. Feel free to look up some new words in the dictionary in order to make your interview more interesting.

1) *¿Quién es tu* _____?

2) *¿Qué te gusta más,* _____ *o* _____?

3) *¿Cuándo* _____?

4) *¿Dónde te gusta* _____?

5) *¿Por qué te gusta* _____?

6) *¿Cómo te gusta* _____?

7) *¿Cuántos/Cuántas* _____ *tienes?*

8) *¿Cuál es tu* _____ *favorito/favorita?*

Lesson 12: Family (*La familia*)

Active Vocabulary Learning

Match the following familial terms in English and Spanish. For detailed instructions on Active Vocabulary Learning, see page 9. Don't forget to copy new words over to your Glossary!

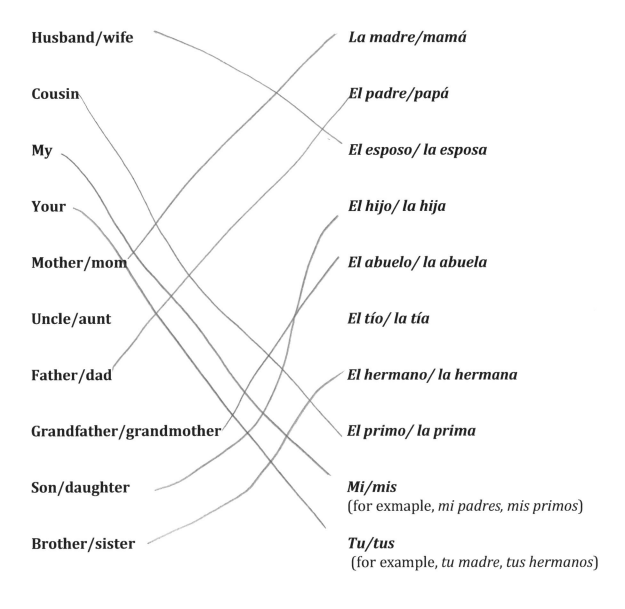

Husband/wife	*La madre/mamá*
Cousin	*El padre/papá*
My	*El esposo/ la esposa*
Your	*El hijo/ la hija*
Mother/mom	*El abuelo/ la abuela*
Uncle/aunt	*El tío/ la tía*
Father/dad	*El hermano/ la hermana*
Grandfather/grandmother	*El primo/ la prima*
Son/daughter	*Mi/mis* (for exmaple, *mi padres, mis primos*)
Brother/sister	*Tu/tus* (for example, *tu madre, tus hermanos*)

Lesson 12 Practice: Family (*La familia*)

Fill in the blank with the correct family member term, or answer the questions in Spanish.

Example: *La hija de tu tía es tu prima.*

Hint: For the purposes of this lesson, we will not consider step family.

1) *La madre de tu madre es tu* __abuela__.

2) *El esposo de tu madre es tu* __padre__.

3) *La hija de tus padres es tu* __hermana__.

4) *Tu madre es la* __esposa__ *de tu padre.*

5) *Mis abuelos están* __casados__ *(casados/divorciados).*

6) *La esposa de tu abuelo es tu* __abuela__.

7) *El hermano de tu padre es tu* __tío__.

8) *El hijo de tu tío es tu* __primo__.

9) *La esposa de tu tío es tu* __tía__.

10) *Los padres de tus padres son tus* __abuelos__.

11) *¿Cuántas hermanas tienes?* __tengo nada__.

12) *¿Cuántas abuelas tienes?* __tengo uno__.

13) *¿Cuántos tíos tienes?* __Tengo cuatro__.

14) *¿Cuántos años tiene tu primo favorito?* __no sé__.

15) *¿De dónde es tu familia?* __Vivimos en California__.

Lesson 13: What's the weather today?
(¿Cómo está el tiempo hoy?)

Active Vocabulary Learning

Match the following weather terms in English and Spanish. For detailed instructions on Active Vocabulary Learning, see page 9. Don't forget to copy new words over to your Glossary!

Note: Seasons are written in lower case in Spanish, although they are capitalized in English.

Lesson 13 Practice: What's the weather today?
(¿Cómo está el tiempo hoy?)

Look online to find the current weather in all of the following places. Include the current season for locations that have seasons. (**Hint:** To determine the season, you will need to know which hemisphere the city is located in.)

Por ejemplo **(for example):**
¿Cómo está el tiempo hoy en Nueva York? – What's the weather today in New York?
Es verano en Nueva York. Está soleado y la temperatura está a 81 grados Fahrenheit/27 centígrados.

    1) *¿Cómo está el tiempo hoy en Denver, Colorado, Estados Unidos?*

    2) *¿Cómo está el tiempo hoy en Montreal, Canadá?*

    3) *¿Cómo está el tiempo hoy en Montevideo, Uruguay?*

    4) *¿Cómo está el tiempo hoy en Ushuaia, Tierra del Fuego, Argentina?*

    5) *¿Cómo está el tiempo hoy en Madrid, España?*

    6) *¿Cómo está el tiempo hoy en San José, Costa Rica?*

    7) *¿Cómo está el tiempo hoy en La Ciudad de México?*

    8) *¿Cómo está el tiempo hoy en Río de Janeiro, Brasil?*

    9) *¿Cómo está el tiempo hoy en Anchorage, Alaska, Estados Unidos?*

    10) *¿Cómo está el tiempo hoy en Londres, Inglaterra?*

    11) *¿Cómo está el tiempo hoy en Quito, Ecuador?*

Lesson 14: Capital Cities of Latin America
(*Las Ciudades Capitales de América Latina*)

Fill in the chart with the *Ciudad Capital* for each country. Then look up the daily weather report for the *Ciudad Capital*. Don't forget the temperature!

Country (El País)	La Ciudad Capital	El Tiempo en la Ciudad Capital
Argentina	Buenos Aires	Está soleado. La temperatura está a 57 grados Fahrenheit/14 centígrados
Bolivia		
Brasil (Note: Portuguese is spoken here.)		
Chile		
Colombia		
Costa Rica		
Cuba		
Ecuador		
El Salvador		
Guatemala		
Honduras		
México		
Nicaragua		
Panamá		
Paraguay		
Perú		
Puerto Rico		
La República Dominicana		
Uruguay		
Venezuela		

Part 3 Quiz

Look online to find the current weather in all of the following places. Answer the following questions using complete sentences in Spanish.

1) *¿Cómo está el tiempo hoy en Almería, España?*

2) *¿Cómo está el tiempo hoy en Dublín, Irlanda?*

3) *¿Cómo está el tiempo hoy en Beijing, China?*

4) *¿Hace más calor en Moscú, Rusia o Asunción, Paraguay?*

5) *¿Hace más frío en Sydney, Australia o Nairobi, Kenia?*

6) *¿Hay una tormenta en Vancouver, Canadá?*

7) *¿Cómo está el tiempo hoy en Berlín, Alemania?*

8) *¿Te gustaría* (would you like) *ir a nadar* (to go swimming) *en Valparaíso, Chile? ¿Por qué* (why) */ por qué no?*

9) *¿Te gustaría ir a esquiar* (to go skiing) *en Colonia, Uruguay? ¿Por qué/Por qué no?*

10) *¿Cómo está el tiempo hoy en El Cairo, Egipto?*

11) *¿Te gustaría volar una cometa* (fly a kite) *en Santo Domingo, República Dominicana? ¿Por qué/Por qué no?*

12) *¿Te gustaría montar en bicicleta* (ride a bicycle) *en Lima, Perú? ¿Por qué/Por qué no?*

Part 3 Writing Activity

Food diary

Record what you ate in Spanish at each meal every day for one week. Look up any new words, and don't forget to copy new words over to your Glossary!

	El desayuno	*El almuerzo*	*La cena*
Lunes			
Martes			
Miércoles			
Jueves			
Viernes			
Sábado			
Domingo			

Part 4: The Verb *Gustar*

No Nonsense Glossary*

Apple	La manzana
Alcaldesa	mayor (female)
Alegría	happiness
Adoraba	loved
Delicado	delicate

*For instructions on building your No Nonsense Glossary, see pages 9-10.

Lesson 15: What do you like to do? (¿Qué te gusta hacer?)

Active Vocabulary Learning

Match the following words in English and Spanish. For detailed instructions on Active Vocabulary Learning, see page 9. Don't forget to copy new words over to your Glossary!

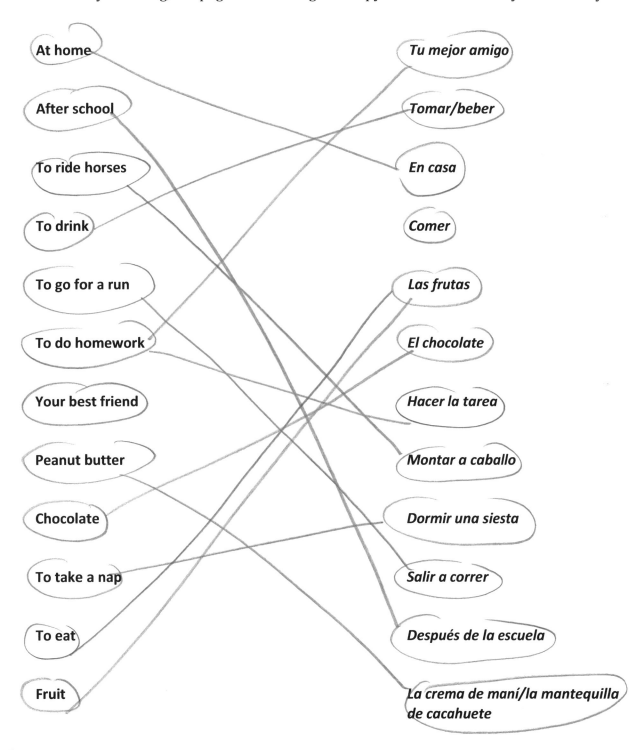

Lesson 15 Grammar: What do you like to do?
(¿Qué te gusta hacer?)

(A mí) **me gusta** – I like	*(A nosostros)* **nos gusta** – We like
(A ti) **te gusta** – You (informal) like	*(A vosotros) os gusta* – You all like (Spain)
(A usted) **le gusta** – You (formal) like	*(A ustedes)* **les gusta** – You all like (Latin America)
(A él) **le gusta** – He likes	*(A ellos)* **les gusta** – they (masculine) like
(A ella) **le gusta** – She likes	*(A ellas)* **les gusta** – they (feminine) like

A mí me gusta – I like

(A mí) me gusta literally means "it is pleasing **to me**," although we tend to translate it as "I like."

Note: *A mí* is optional, because *me* already means "to me."

The verb *Gustar*

Gustar is conjugated to match the thing the person likes.
Me gusta la manzana. (*gusta* because *la manzana* is singular) – I like the apple.
Me gustan las manzanas. (*gustan* because *las manzanas* is plural) – I like apples.

Grammatically speaking, the person is the object, and the thing the person likes is the subject of the sentence.

If it is followed by an infinitive, use *gusta*.
Me gusta viajar. – I like to travel.

Variations

Me gusta mucho – I like it a lot
No me gusta nada – I don't like it at all
Me encanta – I love it, or literally, "it enchants me"
A mí también / a mí tampoco – me too / me neither

Lesson 15 Practice: What do you like to do?
(¿Qué te gusta hacer?)

Answer the following questions using complete sentences in Spanish. If you don't know a word, look it up and be sure to copy over any new words to your Glossary!

1) ¿Qué te gusta comer en Navidad?

2) ¿Qué te gusta hacer los fines de semana?

3) ¿Qué le gusta comer a tu mejor amigo/amiga en su cumpleaños?

4) ¿Qué te gusta beber?

5) ¿Qué te gusta hacer los domingos?

6) ¿Qué te gusta hacer los lunes por la mañana?

7) ¿Qué te gusta hacer en casa?

8) ¿Qué te gusta hacer los sábados por la tarde?

9) ¿Qué te gusta hacer en la escuela?

10) ¿Qué te gusta hacer después de la escuela?

11) ¿Qué te gusta más, comer fruta o comer chocolate?

12) ¿Qué te gusta más, hacer la tarea o montar a caballo?

13) ¿Qué te gusta más, dormir una siesta o salir a correr?

Lesson 15 Practice: *Gustar* Preference Chart

Fill in the chart with things you like, like a lot, don't like and don't like at all. Write at least 5 sentences per box.

Remember, you can like a noun (*Me gusta el helado* – I like ice cream) or a verb (*Me gusta caminar* – I like to walk). If you like a plural noun, don't forget to change it to *gustan* (*Me gustan las papas fritas* – I like potato chips).

Me gusta ___. Me gusta el helado. Me gustan las papas fritas.	Me gusta mucho ___. Me gusta mucho caminar.
No me gusta ___. No me gusta el café.	No me gusta nada ___ (I don't like ___ at all). No me gusta nada hacer la tarea.

Lesson 16: Questions with *Gustar* (*Me/Te/Nos*)

Principles

- Always use **_gusta_** before infinitives.
  Me gusta caminar. – I like to walk.

- Always use **_gusta_** before singular nouns.
  Me gusta la película Los Piratas del Caribe. – I like the movie Pirates of the Caribbean.

- Always use **_gustan_** before plural nouns.
  Me gustan las papas fritas. – I like potato chips.

- For *me*, *te* and *nos*, you do not need to say ***a mí***, ***a ti*** or ***a nosotros*** (although you can say it for emphasis if you want to).

- Place the question word at the very beginning of the sentence.
  ***¿Por qué* te gusta esquiar**? – <u>Why</u> do you like to ski?

- **Note:** For questions beginning with "do" in English, you do not need to translate the "do" into Spanish. Be sure to use the upside-down question mark (¿) to signal that the sentence is a question.

Exercise

Translate the following questions into Spanish. Then answer the questions using complete sentences in Spanish. If you don't know a word, look it up and be sure to copy over any new words to your Glossary!

Example 1: Do you like coffee?

¿Te gusta el café?
Sí, me gusta el café.

Example 2: Why do you like coffee?

¿Por qué te gusta el café?
Me gusta el café porque es rico. (I like coffee because it's delicious.)

1) Do you like to play soccer?

2) When do you like to play soccer?

3) Do you like to drink soda?

4) Why do you like to drink soda?

5) Do you like to ski?

6) Where do you like to ski?

7) Do you like to run?

8) Why do you like to run?

9) Do you like movies?

10) Which movie do you like better, _____ or _____?

11) Do you like to eat peanut butter?

12) What do you like to eat with (*con*) peanut butter?

13) Do you like to take naps?

14) When do you like to take naps?

Lesson 17: Questions with *Gustar* (*Le/Les*)

Active Vocabulary Learning

Match the months in English and Spanish. For detailed instructions on Active Vocabulary Learning, see page 9. Don't forget to copy new words over to your Glossary!

To play tennis	*Cenar*
To swim	*Jugar videojuegos*
To go to the beach	*Tomar sopa caliente*
To play videogames	*Los niños*
To watch horror movies	*Comer comida china*
To go to parties	*Jugar tenis*
To sleep	*El gato*
To eat breakfast	*Dormir*
To eat lunch	*Ver películas de terror*
To eat dinner	*Ir a fiestas*
To have (drink) hot soup	*Ir a la playa*
To eat Chinese food	*Fresas con chocolate*
To drink green tea	*El perro*
Babies	*Desayunar*
Kids	*Tomar/beber té verde*
Dog	*Los bebés*
Cat	*Almorzar*
Chocolate covered strawberries	*Nadar*
To play soccer	*Jugar fútbol*

Lesson 17 Grammar: Questions with *Gustar* (*Le/Les*)

Principles

- For **le** or **les,** it is not always clear who we're talking about, because it could be "he," "she," "it," "you formal," "you guys" or "they."

- **[Question word] + *le/les gusta(n)* + [noun/verb] + [*a whoever*] ?**

    - ***¿Cuándo le gusta bailar a tu hermana?*** – When does your sister like to dance?

- If you are asking "**who**" likes something:
  ¿*A quién le gusta...?*

    - ***¿A quién le gusta bailar?*** – Who likes to dance?

Exercise

Translate the following questions into Spanish. Then answer your questions. If you don't know, make up a creative answer. Feel free to look up some new words in the dictionary in order to make your interview more interesting.

1) Does Miguel like to swim?

2) Where does Miguel like to swim?

3) Does your best friend like to play tennis?

4) Why does your best friend like to play tennis?

5) Do Marcos and Susana like to eat Chinese food?

6) Where do Marcos and Susana like to eat Chinese food?

7) Who likes to drink hot soup after skiing?

8) Who likes to go to school on Saturdays?

9) Who doesn't like to play videogames in the afternoon?

10) Why doesn't your father like to drink green tea?

11) What do the cats like to do on Sunday mornings?

12) When do the kids like to eat ice cream?

13) With whom does your best friend like to eat lunch?

14) Where does the dog like to sleep?

15) What do your grandparents like to eat for breakfast?

16) At what time does your son like to eat dinner?

17) At what time do the babies like to sleep?

18) Who likes to go to parties on Friday nights?

19) Why doesn't your cousin like to watch horror movies?

20) Who likes to go to the beach in the winter?

21) *Inventa tu propia pregunta.* (Make up your own question.)

Lesson 18: More Practice with "What do you like to do?"

Answer the following questions using complete sentences in Spanish. If you don't know a word, look it up and be sure to copy over any new words to your Glossary!

1) *¿Qué te gusta hacer los sábados por la noche?*

2) *¿Qué te gusta hacer los domingos por la mañana?*

3) *¿Qué te gusta hacer cuando hace mucho calor?*

4) *¿Qué le gusta hacer a tu madre cuando hace frío?*

5) *¿Qué le gusta hacer a tu padre en el verano?*

6) *¿Qué les gusta hacer a los perros?*

7) *¿Qué le gusta hacer a tu mejor amigo después de la escuela?*

8) *¿Qué te gusta hacer en tu cumpleaños?*

9) *¿Qué te gusta comer en el desayuno?*

10) *¿A dónde te gusta ir de vacaciones?*

11) *¿Cuál estación del año te gusta más, el invierno o el verano?*

12) *¿Qué les gusta hacer a tus abuelos en el otoño?*

Part 4 Quiz

Translate the following questions into Spanish. Then respond to the questions in Spanish. Don't be afraid to look up words you don't know, even though this is a quiz. This quiz is focused on grammar, so it's ok if some of the vocabulary is new to you.

1) When do you like to play soccer?

2) Do you like to drink soda?

3) Do you like to ski in the winter?

4) Who likes to eat at a restaurant on Friday nights?

5) Who *doesn't* like to eat chocolate covered strawberries for dessert?

6) Where do you like to go running, the park or the gym?

7) When does your mom like to drink coffee, in the morning or at night?

8) Why don't you like to watch movies in the morning?

9) Who likes to go hiking on the weekends?

10) When do you like to do your homework, on Monday mornings or Sunday nights?

11) Where do the kids like to play, at school or at home?

12) Why doesn't Pepe like to go shopping at the mall?

13) What do your cats like to do on Tuesday evenings?

14) Does your dad like to read magazines or watch tv?

15) Who likes to eat ice cream when it's raining?

16) Do you like to cook breakfast?

17) Why don't you like to share your pizza with me?

18) How many hours do you like to sleep?

Part 4 Writing Activity

Gustar Questions Game

Come up with 10 unique questions about yourself or starting with "who".

Example 1: ¿Cuál actor me gusta más, Brad Pitt o Tom Cruise?

Example 2: ¿A quién le gusta más el sushi, a nuestro hijo o a tu madre?

Write down your own answer to the question. Be prepared to ask your questions to your friend, family member or study partner and see how many answers they can get right!

1)

2)

3)

4)

5)

6)

7)

8)

9)

10)

Part 5: The Simple Future & Possessive Adjectives/Pronouns

No Nonsense Glossary*

Apple	La manzana

*For instructions on building your No Nonsense Glossary, see pages 9-10.

Lesson 19: Simple Future: ir + a + infinitive

It's time to conjugate your first verb! Take some time to study the organization of the chart below, as you will be seeing many verb charts organized like this in the future.

Singular		
1st person singular	**Yo**	I
2nd person singular	**Tú**	You (informal)
	Usted	You (formal)
3rd person singular	**Él**	He
	Ella	She

Plural		
1st person plural	**Nosotros**	We
2nd person plural	**Vosotros**	You all (Spain)
	Ustedes	You all (Latin America)
3rd person plural	**Ellos**	They (masculine)
	Ellas	They (feminine)

Ir + a = to go/going to

Yo	**voy**	Nosotros	**vamos**
Tú	**vas**	Vosotros	**vais**
Usted	**va**	Ustedes	**van**
Él / Ella	**va**	Ellos / Ellas	**van**

Ir + a + infinitive (to talk about the future)

¿Qué vas a cenar hoy? – What are you going to eat for dinner today?
　　(Yo) voy a cenar comida mexicana. – I am going to eat Mexican food.
¿Qué vas a hacer este fin de semana? – What are you going to do this weekend?
　　(Yo) voy a ir de vacaciones. – I am going to go on vacation.

¿Qué vas a hacer...
　... hoy?
　... mañana?
　... hoy por la tarde?
　... hoy por la noche?
　... mañana por la tarde?
　... mañana por la noche?
　... este fin de semana?
　... el lunes?
　... el martes?
　... el miércoles?
　... el jueves?
　... el viernes?
　... el sábado?
　... el domingo?

Voy a...
　... *nadar* (to swim)
　... *jugar voleibol* (to play volleyball)
　... *cantar* (to sing)
　... *caminar* (to walk)
　... *descansar* (to rest)
　... *dormir* (to sleep)
　... *pasar tiempo con amigos* (to spend time with friends)
　... *estar con mi familia* (to spend time with family)
　... *escuchar música* (to listen to music)
　... *jugar baloncesto* (to play basketball)
　... *hablar por teléfono* (to talk on the phone)
　... *bailar* (to dance)
　... *ir de vacaciones* (to go on vacation)

Lesson 19 Practice: Simple Future

Respond to the following questions using complete sentences in Spanish. If you don't know a word, look it up and be sure to copy over any new words to your Glossary!

1) *¿Qué vas a hacer hoy por la noche?*

2) *¿Qué vas a hacer mañana?*

3) *¿Qué vas a hacer el jueves?*

4) *¿Qué vas a hacer el viernes por la tarde?*

5) *¿Qué vas a hacer este fin de semana?*

6) *¿Qué va a hacer tu mejor amigo mañana?*

7) *¿Qué va a hacer tu perro/gato hoy por la noche?*

8) *¿A dónde va a ir tu familia de vacaciones el verano que viene?*

9) *¿Qué vas a cenar hoy?*

10) *¿Qué vas a hacer _____ (fill in the blank)?*

Lesson 20: When do you...? (¿Cuándo...?)

Principles

- On a certain day – "On Monday"
  You do not need to say **en** before a day of the week. Even though we say "on Monday" in English, in Spanish we go straight to **el lunes**.
  Example: ***(Yo) voy a la fiesta de Jorge el lunes***. – I am going to Jorge's party on Monday.

- On a certain day (repetitive) – "On Sundays"
  Use **los** before the day, instead of **el**.
  Example: ***(Yo) voy al gimnasio los domingos***. – I go to the gym on Sundays.

- On a certain day at a specific time – "On Fridays at 10:00 pm"
  El/los [day] a las [time] de la mañana/tarde/noche
  Example: ***(Yo) voy a bailar los viernes a las 10:00 de la noche***. – I go dancing on Fridays at 10:00 pm.

- On a certain day at a non-specific time – "On Saturday mornings"
  El/los [day] por la mañana/tarde/noche
  Example: ***(Yo) tomo café los sábados por la mañana***. – I drink coffee on Saturday mornings.

- During a certain season – "In the summer"
  En el/la [season]
  Example: ***Voy a hacer senderismo en las montañas en el verano.*** – I go hiking in the mountains in the summer.

Bonus Vocabulary

This Tuesday – *Este martes*
This weekend – *Este fin de semana*
This week – *Esta semana*
This coming weekend – *El fin de semana que viene*
Next weekend – *El próximo fin de semana*
Last weekend – *El fin de semana pasado*

Last night – *Anoche*
Everyday – *Todos los días*
Always – *Siempre*
Never – *Nunca*
Before – *Antes de*
After – *Después de*

Lesson 20 Practice: When do you…? (¿Cuándo…?)

Active Vocabulary Learning

Match the following words in English and Spanish. For detailed instructions on Active Vocabulary Learning, see page 9. Don't forget to copy new words over to your Glossary!

Students	*Ir al gimnasio*
To eat cake	*Ir a la piscina*
To drink wine	*Comer pastel*
To go to work	*Estudiar para el examen*
To go to the gym	*Ir al trabajo*
To go to the library	*Comer en un restaurante*
To study for the test	*Los estudiantes*
To go to the pool	*Tomar/beber vino*
To eat out at a restaurant	*Ir a la biblioteca*

Bonus Vocabulary

This – *este/esta*
These – *estos/estas*

That – *ese/esa*
Those – *esos/esas*

Respond to the following questions using complete sentences in Spanish, using the days/times suggested. If you don't know a word, look it up and be sure to copy over any new words to your Glossary!

1) *¿Cuándo va a la escuela tu hermano?* Everyday at 8:00 a.m.

2) *¿Cuándo vas a ir a la fiesta de tu mejor amigo?* Friday at 7:30 p.m.

3) *¿Cuándo va a hacer la tarea Juanito?* Monday morning

4) *¿Cuándo van a estudiar para el examen los estudiantes?* This coming Wednesday

5) *¿Cuándo va la piscina Tomás?* Thursdays at 5:15 p.m.

6) *¿Cuándo vas al gimnasio?*

7) *¿Cuándo vas a la escuela/al trabajo?*

8) *¿Cuándo vas a la biblioteca?*

9) *¿Cuándo vas a almorzar?*

10) *¿Cuándo vas a comer a un restaurante con tu familia?*

11) *¿Cuándo vas a esquiar?*

12) *¿Cuándo vas a beber vino?*

13) *¿Cuándo vas a comer pastel?*

14) *¿Cuándo vas a tomar té caliente?*

Lesson 21: Practice with Simple Future questions

Translate these sentences into Spanish. If you don't know a word, look it up and be sure to copy over any new words to your Glossary!

1) Where are you going tonight?
   Note: When a question is about where someone is going, we say *a dónde* instead of *dónde*, because the verb *ir* always needs to have the preposition *a* (to) associated with it, but a sentence cannot end with a preposition in Spanish.

2) When are you going to ride a skateboard?

3) Why are you going to eat chocolate for dinner?

4) Who are you going to the movies with?
   Note: As we saw in #1, a sentence cannot end with a preposition in Spanish, so the preposition *con* (with) will need to come at the beginning of the sentence. This would be like saying "with whom are you going to the movies," which is traditionally considered to be proper English grammar as well.

5) Where are you going to eat tonight?

6) What are you going to write?

7) How are you going to dance at the party?

8) Where are you going to sing?

9) Who is going to go shopping?

10) When are you go to travel to El Salvador?

Lesson 22: Possessive Adjectives (*Los adjetivos posesivos*)

Principles

- Possessive adjectives come before a noun, as in **mi abuela** (my grandmother). These are not the same as possessive pronouns, which replace a noun, as in "mine."

- Possessive adjectives match the noun they describe in number (**mi casa, mis casas**). **Nuestro** and **vuestro** also match the noun in gender (**nuestro amigo, nuestra casa**).

- There is no **'s** in Spanish! Instead, we say **[the thing] de [whoever]**
Lisa's husband – **el esposo de Lisa** (literally, the husband of Lisa)
Your all's car– **el auto de ustedes** (literally, the car of y'all)

Bonus Vocabulary

Mi/s – my
Tu/s – your
Su/s – his/her/your formal

Nuestro/a/os/as – our
Vuestro/a/os/as – your all's (Spain)
Su/s – their/your all's (Latin America)

Exercise

Translate these sentences into Spanish. If you don't know a word, look it up and be sure to copy over any new words to your Glossary!

Remember that adjectives need to match nouns in gender and quantity.

Soon, we will be learning the Present Tense, but for the purpose of this exercise, you will you the following two forms of the verb *ser* (to be).

Is – **es**
Are – **son**

> **Example 1:** His book is new.
> *Su libro es nuevo.*

> **Example 2:** My pants are red.
> *Mis pantalones son rojos.*

1) My cat is gray.

2) Marisol's shirt is red.

3) Our house is green.

4) Their uncle is Julio.

5) His favorite food is _____.

6) Her favorite day is Sunday.

7) Our lemons are yellow.

8) Their grandparents are from Mexico.

9) His parents are 87 years old. (Don't forget to use *tener* to talk about age!)

10) Your (formal) wife is 54 years old.

11) Joaquina's brother is my friend.

12) Our sister is from Chile.

13) Your all's car is blue.

14) My dogs are black.

15) Isabel's grandfather's name is Diego.

Lesson 23: Possessive Pronouns
(*Los pronombres posesivos*)

A possessive pronoun takes the place of a noun.

- **Mine** – *(el) mío/(la) mía/(los) míos/(las) mías*
- **Yours** – *(el) tuyo/(la) tuya/(los) tuyos/(las) tuyas*
- **His/Hers/Usted's** – *(el) suyo/(la) suya/(los) suyos/las suyas*
- **Ours** – *(el) nuestro/(la) nuestra/(los) nuestros/(las) nuestras*
- Your all's (Spain) – *(el) vuestro/(la) vuestra/(los) vuestros/(las) vuestras*
- **Theirs/Your all's (Latin America)** – *(el) suyo/(la) suya/(los) suyos/(las) suyas*

Note: pronoun matches object in gender and quantity!

Principles

Use the article (*el, la, los, las*) if the possessive pronoun is being used as the subject of the sentence (the person or thing doing the verb).

Tu vestido es largo. ***El mío*** *es corto.* – Your dress is long. **Mine** is short.

(***El mío*** is masculine and singular to match *vestido*. Remember that adjectives, such as *corto*, also match nouns in gender and quantity.)

Las camisetas de ustedes son rojas. ***Las nuestras*** *son azules.* –
Your all's shirts are red. **Ours** are blue.

You do not need the article (*el, la, los, las*) if you are saying "it's mine" and "mine" is not the subject of the sentence.

¿De quién es esta chaqueta? Es ***mía***. – Whose jacket is this? It's **mine**.

¿De quién es este coche? Es ***nuestro***. – Who's car is this? It's **ours**.

Lesson 23 Practice: Possessive Adjectives and Pronouns
(*Los adjetivos y pronombres posesivos*)

Translate these sentences into Spanish. If you don't know a word, look it up and be sure to copy over any new words to your Glossary!

1) My sock

2) Your house

3) His shirt

4) Our pizza

5) Their apples

6) Your car is blue.

7) His hair is black.

8) Our garden is small.

9) Their bananas are yellow.

10) Whose salad is this? It's his.

11) Whose dog is that? It's ours.

12) Whose potatoes are these? They're yours.

13) Whose ice cream is this? It's mine!

Part 5 Quiz

Answer the questions with complete sentences in Spanish.

1) *¿Qué vas a hacer mañana?*

2) *¿Cómo estás hoy?*

3) *¿Te gusta hacer la tarea?*

4) *¿Cuál es tu número de teléfono?*

5) *¿Qué va a hacer tu madre mañana?*

6) *¿Quién es tu profesor favorito?*

7) *¿Cuántos años tienes?*

8) *¿De dónde es tu abuela?*

9) *¿Qué va a hacer tu familia este fin de semana?*

10) *¿Cómo se llama tu tío favorito?*

11) *¿Cuándo es el cumpleaños de tu hermano/a?*

12) *¿Qué van a hacer tus padres hoy por la noche?*

13) *¿Te gustan más las frutas o los chocolates?*

14) *¿Cuántos años tiene tu mejor* (best) *amigo/amiga?*

Part 5 Writing Activity

Write a sentence using each infinitive (the middle column), and using the words on the right and left to help you. You may use more than one infinitive in a sentence, if you choose. You may also use any other words you'd like. Then, translate these sentences into Spanish. If you don't know a word, look it up and be sure to copy over any new words to your Glossary!

Me gusta	*dibujar*	*con amigos*
Te gusta	*hablar*	*con mi familia*
Me encanta	*patinar*	*los domingos*
Te encanta	*estar*	*en/a mi casa*
Me gusta mucho	*ser*	*en/a la escuela*
A mi mamá le gusta	*escribir*	*en/a Costa Rica*
A mi hermano/a le gusta	*cantar*	*música*
A los perros les gusta	*bailar*	*tu nombre*
No me gusta	*caminar*	*en el coro*
No me gusta nada	*correr*	*en mi cuaderno*
Voy a	*comer*	*a Europa*
No voy a	*vivir*	*comida china*
	recordar	
	descansar	
	escuchar	
	viajar	

1) <u>Me gusta comer comida china.</u>

2) _____

3) _____

4) _____

5) _____

6) _____

7) _____

8) _____

9) _____

10) _____

11) _____

12) _____

Section II: The Present Tense

Part 6: The Present Tense (1ˢᵗ Half)

No Nonsense Glossary*

Apple	La manzana

*For instructions on building your No Nonsense Glossary, see pages 9-10.

Lesson 24: The Verb *Ser* in the Present Tense

The Present Tense (*el presente*) describes actions that are happening in the present (I am going to the store), or actions that happen habitually (I usually go to the store on Sundays).

Ser – to be (permanent)

Yo	**soy**	Nosotros	**somos**
Tú	**eres**	Vosotros	sois
Usted	**es**	Ustedes	**son**
Él / Ella	**es**	Ellos / Ellas	**son**

Uses

- **Physical traits** (height, skin color, hair color, etc.)
  Yo soy alto(a)/bajo(a). – I am tall/short.
  Yo soy pelirrojo(a). – I am a redhead.

- **Race/ethnicity/nationality**
  Tú eres hispano(a). – You are Hispanic.
  Note: Race, ethnicity and nationality are not capitalized in Spanish.

- **Religion**
  Usted is cristiano. – You (formal) are Christian.
  Él es musulmán. – He is Muslim.
  Ella es judía. – She is Jewish.
  Ella es budista. – She is Buddhist.
  Note: Religious adjectives are not capitalized in Spanish.

- **Political affiliation**
  Nosotros somos demócratas. – We are Democrats.
  Nosotros somos republicanos. – We are Republicans.
  Note: Political affiliations are not capitalized in Spanish.

- **Career/job**
  Ustedes son abogados. – You all are lawyers.

- **Relationships between people**
  Él es mi marido. – He is my husband.

Lesson 24 Practice: The Verb *Ser* in the Present Tense

Fill in the blanks with the correct form of *ser*. Then, translate these sentences into English. If you don't know a word, look it up and be sure to copy it over to your Glossary!

1) *Ella _____ mi hermana.*

2) *(Nosotros) _____ hermanas.*

3) *Tú _____ de Colorado.*

4) *(Yo) _____ simpática.*

5) *¿De dónde _____ (tú)?*

6) *¿De dónde _____ tu padre?*

7) *Mi padre _____ de España.*

8) *Él _____ mi abuelo.*

9) *(Nosotros) _____ amigos.*

10) *Ustedes _____ de México.*

11) *Usted _____ mi profesora.*

12) *¿(Tú) _____ canadiense?*

Lesson 25: The Verb *Estar* in the Present Tense

Estar – to be (temporary)

Yo	**estoy**	Nosotros	**estamos**
Tú	**estás**	Vosotros	*estáis*
Usted	**está**	Ustedes	**están**
Él Ella	**está**	Ellos Ellas	**están**

Uses

- **Location**
  La leche está en el refrigerador. – The milk is in the refrigerator.

- **How someone is feeling** *(happy, sad, tired, well, sick, etc.)*
  Estoy bien. – I am well.
  Estás cansado(a). – You are tired.
  Él está enfermo. – He is sick.
  Estamos felices. – We are happy.
  Están tristes. – They are sad.

Lesson 25 Practice: The Verb *Estar* in the Present Tense

Fill in the blanks with the correct form of *estar*. Then, translate these sentences into English. If you don't know a word, look it up and be sure to copy it over to your Glossary!

1) ¿Cómo _____ (tú)?

2) (Yo) _____ muy bien, gracias.

3) (Nosotros) _____ cansados.

4) (Yo) _____ feliz.

5) ¿Ellos _____ felices?

6) ¿Dónde _____ el diccionario?

7) Mis hermanas _____ tristes.

8) (Nosotros) _____ en la clase de español.

9) Usted _____ en casa.

10) Ustedes _____ en el parque.

11) (Yo) _____ emocionada.

12) El helado _____ en el congelador.

Lesson 26: *Estar* and Location

Active Vocabulary Learning

Match the following words in English and Spanish. For detailed instructions on Active Vocabulary Learning, see page 9. Don't forget to copy new words over to your Glossary!

Backpack	*La puerta*
Computer	*El sacapuntas*
Trash can	*La ventana*
Poster	*La bandera*
Computer screen	*El cartel*
Pencil sharpener	*La silla*
Flag	*La computadora*
Desk	*El escritorio/el pupitre*
Window	*El bote de basura*
Clock	*El teclado*
Chair	*El reloj*
Keyboard	*La mochila*
Door	*La pantalla de la computadora*

Bonus Vocabulary

On top of – *encima de*
Under/below – *debajo de*
Next to – *al lado de*
Behind – *detrás de*

In front of – *delante de*
Here – *aquí*
There – *allí*

Translate these sentences into Spanish. If you don't know a word, look it up and be sure to copy over any new words to your Glossary!

1) The computer is on top of the desk.

2) The chair is under the table.

3) Where is my backpack?

4) Your backpack is here.

5) The keyboard is in front of the computer screen.

6) The clock is below the window.

7) Where is the trash can?

8) Pilar's poster is behind the door.

9) Fernando's pencil sharpener is on top of the table.

10) The American flag is next to the clock.

11) My desk is in front of your desk.

12) Emilio's chair is there.

Lesson 27: What are these people like?
(¿Cómo son estas personas?)

Active Vocabulary Learning

Match the following words in English and Spanish. For detailed instructions on Active Vocabulary Learning, see page 9. Don't forget to copy new words over to your Glossary!

Disorganized	*Ordenado(a)*
Creative	*Sociable*
Patient	*Paciente*
Silly	*Deportista*
Serious	*Perezoso(a)*
Sociable	*Desordenado(a)*
Organized	*Creativo(a)*
Impatient	*Trabajador(a)*
Athletic	*Tímido(a)*
Lazy	*Talentoso(a)*
Hardworking	*Estudioso(a)*
Studious	*Impaciente*
Talented	*Gracioso(a)*
Shy	*Serio(a)*

Respond to the following questions using complete sentences in Spanish. If you don't know a word, look it up and copy it over to your Glossary! Be sure to use the correct form of the adjective (matching the noun in gender and quantity, when necessary).

1) *¿Cómo eres (tú), ordenado o desordenado?*

2) *¿Cómo eres (tú), sociable o tímido?*

3) *¿Cómo eres (tú), serio o gracioso?*

4) *¿Cómo es tu madre, paciente o impaciente?*

5) *¿Cómo es tu padre?*

6) *¿Cómo es tu perro, deportista o perezoso?*

7) *¿Cómo son los Broncos de Denver (o tu equipo preferido de fútbol), talentosos o perezosos?*

8) *María es deportista. ¿A María qué le gusta hacer?*

9) *Tomás es estudioso. ¿A Tomás qué le gusta hacer?*

10) *Cristina y Susana son trabajadoras. ¿A ellas qué les gusta hacer?*

11) *A la abuela le gusta mucho dormir. ¿Cómo es la abuela?*

12) *A Nacho no le gusta hablar con amigos. ¿Cómo es Nacho?*

13) *A mí me gusta dibujar, escribir poesía y tocar la guitarra. ¿Cómo soy yo?*

Lesson 28: Conjugating –ar Verbs in Present Tense

The Present Tense (*el presente*) is used to talk about things that are happening in the present (example: I am going to school) or things that happen habitually (example: I go to the gym on Sundays).

Singular		
1st person singular	**Yo**	I
2nd person singular	**Tú**	You (informal)
	Usted	You (formal)
3rd person singular	**Él** / **Ella**	He / She

Plural		
1st person plural	**Nosotros**	We
2nd person plural	**Vosotros** / **Ustedes**	You all (Spain) / You all (Latin America)
3rd person plural	**Ellos** / **Ellas**	They (masculine) / They (feminine)

To conjugate a verb, take the infinitive (the form of the verb ending in –ar, –er or –ir). Remove the –ar, –er or –ir ending and add the appropriate ending listed below.

–ar verbs
(Shown with the verb *hablar* – to speak)

Yo	habl**o**	Nosotros	habl**amos**
Tú	habl**as**	Vosotros	habl**áis**
Usted	habl**a**	Ustedes	habl**an**
Él / Ella	habl**a**	Ellos / Ellas	habl**an**

Examples:
- *Yo **hablo** con mis amigos todos los días.* – I **speak** with my friends everyday.
- *Tú **hablas** con tu madre los fines de semana.* – You **speak** with your mother on weekends.

What other –ar verbs do you know?

1)

2)

3)

4)

5)

6)

Active Vocabulary Learning

Match the following words in English and Spanish. For detailed instructions on Active Vocabulary Learning, see page 9. Don't forget to copy new words over to your Glossary!

To walk	*Nadar*
To sing	*Bailar*
To swim	*Estudiar*
To ride	*Esquiar*
To draw	*Practicar*
To dance	*Cantar*
To listen	*Dibujar*
To practice	*Escuchar*
To rest	*Enseñar*
To speak	*Descansar*
To teach	*Montar*
To ski	*Caminar*
To dance	*Hablar*

Lesson 28 Practice: Conjugating –ar Verbs in Present Tense

Fill in the blanks with the correct conjugation of the verb in parentheses. Then, translate these sentences into English. If you don't know a word, look it up and be sure to copy over any new words to your Glossary!

1) *(Yo) _____ (nadar) en el océano.*

2) *(Tú) _____ (cantar) muy bien.*

3) *Él _____ (caminar) a la casa.*

4) *Mariana _____ (descansar) este fin de semana.*

5) *(Nosotros) _____ (escuchar) música por la noche.*

6) *Ustedes _____ (hablar) con la profesora de español.*

7) *Ellos _____ (bailar) los domingos.*

8) *Elena _____ (tomar) café con leche.*

9) *Usted _____ (sacar) buenas fotos.*

10) *Samuel _____ (tocar) el piano.*

Translate these sentences into Spanish. If you don't know a word, look it up and be sure to copy over any new words to your Glossary!

1) I listen to music.

2) My mother sings.

3) Your sister swims.

4) I dance at home.

5) I talk with my friends.

6) Stefanie rests on Sundays.

7) We talk on the phone.

8) They walk to school.

9) The kids swim in the pool.

10) I don't dance with my backpack.

Lesson 29: What do these people do?
(¿Qué hacen estas personas?)

Hacer – to do/ make

Yo	hago	Nosotros	hacemos
Tú	haces	Vosotros	hacéis
Usted	hace	Ustedes	hacen
Él / Ella	hace	Ellos / Ellas	hacen

Choose an appropriate verb from the word bank to answer each question. Conjugate the verb and write a complete sentence.

Word bank: *nadar, bailar, estudiar, esquiar, practicar, cantar, celebrar, dibujar, escuchar, enseñar, descansar, montar, caminar, hablar*

1) ¿Qué haces (tú) en la escuela?

2) ¿Qué hace Josefina en el océano?

3) ¿Qué haces (tú) en el sofá?

4) ¿Qué hacen los niños en el coro?

5) ¿Qué hacemos (nosotros) en el parque?

6) ¿Qué hacen los amigos por teléfono?

7) ¿Qué hago (yo) en la fiesta?

8) ¿Qué hace la profesora en la escuela?

9) ¿Qué hacen los Broncos de Denver (o tu equipo preferido de fútbol) antes de un partido importante?

Respond to the following questions in Spanish, using –ar verbs in the present tense. If you don't know a word, look it up and be sure to copy over any new words to your Glossary!

1) *Juan es un estudiante. ¿Qué hace Juan?*

2) *María es una atleta de los Juegos Olímpicos de Invierno. ¿Qué hace María?*

3) *Carlos es profesor. ¿Qué hace Carlos?*

4) *Linda y Susana son bailarinas. ¿Qué hacen ellas?*

5) *(Nosotros) somos cantantes. ¿Qué hacemos (nosotros)?*

6) *Victoria es recepcionista. ¿Qué hace Victoria?*

7) *(Nosotros) somos artistas. ¿Qué hacemos (nosotros)?*

8) *Manuel es atleta. ¿Qué hace Manuel?*

9) *José y Patricia son <u>salvavidas</u>* (lifeguards). *¿Qué hacen ellos?*

10) *Mario es ciclista. ¿Qué hace Mario?*

11) *Inventa to propia pregunta* (Create your own question).

Part 6 Quiz

Translate these sentences into Spanish.

1) The chair is under the table.

2) The apple is on top of the desk.

3) I listen to music.

4) My mother sings.

5) Your sister swims.

Respond to the following questions using complete sentences in Spanish.

6) *¿Qué haces tú para tu cumpleaños?*

7) *¿Qué hacemos nosotros en las montañas en el invierno?*

8) *¿Qué hacen los artistas en París?*

9) *¿Cómo eres tú, ordenado o desordenado?*

10) *¿Cómo eres tú, sociable o tímido?*

Part 6 Writing Activity

My Family & Friends

Write a short paragraph in Spanish about your family and/or friends. Refer to pages 51-52 for ideas about how to talk about what people like to do, and page 79 for ideas about how to talk about what people are like.

- Write at least 5 sentences for each person.

- Write about a least 4 people, including yourself.

- Don't forget to use the correct form of the verb *ser*!

Yo	Persona #2:_____
Persona #3:_____	**Persona #4:**_____

Part 7: The Present Tense (2nd Half)

No Nonsense Glossary*

Apple	La manzana

*For instructions on building your No Nonsense Glossary, see pages 9-10.

Lesson 30: Conjugating –er/–ir Verbs in the Present Tense

To conjugate a verb, take the infinitive (the form of the verb ending in –ar, –er or –ir). Remove the –ar, –er or –ir ending and add the appropriate ending listed below.

–er verbs
(Shown with the verb *comer* – to eat)

Yo	com**o**	Nosotros	com**emos**
Tú	com**es**	Vosotros	com**éis**
Usted	com**e**	Ustedes	com**en**
Él / Ella	com**e**	Ellos / Ellas	com**en**

–ir verbs
(Shown with the verb *vivir* – to live)

Yo	viv**o**	Nosotros	viv**imos**
Tú	viv**es**	Vosotros	viv**ís**
Usted	viv**e**	Ustedes	viv**en**
Él / Ella	viv**e**	Ellos / Ellas	viv**en**

Examples

- *(Yo)* **como** *el desayuno todos los días.* – I **eat** breakfast everyday.

- *(Tú)* **comes** *comida italiana.* – You **eat** Italian food.

- *(Nosotros)* **vivimos** *en los Estados Unidos.* – We **live** in the United States.

- *Ustedes* **viven** *en Canadá.* – Y'all **live** in Canada.

- *El profesor* **comparte** *el libro con el estudiante.* – The teacher **shares** the book with the student.

- *(Yo)* **comparto** *palomitas con mi hermano.* – I **share** popcorn with my brother.

Using Conjugated Verbs & Infinitives

- When using a conjugated verb followed by another verb, the second verb remains in the infinitive form. You have already seen this with the verb *gustar* (*Me gusta esquiar* – I like to ski). *Gusta* is conjugated and *esquiar* remains in the infinitive form.

- Spanish infinitives, such as *comer*, can be translated into English as "to eat" or "eating," depending on the context.

    Example: *(Yo) prefiero* **comer** *ensaladas.* – I prefer **to eat** salads. OR I prefer **eating** salads.

Common Irregular Verbs in the Present Tense

These verbs are irregular and will need to be memorized. There are others but these are a few of the most common ones. You have already seen some of these in previous activities.

Tener – to have

Yo	tengo	Nosotros	tenemos
Tú	tienes	Vosotros	tenéis
Usted	tiene	Ustedes	tienen
Él / Ella	tiene	Ellos / Ellas	tienen

Hacer – to do/make

Yo	hago	Nosotros	hacemos
Tú	haces	Vosotros	hacéis
Usted	hace	Ustedes	hacen
Él / Ella	hace	Ellos / Ellas	hacen

Dar – to give

Yo	doy	Nosotros	damos
Tú	das	Vosotros	dais
Usted	da	Ustedes	dan
Él / Ella	da	Ellos / Ellas	dan

Ser – to be (permanent)

Yo	soy	Nosotros	somos
Tú	eres	Vosotros	sois
Usted	es	Ustedes	son
Él / Ella	es	Ellos / Ellas	son

Estar – to be (temporary)

Yo	estoy	Nosotros	estamos
Tú	estás	Vosotros	estáis
Usted	está	Ustedes	están
Él / Ella	está	Ellos / Ellas	están

Ir – to go

Yo	voy	Nosotros	vamos
Tú	vas	Vosotros	vais
Usted	va	Ustedes	van
Él / Ella	va	Ellos / Ellas	van

Common Verbs with Irregular *Yo* Forms

These common verbs have irregular **yo** forms that will need to be memorized.

Conocer – conozco (to know a person or place)
Decir – digo (to say/tell)
Hacer – hago (to do/make)
Oír – oigo (to hear)

Poner – pongo (to put/set)
Saber – sé (to know)
Salir – salgo (to go out)
Seguir – sigo (to continue)

Tener – tengo (to have)
Traer – traigo (to bring)
Venir – vengo (to come)
Ver – veo (to see)

Lesson 30 Practice: Conjugating –er/–ir Verbs in the Present Tense

Active Vocabulary Learning

Match the following words in English and Spanish. For detailed instructions on Active Vocabulary Learning, see page 9. Don't forget to copy new words over to your Glossary!

Ice tea	*El café*
French fries	*El tocino*
Orange juice	*El té helado*
Scrambled eggs	*La galleta*
Sausage	*La leche*
Bacon	*La manzana*
Cookie/cracker/biscuit	*El sándwich de jamón y queso*
Coffee	*El perro caliente*
With you/with me	*Las papas fritas*
Milk	*Los huevos revueltos*
Ham and cheese sandwich	*Contigo/conmigo*
Lemonde	*La banana/el plátano*
Soda/pop	*El refresco*
Hot dog	*La salchicha*
Apple	*El jugo de naranja*
Banana	*La limonada*

Respond to the following questions using complete sentences in Spanish. If you don't know a word, look it up and be sure to copy over any new words to your Glossary!

1) *¿Qué comes (tú) en el desayuno, generalmente?*

2) *¿Qué come tu padre en el almuerzo?*

3) *¿En tu familia, ustedes comen salchichas y tocino?*

4) *¿Tu mamá come perros calientes?*

5) *¿(Tú) comes galletas en el desayuno?*

6) *¿Los bebés beben té helado?*

7) *¿(Tú) compartes tu pizza con tu hermano?*

8) *¿Tu hermano comparte sus papas fritas contigo?*

9) *¿(Tú) bebes café?*

Fill in the blank with the verb that makes the most sense. Don't forget to conjugate the verb!

10) *Los bebés _____ leche.*

11) *(Yo) _____ una manzana.*

12) *(Tú) _____ un sándwich de jamón y queso.*

13) *(Nosotros) _____ un refresco.*

14) *Victoria _____ huevos revueltos en el desayuno.*

15) *Ustedes _____ jugo de naranja.*

Lesson 31: Practice with the Present Tense

Conjugate the following verbs for the subjects suggested in parentheses.

1) *ser (yo)* –

2) *compartir (él)* –

3) *comer (ustedes)* –

4) *beber (nosotros)* –

5) *estar (ellos)* –

6) *ser (nosotros)* –

7) *creer (yo)* –

8) *comer (tú)* –

9) *deber (usted)* –

10) *compartir (tú)* –

11) *ser (ella)* –

12) *estar (ustedes)* –

13) *hablar (ellas)* –

14) *bailar (ella)* –

15) *tener (yo)* –

Translate the following sentences into Spanish.

16) You share a hot dog with your friend.

17) The kids eat bananas for lunch.

18) The teacher eats a ham and cheese sandwich.

Fill in the blank with the correct conjugation of the verb in parentheses.

1) *(Tú)* _____ *(comer) una pizza.*

2) *Tus amigas* _____ *(estar) en tu casa.*

3) *Mi madre* _____ *(hablar) por teléfono.*

4) *La abuela* _____ *(cantar) en el concierto.*

5) *(Nosotros)* _____ *(bailar) en la escuela.*

6) *Usted* _____ *(ser) de México.*

7) *Ustedes* _____ *(comer) en la cafetería.*

8) *(Nosotros)* _____ *(hablar) mucho.*

9) *(Yo)* _____ *(tener) quince años.*

10) *¿Qué* _____ *(comer) (tú) en la cena?*

11) *¿Por qué no* _____ *(hablar) (tú) con el muchacho guapo?*

12) *A ustedes les* _____ *(gustar) comida china.*

Translate these sentences into Spanish. Remember to conjugate the verbs correctly. If you don't know a word, look it up and copy it over to your Glossary!

1) I swim in the blue water.

2) We listen to music in the park.

3) You eat a lot!

4) I travel to Santiago, Chile every summer.

5) He doesn't like to run at all!

6) Where do you go to play tennis?

7) What time are you going to go to the party?

8) We like to rest on Sunday evenings.

9) What do you like better, living with family or friends?

10) What are you going to do today?

Lesson 32: More Practice with the Present Tense

Conjugate the following verbs for the subjects suggested in parentheses.

1) *ser (yo)* –

2) *ir (él)* –

3) *comer (ustedes)* –

4) *montar (nosotros)* –

5) *estar (ellos)* –

6) *ser (nosotros)* –

7) *ir (yo)* –

8) *viajar (tú)* –

9) *deber (usted)* –

10) *vivir (tú)* –

11) *ser (ella)* –

12) *ir (ustedes)* –

13) *caminar (ellas)* –

14) *bailar (ella)* –

15) *tener (yo)* –

Translate these sentences into Spanish. If you don't know a word, look it up and be sure to copy over any new words to your Glossary!

16) You are going to ski in the mountains with your friends on Saturday.

17) You (formal) should go shopping with your mom this weekend.

18) I am going to travel to the countryside tomorrow.

19) Y'all are going to watch a movie at home.

20) They are going to eat at a restaurant on Friday.

21) Luisa dances on Tuesday afternoons.

22) Y'all eat a lot of bacon.

23) I have homework every night.

24) You live with your family.

25) We are going to ride bicycles tomorrow afternoon.

26) Carolina is intelligent, and Roberto is kind.

27) Do you travel to Lima, Perú every year?

28) Y'all are going to walk in the park this afternoon.

29) The kids are happy, because today is José's birthday.

30) I am going to run with my dog today.

31) At what time are you and your family going to eat dinner?

32) When are you going to travel to Bogotá, Colombia?

33) What are you going to do this weekend?

Conjugate the following verbs for the subjects suggested in parentheses.

1) *ir (yo)* –

2) *ir (él)* –

3) *ir (nosotros)* –

4) *ir (tú)* –

5) *beber (ellos)* –

6) *comer (él)* –

7) *ver (ellos)* –

8) *cantar (él)* –

9) *correr (ellos)* –

10) *gustar (los libros)* –

Translate these sentences into Spanish. If you don't know a word, look it up and be sure to copy over any new words to your Glossary!

11) I am going to a restaurant to (*para*) eat bread.

12) We are going to the movies to watch a film.

13) You are going to Seville next week.

14) Where is Sergio going tomorrow?

15) Who is going to drink the coffee on top of the table?

16) Ana eats vegetables every day.

17) My parents drink soda every day.

18) The kids run in the park after school.

19) I like soccer.

20) Francisco sings at the club on Thursday nights.

21) My grandparents always watch television in the morning.

22) Why are you going to ride a bike at the beach?

23) Who are you going to the movies with?

Lesson 33: Stem-changing Verbs in the Present Tense

In the Present Tense, there are certain verbs that are known as "Stem-Changing Verbs" (sometimes called "Shoe Verbs"). These verbs follow three patterns of stem changes, which you will see below. The stem change will affect all forms of the verb in the Present Tense, except for *nosotros* and *vosotros*.

Common Stem-Changing Verbs in the Present Tense

e – ie
Sentir – to feel

Yo	s**ie**nto	Nosotros	sentimos
Tú	s**ie**ntes	Vosotros	sentís
Usted	s**ie**nte	Ustedes	s**ie**nten
Él / Ella	s**ie**nte	Ellos / Ellas	s**ie**nten

e – i
Pedir – to ask for/order

Yo	p**i**do	Nosotros	pedimos
Tú	p**i**des	Vosotros	pedís
Usted	p**i**de	Ustedes	p**i**den
Él / Ella	p**i**de	Ellos / Ellas	p**i**den

o – ue
Poder – to be able to

Yo	p**ue**do	Nosotros	podemos
Tú	p**ue**des	Vosotros	podéis
Usted	p**ue**de	Ustedes	p**ue**den
Él / Ella	p**ue**de	Ellos / Ellas	p**ue**den

Common Verbs with the e – ie Pattern
Cerrar – to close
Empezar – to start
Querer – to want/love
Sentir – to feel
Preferir – to prefer

Common Verbs with the e – i Pattern
Decir – to say/tell
Pedir – to ask for/order
Servir – to serve

Common Verbs with the o – ue Pattern
Almorzar – to eat lunch
Morir – to die
Poder – to be able to

Lesson 33 Practice: Stem-changing Verbs in the Present Tense

List out the conjugations for the following Stem-Changing verbs.

Almorzar (o to ue) (to eat) –

Poder (o to ue) (to be able to) –

Recordar (o to ue) (to remember) –

Querer (e to ie) (to want/love) –

Empezar (e to ie) (to start) –

Pedir (e to i) (to order/ask for) –

Fill in the blank with the correct conjugation of the verb in parentheses. Then, translate the sentences into Spanish. If you don't know a word, look it up and be sure to copy over any new words to your Glossary!

1) *(Tú) _____ (almorzar) con tu padre.*

2) *(Yo) _____ (querer) comer comida italiana.*

3) *La clase de inglés _____ (empezar) a las 10:45.*

4) *Las hermanas _____ (querer) tomar café con leche.*

5) *El abuelo no _____ (recordar) muchas cosas.*

6) *(Yo) _____ (empezar) a estudiar a las 9:00 de la noche.*

7) *Cuando (nosotros) _____ (almorzar) en la cafetería, _____ (comer) mucho.*

8) *Ustedes _____ (recordar) el vocabulario importante.*

9) *Mi abuela _____ (tener) 96 años.*

10) *El 21 de marzo _____ (empezar) la primavera.*

11) *¡(Tú) _____ (poder) aprender el español!*

12) *Cuando voy a un restaurante mexicano, (yo) siempre _____ (pedir) tacos con carne.*

Lesson 34: Practice with Regular & Irregular Verbs in the Present Tense

Respond to the following questions using complete sentences in Spanish. If you don't know a word, look it up and be sure to copy over any new words to your Glossary!

1) *¿Cuántos años tienes?*

2) *¿Cuántas hamburguesas puedes comer?*

3) *¿Cuántos años tiene tu perro/gato?*

4) *¿A dónde vas mañana?*

5) *¿A qué hora haces la tarea?*

6) *¿Tu mamá va al trabajo los sábados?*

7) *¿Qué vas canar hoy?*

Translate the following sentences into Spanish.

8) I have 2 dogs.

9) I can eat 12 sausages!

10) My friend goes to school every day.

11) I am studious.

12) I eat bacon when I do my homework.

Part 7 Quiz

Translate the following sentences into Spanish.

1) I listen to music.

2) My mother sings.

3) My grandfather doesn't remember things.

4) My sister can (is able to) swim.

5) Spanish class starts at 10:15 a.m.

6) My father wants to eat Mexican food.

7) I want to dance at home.

8) I like to be with friends.

9) The sisters eat lunch at noon.

10) I rest on Sundays.

11) We talk on the phone.

12) They walk to school.

13) We eat lunch at the cafe.

14) My grandmother is 99 years old.

Part 7 Writing Activity

My Short Story (*Mi Cuento*)

Write a short story of at least 10 sentences in Spanish. Include at least 5 verbs that you know, and be sure to conjugate them correctly. You may also want to include:

- dates
- family members
- colors
- times of day
- description of where people are from/how old they are

Part 8: Practice the Present Tense with Vocabulary Themes

No Nonsense Glossary*

Apple	La manzana

*For instructions on building your No Nonsense Glossary, see pages 9-10.

Lesson 35: Classes in School
(*Las clases en la escuela/el colegio*)

Match the following words in English and Spanish. For detailed instructions on Active Vocabulary Learning, see page 9. Don't forget to copy new words over to your Glossary!

Math class	*La clase de historia*
Science class	*La Segunda Guerra Mundial*
Chemistry class	*La clase de ciencias sociales*
Social Studies class	*La clase de música*
Classroom	*La clase de matemáticas*
Gym class	*La aula/el salón de clase*
Boring	*La clase de inglés*
History class	*La clase de educación física*
Interesting	*La clase de ciencias naturales*
Music class	*Aburrido(a)*
World War II	*Divertido(a)*
Fun	*Fácil/ difícil*
English class	*La clase de química*
Easy/ difficult	*Interesante*

Bonus Vocabulary

1st period – *la primera hora*
2nd period – *la segunda hora*
3rd period – *la tercera hora*
4th period – *la cuarta hora*
5th period – *la quinta hora*

6th period – *la sexta hora*
7th period – *la séptima hora*
8th period – *la octava hora*
9th period – *la novena hora*
10th period – *la décima hora*

Respond to the following questions using complete sentences in Spanish. If you don't know a word, look it up and be sure to copy over any new words to your Glossary!

1) *¿En qué clase estudias álgebra?*

2) *¿En qué clase usas la computadora?*

3) *¿En qué clase estudias biología?*

4) *¿En qué clase estudias literatura?*

5) *¿En qué clase estudias la Segunda Guerra Mundial?*

6) *¿En qué clase estudias una lengua nueva?*

7) *¿A qué hora almuerzas?*

8) *¿Qué clase tienes en la quinta hora?*

9) *¿Qué clase tienes en la primera hora?*

10) *¿Qué clase tienes en la segunda hora?*

11) *¿Cuál clase te gusta más, la clase de ciencias naturales o la clase de ciencias sociales?*

12) *¿Cuál es tu clase favorita? ¿Por qué?*

13) *A mí me gusta mucho la clase de español. ¿Y a ti? ¿Por qué o por qué no?*

14) *No me gusta nada la clase de matemáticas. ¿Y a ti? ¿Por qué o por qué no?*

Lesson 36: Things at school
(*Las cosas en la escuela*)

Match the following words in English and Spanish. For detailed instructions on Active Vocabulary Learning, see page 9. Don't forget to copy new words over to your Glossary!

Elementary school	*La calculadora*
Middle School	*El libro*
High School	*El cuaderno*
Paper	*La secundaria*
Calculator	*La goma de borrar*
Pencil	*La mochila*
Book	*El papel*
Eraser	*El diccionario*
Pen	*El lápiz*
Notebook	*La carpeta*
Backpack	*La primaria*
Folder	*La biblioteca*
Bookstore	*El bolígrafo*
Library	*El colegio/ la preparatoria*
Dictionary	*La librería*

Respond to the following questions with complete sentences in Spanish, using the locations suggested in English.

1) ¿Dónde está el libro? (in the library)

2) ¿Dónde está la calculadora? (in my backpack)

3) ¿Dónde está el diccionario? (in the bookstore)

4) ¿Dónde está el bolígrafo? (in the folder)

5) ¿Dónde está el papel? (in the notebook)

6) ¿Dónde está la goma de borrar? (on the pencil)

7) ¿Dónde está la biblioteca? (in the high school)

8) ¿Dónde está tu mochila? (at home)

Respond to the following questions using complete sentences in Spanish. If you don't know a word, look it up and be sure to copy over any new words to your Glossary!

1) ¿Necesitas una regla en la clase de matemáticas?

2) ¿Quieres un diccionario para tu cumpleaños?

3) ¿Tienes una calculadora?

4) ¿Ves la televisión por la noche?

5) ¿Tu madre necesita una regla cuando come?

6) ¿Necesitamos un cuaderno en la clase de inglés?

7) ¿Tu hermana quiere una mochila para Navidad?

8) ¿Tu padre necesita una goma de borrar?

9) ¿Te gustan más los bolígrafos o los lápices?

Lesson 37: Hobbies (*Los pasatiempos*)

Active Vocabulary Learning

Match the following words in English and Spanish. For detailed instructions on Active Vocabulary Learning, see page 9. Don't forget to copy new words over to your Glossary!

Soccer game	*Ir a la playa*
To play golf	*Ir al baile*
To go to the concert	*La lección de piano*
To go to the dance	*Ir al cine*
The mall	*El partido de fútbol*
To go to the beach	*Jugar deportes*
Jewelry store	*Jugar golf*
Piano lesson	*El centro comercial*
To go to the movies	*Ir al concierto*
The kid/boy	*El muchacho*
To play sports	*La joyería*

Respond to the following questions with complete sentences in Spanish, using the days/times suggested in parentheses. If you don't know a word, look it up and be sure to copy over any new words to your Glossary!

1) ¿A qué hora vas a jugar fútbol? (5:00 pm)

2) ¿A qué hora van tú y tu familia a la playa? (11:00 am)

3) ¿A qué hora va tu hermana a la lección de piano? (3:30 pm)

4) ¿A qué hora van tus amigos a jugar golf? (4:15 pm)

5) ¿A qué hora vas a comer en el restaurante? (6:30 pm)

6) ¿Cuándo vas al concierto con tus amigos? (Saturday, 8:00 pm)

7) ¿Cuándo va Julián al trabajo? (Mondays, 9:15 am)

8) ¿Cuándo vas a ir a la fiesta de tu amiga? (Friday, 7:30 pm)

9) ¿Cuándo van ustedes al gimnasio? (Thursdays, 5:30 pm)

10) ¿Cuándo desayunas? (everyday, 8:00 am)

11) *¿Cuándo van los muchachos a ver el partido de fútbol?* (Sunday, 1:30 pm)

12) *¿Cuándo vas a ir al baile?* (Saturday, 9:30 pm)

13) *¿Cuándo haces la tarea?* (Sundays, 8:00 pm)

14) *¿Cuándo juegas videojuegos?* (everyday, 4:15 pm)

15) *¿Cuándo juegas deportes?* (on the weekends)

16) *¿Cuándo estudias español?* (always!)

17) *¿Cuándo vas a la biblioteca?* (never)

18) *¿Cuándo almuerzas?* (everyday, noon)

19) *¿Cuándo nadas en la piscina?* (sometimes, in the afternoon)

20) *¿Cuándo vas al cine?* (this evening)

Lesson 38: Colors and Clothing (*Los colores y la ropa*)

Active Vocabulary Learning

Match the following words in English and Spanish. For detailed instructions on Active Vocabulary Learning, see page 9. Don't forget to copy new words over to your Glossary!

T-shirt	*La sudadera*
Socks	*La blusa*
Jeans	*Los pantalones*
Blouse	*La camiseta*
Skirt	*Largo/corto*
Boots	*Demasiado*
Coat	*El abrigo*
Sweatshirt	*Los jeans/vaqueros/ pantalones de mezclilla*
Long/short	*Los zapatos*
Dress	*Las botas*
Pants	*Grande/chico*
Too	*El vestido*
Shoes	*La falda*
Raincoat	*El suéter*
Large/small	*Los calcetines*
Sweater	*El impermeable*

Translate these sentences into Spanish. If you don't know a word, look it up and be sure to copy over any new words to your Glossary!

1) Do you like Mr. Gomez's pink pants?

2) The girl is wearing (*tiene puesta*) a short skirt.

3) Her boots are black.

4) I like red dresses.

5) Mrs. Gonzalez *is wearing* (*tiene puesto*) a purple sweater with orange jeans.

6) Carla likes to wear (*ponerse*) big sweatshirts.

7) Which blouse do you like better, the black one (*la negra*) or the white one (*la blanca*)?

8) Your white boots are beautiful!

9) Joaquín likes to wear (*ponerse*) green socks.

10) His yellow t-shirt is too small.

Lesson 39: Weather (*El Tiempo*)

Respond to the following questions using complete sentences in Spanish. If you don't know a word, look it up and be sure to copy over any new words to your Glossary!

1) ¿Qué ropa te pones cuando hace calor? (*Me pongo* – I wear)

2) ¿Qué ropa te pones cuando hace frío?

3) ¿Qué ropa te pones cuando llueve?

4) ¿Qué ropa te pones cuando nieva?

5) ¿Qué bebes cuando hace mucho calor?

6) ¿A dónde van ustedes cuando llueve?

7) Es domingo y hace mucho frío. Son las 6:00 de la mañana y nieva. ¿Qué vas a hacer (tú)?

8) Es mediodía y hace calor. Es lunes. ¿Qué hace tu hermano?

9) Son las 4:00 de la tarde y es verano. ¿Qué hace el profesor?

10) Son las 2:00 de la tarde y hace mucho calor. ¿Qué hacen los gatos?

11) Es Navidad y hace mucho frío. ¿Qué come tu mamá?

12) Es verano y vas a jugar mucho fútbol. ¿Qué vas a beber?

13) Es enero en Buenos Aires. ¿Qué ropa vas a ponerte? (*Me voy a poner* – I'm going to wear…)

Lesson 40: Food & Utensils (*La comida y los cubiertos*)

Active Vocabulary Learning

Match the following words in English and Spanish. For detailed instructions on Active Vocabulary Learning, see page 9. Don't forget to copy new words over to your Glossary!

Bakery/pastery shop	*El pastel*
Barbeque	*Las verduras frescas*
Soup	*La pastelería*
Cake	*La ensalada de frutas*
To be hungry	*El asado*
Meat	*La verdulería*
Fresh vegetables	*La carne*
Fruit salad	*La cuchara*
Spaghetti	*Tener hambre*
Vegetable stand	*El supermercado*
Fruit stand	*El cuchillo*
Steak	*El espagueti*
Supermarket	*La frutería*
Fork	*La sopa*
Knife	*El tenedor*
Spoon	*La carnicería*
Butcher/butcher's shop	*El bistec*

Respond to the following questions using complete sentences in Spanish. If you don't know a word, look it up and be sure to copy over any new words to your Glossary!

1) *Tengo hambre. ¿A dónde puedo ir?*

2) *Voy a hacer una sopa, y necesito verduras frescas. ¿A dónde puedo ir?*

3) *Voy a hacer un asado, y necesito varios tipos de carne. ¿A dónde puedo ir?*

4) *Voy a una fiesta de cumpleaños, y necesito un pastel. ¿A dónde puedo ir?*

5) *Voy a hacer una ensalada de frutas, y necesito frutas frescas. ¿A dónde puedo ir?*

6) *Voy a comer el espagueti. ¿Necesito cuchara, tenedor o cuchillo?*

7) *Voy a comer un bistec. ¿Necesito cuchara, tenedor o cuchillo?*

8) *Voy a comer un pastel. ¿Necesito cuchara, tenedor o cuchillo?*

9) *Voy a tomar una sopa. ¿Necesito cuchara, tenedor o cuchillo?*

10) *Voy a comer una ensalada. ¿Necesito cuchara, tenedor o cuchillo?*

Lesson 41: Food & Health (*La comida y la salud*)

Active Vocabulary Learning

Match the following words in English and Spanish. For detailed instructions on Active Vocabulary Learning, see page 9. Don't forget to copy new words over to your Glossary!

Ice cream	*El queso*
To be good/bad for your health	*Ser bueno(a)/malo(a) para la salud*
Apple juice	*El té caliente*
Delicious/disgusting	*El jugo de manzana*
A glass of wine	*Hacer ejercicio*
Cheese	*La hamburguesa*
Hot tea	*La grasa*
Carrots	*Una copa de vino*
To exercise	*La mantequilla*
Hamburger	*El helado*
Butter	*Delicioso(a)/asqueroso(a)*
Fat (dietary)	*Las zanahorias*

Translate these sentences into Spanish. If you don't know a word, look it up and be sure to copy over any new words to your Glossary!

1) I share strawberries with my friend, because they are delicious.

2) I don't drink a lot of coffee, because it's not good for my health.

3) I eat ice cream in the summer, because I like it a lot.

4) You drink orange juice for breakfast, because it's good for your health.

5) My friend doesn't eat a lot of butter, because it's bad for his health.

6) The kids eat bacon at lunch, because it's delicious.

7) I don't drink apple juice at dinner, because it's disgusting.

Respond to the following sentences using complete sentences in Spanish.

8) *¿Comes muchas grasas? ¿Por qué?*

9) *¿Cuántas hamburguesas comes cuando tienes hambre?*

10) *¿Haces ejercicio para mantenerte saludable? ¿Por qué?*

11) *¿Cuándo comes zanahorias? ¿Por qué?*

12) *¿Cuándo comes pastel? ¿Por qué?*

13) *¿Cuándo bebes té caliente? ¿Por qué?*

14) *¿Cuándo bebe café tu mamá? ¿Por qué?*

Lesson 42: Your Room (*Tu dormitorio*)

Active Vocabulary Learning

Match the following words in English and Spanish. For detailed instructions on Active Vocabulary Learning, see page 9. Don't forget to copy new words over to your Glossary!

Window	*Las cortinas*
Rug	*La almohada*
Curtains	*La alfombra*
Alarm clock	*La colcha*
Painting	*La lámpara*
Pillow	*El despertador*
Bed	*El armario/guardarropa*
Bedspread/comforter	*El cuadro*
Mirror	*La mesita*
Bedroom	*La cómoda*
Lamp	*El espejo*
Closet	*La ventana*
Night table	*La cama*
Wardrobe/armoire	*El clóset*
Dresser/bureau	*El dormitorio*

Respond to the following questions using complete sentences in Spanish. If you don't know a word, look it up and be sure to copy over any new words to your Glossary!

1) *¿Tienes un espejo en tu dormitorio? ¿Cómo es? ¿Grande o pequeño? ¿Cuadrado o redondo?*

2) *¿Cuántas almohadas tienes en tu cama? ¿Cómo son?*

3) *¿De qué color es tu colcha?*

4) *¿Tienes una alfombra en tu dormitorio? ¿De qué color es?*

5) *¿Cuántas ventanas tienes en tu dormitorio?*

6) *¿De qué color son las cortinas?*

7) *¿Tienes un despertador? ¿De qué color es? ¿A qué hora suena?*

8) *¿Tienes cuadros en tu dormitorio? ¿Cuántos? ¿Cómo son?*

9) *¿Cuántas lámparas tienes en tu dormitorio? ¿De qué color son? ¿Dónde están?*

10) *¿Tienes un clóset grande o pequeño?*

11) *¿Dónde pones las camisetas? (Yo pongo…)*

12) *¿Dónde pones los calcetines?*

13) *¿Dónde pones los zapatos?*

14) *¿Dónde pones los pantalones?*

15) *¿Dónde está tu cama?*

16) *¿Dónde está la mesita?*

17) *¿Dónde está la cómoda?*

18) *¿Dónde está la puerta?*

19) *Inventa tu propia pregunta…*

20) *Inventa tu propia pregunta…*

Lesson 43: At Home (*En casa*)

Active Vocabulary Learning

Match the following words in English and Spanish. For detailed instructions on Active Vocabulary Learning, see page 9. Don't forget to copy new words over to your Glossary!

Refrigerator	*El patio*
Sofa	*El refrigerador*
Table	*El sótano*
Chair	*Grande/pequeño(a)*
Stove	*Ver la tele*
Basement	*El sofá*
Washing machine	*El comedor*
Patio	*La cocina*
Room	*El jardín*
To watch t.v.	*La chimenea*
To wash the dishes	*La mesa*
Dining room	*La sala*
Kitchen	*El televisor*
Living room	*La estufa*
Yard/garden	*La silla*
Fireplace/hearth	*El cuarto*
Big/small	*La lavadora*
Television (the appliance itself)	*Lavar los platos*

Respond to the following questions using complete sentences in Spanish. If you don't know a word, look it up and be sure to copy over any new words to your Glossary!

Note: The word *hay* means there is/there are. It can be used in a question, and also in the answer to the same question.

Example: *¿Cuántos baños hay en tu casa?* – How many bathrooms are there in your house?
Hay dos baños en mi casa. – There are 2 bathrooms in my house.

1) *¿Cuántos dormitorios hay en tu casa?*

2) *¿Dónde está el refrigerador?*

3) *¿Dónde está el sofá? ¿De qué color es el sofá?*

4) *¿Cuántas ventanas hay en tu dormitorio?*

5) *¿Dónde está la estufa?*

6) *En tu casa, ¿hay un sótano?*

7) *En tu casa, ¿hay un patio? ¿Cuántas sillas y mesas hay en tu patio?*

8) *¿Dónde está la lavadora? ¿De qué color es?*

9) *¿Cómo es tu jardín, grande o pequeño?*

10) *En tu casa, ¿hay una chimenea? ¿Dónde está?*

11) *¿Dónde está el televisor?*

12) *¿Qué haces en la sala?*

13) *¿Qué haces en la cocina?*

14) *¿Qué haces en el patio?*

15) *¿Qué hace tu familia en el comedor?*

16) *¿Quién de tu familia lava los platos? ¿Dónde lavan los platos?*

17) *¿Dónde haces la tarea?*

18) *¿Dónde ves la tele?*

19) *¿Dónde usas la computadora?*

20) *¿Dónde desayunas?*

21) *¿De qué color es tu dormitorio?*

22) *¿De qué color es el comedor?*

23) *¿Cuántas sillas hay en el comedor?*

24) *¿Cuál es tu cuarto favorito de la casa?*

Part 8 Quiz

Respond to the following questions with complete sentences in Spanish.

1) *¿A qué hora almuerzas cuando estás en la escuela/el trabajo?*

2) *¿Cuándo es tu cumpleaños?*

3) *¿Cómo está el tiempo hoy?*

4) *¿Necesitas un cuaderno en la clase de ciencias sociales?*

5) *¿Necesitas un bolígrafo en la clase de educación física?*

6) *¿Cuál es la fecha de hoy?*

7) *¿Qué hora es?*

8) *¿Qué te gusta hacer durante el fin de semana?*

9) *¿Te gusta más trabajar o jugar deportes?*

10) *A mí no me gusta nada correr. ¿Y a ti?*

11) *A mí me gusta jugar videojuegos. ¿Y a ti?*

12) *¿Cómo eres, tímido o sociable?*

13) *¿Cómo es tu madre, ordenada o desordenada?*

14) *No me gusta ni pasar tiempo con amigos, ni hablar por teléfono, pero me gusta mucho estudiar. Yo soy _____.*

15) *¿Cuál clase tienes en la cuarta hora?*

16) *¿Cuál clase tienes en la segunda hora?*

17) *No me gusta nada la clase de matemáticas. Es muy _____.*

18) *La clase de música es divertida y también _____.*

Translate the following sentences into Spanish.

19) The flag is next to the clock.

20) The chair is behind the desk.

21) Where is the trash can in this classroom?

22) The apple juice is on top of the table.

23) I eat sausage and eggs for breakfast.

24) I share a pizza with my friend.

25) I am creative.

26) You are lazy.

27) I like to listen to music and eat a ham and cheese sandwich.

Part 8 Writing Activities

What do you eat every day? (¿Qué comes todos los días?)

Write a complete sentence in the present tense describing what you generally eat on each day of the week. (This is just practice, so don't worry if you don't always eat the same thing every week!)

Example: *El domingo <u>como una pizza.</u>*

El lunes _____.

El martes _____.

El miércoles _____.

El jueves _____.

El viernes _____.

El sábado _____.

El domingo _____.

What clothing do you wear every day?
(¿Qué ropa te pones todos los días?)

Write a complete sentence in the present tense describing what you generally wear on each day of the week. (This is just practice, so don't worry if you don't always wear the same thing every week!)

Example: *El domingo* <u>yo me pongo shorts rojos, camiseta blanca, calcetines amarillos y tenis blancos.</u>

El lunes _____.

El martes _____.

El miércoles _____.

El jueves _____.

El viernes _____.

El sábado _____.

El domingo _____.

What do you do every day? (¿Qué haces todos los días?)

Write a complete sentence in the present tense describing what you are doing or generally do on each day of the week.

Example: *El domingo* celebro el cumpleaños de mi hermana.

El lunes _____.

El martes _____.

El miércoles _____.

El jueves _____.

El viernes _____.

El sábado _____.

El domingo _____.

Section III: Beyond the Present Tense

Part 9: The Preterite Tense

No Nonsense Glossary*

Apple	La manzana

*For instructions on building your No Nonsense Glossary, see pages 9-10.

Lesson 44: Conjugating Regular Verbs in Preterite Tense

The Preterite Tense (*el pretérito*) is used to talk about the past. You will see that there is more than one past tense in Spanish, but let's focus on learning the Preterite for now. Think of it as the past tense for actions that have been fully completed in the past (example: I ate ice cream last night.).

To conjugate a verb, take the infinitive (the form of the verb ending in –ar/–er/–ir). Remove the –ar/–er/–ir ending and add the appropriate ending listed below.

–ar verbs
(Shown with the verb *hablar* – to speak)

Yo	habl**é**	Nosotros	habl**amos**
Tú	habl**aste**	Vosotros	habl**asteis**
Usted	habl**ó**	Ustedes	habl**aron**
Él / Ella	habl**ó**	Ellos / Ellas	habl**aron**

–er verbs
(Shown with the verb *comer* – to eat)

Yo	com**í**	Nosotros	com**imos**
Tú	com**iste**	Vosotros	com**isteis**
Usted	com**ió**	Ustedes	com**ieron**
Él / Ella	com**ió**	Ellos / Ellas	com**ieron**

–ir verbs
(Shown with the verb *vivir* – to live)

Yo	viv**í**	Nosotros	viv**imos**
Tú	viv**iste**	Vosotros	viv**isteis**
Usted	viv**ió**	Ustedes	viv**ieron**
Él / Ella	viv**ió**	Ellos / Ellas	viv**ieron**

Ejemplo: Yo **hablé** con mi abuela ayer. – I **spoke** with my grandmother yesterday.

Common Irregular Verbs in the Preterite Tense

Decir – to say/tell

Yo	**dije**	Nosotros	**dijimos**
Tú	**dijiste**	Vosotros	*dijisteis*
Usted	**dijo**	Ustedes	**dijeron**
Él / Ella	**dijo**	Ellos / Ellas	**dijeron**

Common verbs with a similar pattern:
Conducir – <u>*conduj*</u> (to drive)
Producir – <u>*produj*</u> (to produce)
Traer – <u>*traj*</u> (to bring)
Traducir – <u>*traduj*</u> (to translate)

Hacer – to do/make

Yo	**hice**	Nosotros	**hicimos**
Tú	**hiciste**	Vosotros	*hicisteis*
Usted	**hizo**	Ustedes	**hicieron**
Él / Ella	**hizo**	Ellos / Ellas	**hicieron**

Common verbs with a similiar pattern:
Querer – <u>*quis*</u> (to want/love)

Ir – to go / *Ser* – to be (permanent)

Yo	**fui**	Nosotros	**fuimos**
Tú	**fuiste**	Vosotros	*fuisteis*
Usted	**fue**	Ustedes	**fueron**
Él / Ella	**fue**	Ellos / Ellas	**fueron**

Dar – to give

Yo	**di**	Nosotros	**dimos**
Tú	**diste**	Vosotros	*disteis*
Usted	**dio**	Ustedes	**dieron**
Él / Ella	**dio**	Ellos / Ellas	**dieron**

Common verbs with a similar pattern:
Ver – <u>*v*</u> (to see)

Poder – to be able to

Yo	**pude**	Nosotros	**pudimos**
Tú	**pudiste**	Vosotros	*pudisteis*
Usted	**pudo**	Ustedes	**pudieron**
Él / Ella	**pudo**	Ellos / Ellas	**pudieron**

Common verbs with a similar pattern:
Poner – <u>*pus*</u> (to put/set)

Estar – to be (temporary)

Yo	**estuve**	Nosotros	**estuvimos**
Tú	**estuviste**	Vosotros	*estuvisteis*
Usted	**estuvo**	Ustedes	**estuvieron**
Él / Ella	**estuvo**	Ellos / Ellas	**estuvieron**

Common verbs with a similar pattern:
Contener – <u>*contuv*</u> (to contain)
Mantener – <u>*mantuv*</u> (to maintain)
Tener – <u>*tuv*</u> (to have)

Verbs Ending in –car/–gar/–zar in the Preterite Tense

There are some verbs that undergo a spelling change in the *Yo* form of the Preterite Tense, but their pronunciation is not affected. There are phonetic reasons for this, but let's not worry about that at this point. For now, you should do your best to memorize these patterns and the affected verbs.

Note: Since this only affects the spelling of verbs, if you are more focused on speaking and understanding Spanish as opposed to writing it, you do not have to make yourself crazy trying to learn this particular rule.

–car verbs (c → qu)
(Shown with the verb *sacar* – to take/ to take out)

Yo	sa**qu**é	Nosotros	sacamos
Tú	sacaste	Vosotros	sacasteis
Usted	sacó	Ustedes	sacaron
Él / Ella	sacó	Ellos / Ellas	sacaron

–gar verbs (g → gu)
(Shown with the verb *entregar* – to hand in)

Yo	entre**gu**é	Nosotros	entregamos
Tú	entregaste	Vosotros	entregasteis
Usted	entregó	Ustedes	entregaron
Él / Ella	entregó	Ellos / Ellas	entregaron

–zar verbs (z → c)
(Shown with the verb *almorzar* – to eat lunch)

Yo	almor**c**é	Nosotros	almorzamos
Tú	almorzaste	Vosotros	almorzasteis
Usted	almorzó	Ustedes	almorzaron
Él / Ella	almorzó	Ellos / Ellas	almorzaron

Lesson 44 Practice: Regular & Irregular Verbs in the Preterite Tense

Fill in the blank using the correct conjugation of the verb in parentheses. Then, translate these sentences into Spanish. If you don't know a word, look it up and be sure to copy over any new words to your Glossary!

1) ¿Qué _____ (comer) (tú) anoche?

2) Lisa _____ (hablar) con su hijo el viernes pasado.

3) Ustedes dos _____ (bailar) en la discoteca anoche.

4) La abuela _____ (cantar) en el coro el fin de semana pasado.

5) ¿(Tú) _____ (dibujar) este dibujo maravilloso?

6) Las hermanas _____ (escribir) una carta a Papa Noel.

7) La semana pasada, (nosotros) _____ (caminar) por el parque.

8) El gato _____ (descansar) anoche.

9) ¿(Tú) _____ (nadar) en la piscina la semana pasada?

10) ¿Qué _____ (cocinar) Luz para el desayuno?

11) ¿A dónde _____ (ir) ustedes ayer?

12) ¿Cuál película _____ (ir) a ver (tú) el sábado pasado?

13) (Yo) me _____ (quedar) en casa anoche.

14) Mi primo _____ (ir) al gimnasio ayer.

15) (Yo) _____ (ir) a las montañas el domingo pasado.

16) ¿Qué _____ (hacer) (tú) ayer?

17) (Yo) no _____ (montar) en bici anoche.

18) 18) ¿Quién _____ (comer) en un restaurante el fin de semana pasado?

Lesson 45: Practice with the Preterite Tense

Conjugate the following verbs for the subjects listed in parentheses.

1) *ir (yo)* –

2) *ir (él)* –

3) *ir (nosotros)* –

4) *ir (tú)* –

5) *beber (ellos)* –

6) *comer (él)* –

7) *ver (ellos)* –

8) *ver (él)* –

9) *correr (ellos)* –

10) *gustar (ella)* –

Translate these sentences into Spanish. If you don't know a word, look it up and be sure to copy over any new words to your Glossary!

In Question #6, you will need to use the **Personal *a***. This is a preposition in Spanish that is used just before the direct object, when the direct object is a person, or an animal that the speaker personifies, such as a pet.

Note: When *a* comes before *el*, the two combine into *al*.

Ejemplos: *Llamé **a** mi prima anoche.* – I called my cousin last night.
*Le di de comer **al** perro esta mañana.* – I fed the dog this morning.

1) You went to La Ciudad de México last year.

2) I went to Costa Rica last week.

3) We went skiing in the mountains last winter.

4) Luís went to the mall to buy a shirt.

5) Sabrina and Patricia ran in the gym last night.

6) The woman on the bus saw a kid on a bicycle.

7) The students drank a lot of coffee before the test.

8) Emiliano liked the Chinese food.
   (**Note:** For a refresher on how to use the verb *gustar*, see page 49. Remember to conjugate gustar in the *ella* form for Chinese food.)

9) The kids saw a movie at the zoo.

10) Sebastián ate all the pizza for breakfast this morning!

Lesson 46: More Practice with the Preterite Tense

Active Vocabulary Learning

Match the following words in English and Spanish. For detailed instructions on Active Vocabulary Learning, see page 9. Don't forget to copy new words over to your Glossary!

To cook	*Dormir*
To swim	*Hacer*
To exercise	*Comprar*
To work	*Cocinar*
To sunbathe	*Esquiar*
To celebrate	*Nadar*
To sleep	*Bailar*
To travel	*Hacer ejercicio*
To buy	*Descansar*
To dance	*Hacer senderismo en las montañas*
To rest	*Trabajar*
To kiss	*Comer*
To eat	*Tomar el sol*
To do/ to make	*Viajar*
To go hiking in the mountains	*Besar*
To ski	*Celebrar*

Respond to the following questions with complete sentences in Spanish. You may use verbs from the Word Bank if you like, but don't forget to conjugate them!

Word bank: *dormir, hacer, comprar, cocinar, esquiar, nadar, bailar, hacer ejercicio, descansar, hacer senderismo en las montañas, trabajar, comer, tomar el sol, viajar, besar, celebrar*

1) *¿Qué hiciste ayer?*

2) *¿Qué comieron ustedes en el desayuno hoy?*

3) *¿A dónde viajó Gabriela el año pasado?*

4) *¿Cuándo hiciste la tarea de español?*

5) *¿Qué hizo Rodrigo en Vail (o los Alpes) el fin de semana pasado?*

6) *¿Qué hicimos en la playa el verano pasado?*

7) *¿Qué compró la viejita en el supermercado?*

8) *¿Qué hice en el gimnasio ayer por la tarde?*

9) *¿Qué hicieron Juan y María en la discoteca?*

10) *¿Qué hicieron ustedes en el Año Nuevo?*

11) *¿Qué hiciste de cenar anoche?*

12) *¿Qué hicieron los gatos en la alfombra?*

13) *¿Qué hizo Silvia en el trabajo el viernes pasado?*

Part 9 Quiz

Conjugate the following verbs in the Preterite tense according to the subjects in parentheses.

1) *caminar (yo)*

2) *vivir (ustedes)*

3) *hacer (ella)*

4) *comer (nosotros)*

Fill in the blank with the correct Preterite conjugation of the verb in paretheses.

5) *¿Qué _____ (comer) tu hermano anoche?*

6) *Teresa _____ (hablar) con su hija el viernes pasado.*

7) *Ustedes dos _____ (ir) a bailar en la discoteca anoche.*

Respond to the following questions with complete sentences in Spanish.

8) *¿Qué hiciste ayer?*

9) *¿Qué desayunaste hoy?*

10) *¿A dónde viajaste el año pasado?*

Part 9 Take-it-Apart Grammar
(for Reading Comprehension)

When you practice reading comprehension in Spanish, it can be tempting to just guess what sentences mean. But there's a problem with this approach: it doesn't help you improve, and can lead to frustration and confusion.

Instead, slow down and practice deconstructing sentences into their grammatical components. Use the Take-It-Apart Grammar formula below to help you!

Take your time, and do not try to hurry and guess the meaning of the sentence. Figuring out all of the pieces of the sentence will allow you a greater understanding of the Spanish language, and will drastically improve your reading comprehension. Eventually, your brain will learn to go through all of these steps on its own, and speed will no longer be an issue.

Note: Sometimes, there may be more than one possible subject (example: he/she/you formal). Choose one and stick with it for the rest of the question.

Ejemplo: ¿Qué viste en el museo ayer?

Step 1: Verbs
Instructions: Search for and write down any conjugated verbs in the conjugated verb box. Then fill out the remaining boxes for that verb.
Hint: If you see multiple verb columns, it means there is more than one conjugated verb!

Conjugated verb	viste
Ending	-iste
Infinitive	ver
Tense	Preterite
Subject	tú
English meaning	to see

Step 2: Translation
Instructions: Answer the following questions and use the information you've gathered to translate the sentence into English. After that, you may be asked to write the original Spanish sentence in a different tense in Spanish and translate the new meaning into English. Think of this as grammatical weightlifting. The more you do, the better you'll get.

Question or statement? <u>question</u>   Question word: <u>Qué</u>

Translation: <u>What did you see in the museum yesterday?</u>

Rewrite in the Simple Future. <u>¿Qué vas a ver en el museo mañana?</u>

New Translation: <u>What are you going to see in the museum tomorrow?</u>

1) *Vamos a ir al parque este fin de semana.*

Conjugated verb	
Ending	
Infinitive	
Tense	
Subject	
English meaning	

Question or statement? _____ Question word: _____

Translation: _____

Rewrite in the Preterite. _____

New Translation: _____

2) *Hoy es el primer día de invierno.*

Conjugated verb	
Ending	
Infinitive	
Tense	
Subject	
English meaning	

Question or statement? _____ Question word: _____

Translation: _____

Rewrite in the Simple Future. _____

New Translation: _____

3) *¿A dónde fuiste el año pasado?*

Conjugated verb	
Ending	
Infinitive	
Tense	
Subject	
English meaning	

Question or statement? _____   Question word: _____

Translation: _____

Rewrite in the Simple Future. _____

New Translation: _____

4) *Hizo toda la tarea.*

Conjugated verb	
Ending	
Infinitive	
Tense	
Subject	
English meaning	

Question or statement? _____   Question word: _____

Translation: _____

Rewrite in the Simple Future. _____

New Translation: _____

5) ¿A qué hora llegas a la escuela, generalmente?

Conjugated verb	
Ending	
Infinitive	
Tense	
Subject	
English meaning	

Question or statement? _____   Question word: _____

Translation: _____

Rewrite in the Preterite. _____

New Translation: _____

6) ¿Quién quiere ir al cine conmigo hoy por la noche?

Conjugated verb	
Ending	
Infinitive	
Tense	
Subject	
English meaning	

Question or statement? _____   Question word: _____

Translation: _____

Rewrite in the Simple Future. _____

New Translation: _____

7) *¿A quién le gusta ponerse vestidos lindos?*

Conjugated verb	
Ending	
Infinitive	
Tense	
Subject	
English meaning	

Question or statement? _____ Question word: _____

Translation: _____

Rewrite in the Preterite. _____

New Translation: _____

8) *No quiero saber si el vaso está lleno o vacío. ¡Quiero un refresco!*

Conjugated verb			
Ending			
Infinitive			
Tense			
Subject			
English meaning			

Question or statement? _____ Question word: _____

Translation: _____

Rewrite in the Simple Future. _____

New Translation: _____

Part 9 Writing Activities

Create Sentences in the Preterite

Write 10 sentences in the preterite. Choose a subject from the 1st column; a verb from the 2nd column and a suggestion from the 3rd and 4th columns (or your own creative invention) to complete the sentence.

Use the correct endings for –ar/–er/–ir verbs! **Note:** one of these verbs is irregular.

Yo	bailar	en el parque	ayer
Tú	enseñar	la Copa Mundial	anoche
El abuelo	comer	mucho dinero en Las Vegas	el fin de semana pasado
Mi mejor amigo	salir	salsa	el año pasado
Los cubanos	ir	la clase	la semana pasada
Ustedes	correr	en la granja	el mes pasado
Los profesores	montar a caballo	en el gimnasio	hace mucho tiempo
Nosotros	ganar	en el sofá	el sábado pasado
Los perros	dormir	con amigos	
El equipo de fútbol alemán	perder	las llaves	
		al cine	
		a un restaurante chino	
		en el hotel	
		en la playa	

Ejemplo: Yo corrí en el parque el sábado pasado. (I ran in the park last Saturday.)

1) _____

2) _____

3) _____

4) _____

5) _____

6) _____

7) _____

8) _____

9) _____

10) _____

Celebrity Interview Skit (*Hacer una Entrevista*)

Choose one person to be the interviewer and the other to be the celebrity. The interviewer will ask the celebrity questions about their trip to your city or hometown. The celebrity (who is from somewhere else) will answer the questions about what things they did in your city, and what they do or don't like about your city. You can pretend the celebrity has been in your city for a week, and they are leaving tomorrow.

You should aim for at least 5 minutes of total dialogue.

If you don't have a study partner, write the script and play both roles yourself!

What to include:
- basic greetings
- questions about the celebrity (where they are from, what they do, etc.)
- when/why they came to your city
- what they did: Preterite Tense
- where/what they ate: Preterite Tense
- what clothing they wore to various events/restaurants: Preterite Tense
- what they like and don't like about your city: Present Tense

Pay attention to which tense you are using. Be as creative as you can!

My Diary (*Mi diario*)

Escribe por lo menos 3 frases para responder a cada pregunta. (Write at least 3 sentences to respond to each question.)

¡No te olvides! (Don't forget!):
- Check which tense you are using to talk about the past and present. For future, remember to use [ir + a + infinitive.]
- Use your vocabulary to talk about weekends.
- Use your food vocabulary to talk about what you ate or are going to eat.
- Use your clothing vocabulary to talk about what you wore or are going to wear.

Helpful words:
- **Después de + infinitive** – after
  Después de esquiar, voy a tomar un té caliente. – After skiing, I am going to drink hot tea.

- **Antes de + infinitive** – before
  Antes de ir a la escuela, desayuné. – Before going to school, I ate breakfast.

- **Después** – after that
  Fuimos a correr. Después, comimos una pizza. – We went for a run. After that, we ate pizza.

How to write the date: *domingo, 20 de abril* – Sunday, April 20th

¿Qué hiciste hoy? _____ (día, número, de mes)

¿A qué hora? _____

¿Qué hiciste ayer? _____ (día, número, de mes)

¿A qué hora? _____

¿Qué hiciste el _____ (fill in a day of the week)?

¿A qué hora? _____

¿Qué vas a hacer mañana? _____ (día, número, de mes)

¿A qué hora? _____

Part 10: Direct/Indirect Object Pronouns & Reflexive Verbs

No Nonsense Glossary*

Apple	La manzana

*For instructions on building your No Nonsense Glossary, see pages 9-10.

Lesson 47: Direct Object Pronouns

Think of a <u>direct object</u> as a thing. It could also be a person, but often it will be a thing. The direct object is the thing the verb is being done to. It is different from the subject, which is whoever/whatever is doing the verb.

   Ejemplos: I am going to buy <u>a new shirt</u>.
       We want to eat <u>the chicken</u>.

The most important direct object pronouns to remember are the third person pronouns: ***lo, la, los, las***. (This is because first and second person object pronouns are the same for direct and indirect object pronouns: ***me, te, nos, os***.)

   In English, ***Lo/La*** = it. ***Los/Las*** = them.

Write the correct direct object pronoun for the following nouns:

1) *el libro:*

2) *la flor bonita:*

3) *los bolígrafos:*

4) *las mesas:*

5) *el pollo:*

6) *unas manzanas rojas:*

7) *los jeans:*

8) *mi hermano menor:*

9) *una camisa nueva:*

10) *unos calcetines:*

11) *una mochila negra:*

In a sentence, place the direct object pronoun directly before the conjugated verb:
   _Lo_ quiero comer. (I want to eat <u>it</u>.)

Or attach the direct object pronoun to the infinitive, if there is one:
   Quiero comer_lo_. (I want to eat <u>it</u>.)

In the examples above, **lo** could refer to any singular masculine noun. For example, **el taco**.

In the following sentences, find the noun, and decide which direct object pronoun could be used to replace it. Then, rewrite the sentence using the direct object pronoun. Finally, translate the sentences into English. If you don't know a word, look it up and be sure to copy over any new words to your Glossary!

Ejemplo: *Papá quiere comprar los jeans.*

Translation: Dad wants to buy the jeans.

Direct Object: los jeans   Direct Object Pronoun: los

New sentence: Papá los quiere comprar. / Papá quiere comprarlos.

Translation: Dad wants to buy them.

1) *Voy a comprar una camisa nueva.*

Translation:

Direct Object: Direct Object Pronoun:

New sentence:

Translation:

2) *Quiero comer unas manzanas rojas.*

Translation:

Direct Object: Direct Object Pronoun:

New sentence:

Translation:

3) *Jorge necesita leer el libro.*

Translation:

Direct Object: Direct Object Pronoun:

New sentence:

Translation:

4) *Pepito perdió unos calcetines.* (*Perder* – to lose)

Translation:

Direct Object: Direct Object Pronoun:

New sentence:

Translation:

5) *¿Quién va a poner las mesas?* (*Poner* – to set)

Translation:

Direct Object: Direct Object Pronoun:

New sentence:

Translation:

6) *Busco a mi hermano menor.* (*Buscar* – to look for)

Translation:

Direct Object: Direct Object Pronoun:

New sentence:

Translation:

7) *¿Vas a ver la película?*

Translation:

Direct Object: Direct Object Pronoun:

New sentence:

Translation:

Lesson 48: Indirect Object Pronouns

Think of an <u>indirect object</u> as a person. It could also be an animal or a thing, but often it will be a person. The indirect object is the thing the verb is being done to or for. It is different from the subject, which is whoever/whatever is doing the verb.

    Ejemplos: *I am going to buy a new shirt for <u>my brother</u>.*
               We want to give the cake to <u>our grandmother</u>.

The most important indirect object pronouns to remember are the third person and *usted/ustedes* pronouns: **le**, **les**. (This is because all other object pronouns are the same for direct and indirect object pronouns: **me**, **te**, **nos**, **os**.)

Generally, in English, **le** = him/her. **Les** = them.

Write the correct indirect object pronoun for the following nouns:

    1) *los niños:*

    2) *la mujer:*

    3) *mi madre:*

    4) *el papá de Juan:*

    5) *la abuela de mi amigo:*

    6) *los profesores:*

    7) *Martín:*

    8) *mi perro:*

    9) *el bebé:*

    10) *los gatos:*

    11) *mis tíos:*

In a sentence, place the indirect object pronoun directly before the conjugated verb:
Le voy a dar un regalo. (I am going to give him/ her/ you formal a gift.)

Or attach the indirect object pronoun to the infinitive, if there is one:
Voy a darle un regalo. (I am going to give him/ her/ you formal a gift.)

In the 2 examples above, we don't know specifically who the *le* is referring to, because it could be **to him, to her** or **to you formal**. Sometimes, when it is not clear from the context, it is necessary to say *le/les* and also specify the person at the end of the sentence.

Ejemplo: *Le voy a dar el regalo a Sara.* (I am going to give the gift to Sara.)

Once it is clear you are talking about Sara, you could leave out her name in the next sentence and just use *le*.

In the following sentences, find the indirect object, and decide which indirect object pronoun could be used to replace it. Then, rewrite the sentence using the indirect object pronoun. Finally, translate the sentences into English.

Ejemplo: *Voy a darle el jugo de manzana a la niña.*

Translation: I am going to give the apple juice to the girl.

Indirect Object: la niña   Indirect Object Pronoun: le

New sentence: Le voy a dar el jugo de manzana. / Voy a darle el jugo de manzana.

Translation: I am going to give her the apple juice.

1) *Quiero hacer un pastel para mi abuela.*

Translation:

Indirect Object: Indirect Object Pronoun:

New sentence:

Translation:

2) *La profesora va a hacer un examen difícil para los estudiantes.*

Translation:

Indirect Object: Indirect Object Pronoun:

New sentence:

Translation:

3) *Ricardo quiere visitar a su amigo en Sevilla.*

Translation:

Indirect Object: Indirect Object Pronoun:

New sentence:

Translation:

4) *Pedro y Sabrina escriben cartas a sus tíos en México.*

Translation:

Indirect Object: Indirect Object Pronoun:

New sentence:

Translation:

5) *Nosotros vamos a regalarle este suéter a nuestra mamá para su cumpleaños.*

(*Regalar* – to give as a gift)

Translation:

Indirect Object: Indirect Object Pronoun:

New sentence:

Translation:

6) *¿Vas a darle el juguete a tu hermana?*

Translation:

Indirect Object: Indirect Object Pronoun:

New sentence:

Translation:

7) *Mi papá va a hacer una reservación para mi mamá.*

Translation:

Indirect Object: Indirect Object Pronoun:

New sentence:

Translation:

Lesson 49: Reflexive Verbs

A reflexive verb is a verb that someone does to him/herself. Another way to think about it is that the subject (the person doing the verb) and the object (whoever the verb is being done to or for) are the same person.

Instead of giving something to someone else, like we've seen in the previous lessons, you might wash your own face. In this case, you would use the reflexive form of the verb *lavar* (to wash). The reflexive form is *lavarse* (to wash oneself).

    ***Ejemplo**: (Yo) me lavo la cara*. – I wash my (own) face.

Note: When using a reflexive verb, you don't need to say *mi cara*, because the **me lavo** makes it clear that the face is mine.

Based on the subject of the verb, you will use the appropriate reflexive pronoun from the chart below.

Reflexive Pronouns

Yo	**me**	*Nosotros*	**nos**
Tú	**te**	*Vosotros*	**os**
Usted	**se**	*Ustedes*	**se**
Él / Ella	**se**	*Ellos / Ellas*	**se**

Passive Voice Construction with *se*

Se + [third person singular/plural conjugation of verb]
- ***La casa se vende.*** – The house is for sale.
    - **Note:** Literally, this means "the house sells itself."
- ***Se venden tacos.*** – Tacos for sale/ Tacos are sold.
- ***Se habla español.*** – Spanish is spoken.

Common Reflexive Verbs

Spanish	English	Notes
Acostarse	To go to bed/ lie down	Present Tense: stem change o → ue
Afeitarse (la barba)	To shave (one's beard)	
Bañarse	To bathe (oneself)	
Caerse	To fall down	Present Tense: Irregular Yo (*caigo*) Preterite: i → y (in 3rd person/Ud(s).
Cepillarse (el pelo/los dientes)	To brush (one's hair/teeth)	
Callarse	To be quiet	
Despertarse	To wake (oneself) up	Present Tense: stem change e → ie
Divertirse	To have fun	Present Tense: stem change e → ie
Dormirse	To fall asleep	Present Tense: stem change o → ue
Ducharse	To take a shower	
Lavarse	To wash (oneself)	
Levantarse	To get (oneself) up	
Perderse	To get lost	Present Tense: stem change e → ie
Ponerse (la ropa)/ vestirse	To put on (clothes)/ get dressed	*Ponerse* – Present Tense: Irregular Yo (*pongo*) *Vestirse* – Present Tense: stem change: e → i
Portarse	To behave	
Probarse (la ropa)	To try on (clothes)	Present Tense: stem change o → ue
Quedarse	To stay	

Ejemplos

- *(Nosotros) nos lavamos las manos.* – We are washing our hands.
- *El señor se afeita la barba.* – The man is shaving his beard.
- *(Yo) me levanto tarde los domingos.* – I get up late on Sundays.
- *(Tú) te pruebas el vestido.* – You are trying on the dress.
- *La científica se queda en un hotel.* – The scientist is staying at a hotel.

Lesson 49 Practice: Reflexive Verbs

Choose whether to conjugate the verbs in the following sentences, or leave them in the infinitive. Then, translate these sentences into English.

Note: Remember that you cannot put two conjugated verbs next to each other. Just like when you learned to use the verb *gustar*, you would conjugate the first verb and leave the second verb in the infinitive. (*Me gusta caminar.* – I like to walk.) With reflexive verbs, you would leave the second verb in the infinitive but use the correct reflexive pronoun to match the subject. (*Vamos a divertirnos.* – We're going to have fun.)

1) *Me gusta _____ (divertirse) en las fiestas.*

2) *Cuando voy a las fiestas, _____ (divertirse) mucho.*

3) *¿(Tú) quieres _____ (acostarse) tarde hoy?*

4) *¿A qué hora _____ tú (acostarse), generalmente?*

5) *¿A qué hora vas a _____ (despertarse) mañana?*

6) *¿A qué hora _____ (tú) (despertarse) cuando estás de vacaciones?*

7) *¿El chico prefiere _____ (bañarse) o _____ (ducharse)?*

8) *El chico _____ (bañarse) los domingos.*

9) *(Nosotros) vamos a _____ (lavarse) las manos.*

10) *(Nosotros) _____ (lavarse) las manos antes de comer.*

11) *Cuando (yo) _____ (quedarse) en un hotel, siempre _____ (levantarse) temprano.*

12) *Los niños no necesitan _____ (afeitarse) las barbas.*

13) *(Nosotros) _____ (divertirse) en la playa.*

14) *Los primos _____ (lavarse) los dientes.*

15) *¿Te vas a _____ (ducharse) antes de la boda?*

16) *Estoy muy cansada. ¡Me quiero _____ (dormirse)!*

Lesson 50: Direct/Indirect Object & Reflexive Pronouns Together

Direct/Indirect Object and Reflexive Pronouns Reference Chart

Direct

Yo	me	Nosotros	nos
Tú	te	Vosotros	os
Usted	lo, la	Ustedes	los, las
Él Ella	lo, la	Ellos Ellas	los, las

Indirect

Yo	me	Nosotros	nos
Tú	te	Vosotros	os
Usted	le	Ustedes	les
Él Ella	le	Ellos Ellas	les

Who or what?
- ¿Dónde está **el libro**?
- (Where is **the book**?)
--- No **lo** puedo encontrar.
--- No puedo encontrar**lo**.

To whom or for whom?
- ¿Vas a dar el regalo **a Sabrina**?
- (Are you going to the gift to Sabrina?)
--- Sí, **le** voy a dar el regalo.
--- Sí, voy a dar**le** el regalo.

Direct/Indirect object pronouns come...
- Before the conjugated verb: ¿**Me** das el libro? – Would you give **me** the book?
- Attached to the infinitive: ¿Puedes dar**me** el libro? – Can you give **me** the book?
- Attached to a command: ¡Da**me** el libro! – Give **me** the book!
  (We will learn about this in Part 11.)

You can use both at once:
- Indirect before Direct: ¿**Me lo** das? – Would you give **it** to **me**?
- If **le/les** comes next to **lo/la/los/las** (¿Le lo das?), the **le** becomes **se**: ¿**Se lo** das?
  - Would you give **it** to **him/her**?

Reflexive Pronouns

Yo	me	Nosotros	nos
Tú	te	Vosotros	os
Usted	se	Ustedes	se
Él Ella	se	Ellos Ellas	se

Use reflexive pronouns when the subject and object of a verb are the same. For example, the subject is doing something to himself. Indirect before Direct, Reflexive first of all!

Lesson 50 Practice: Using Direct/Indirect Object Pronouns Together

It is possible to use both indirect and direct object pronouns together. When this happens, be sure to put the **indirect before direct**!

When *le/les* lands next to *lo/la/los/las* (basically, whenever there are two pronouns in a row beginning with "**L**"), the *le/les* turns into *se*.

> For example: *Le voy a dar un regalo.*
> Becomes: *[Le] lo voy a dar.* Or, *Voy a dar[le]lo.* But wait, there's more!
> Becomes: *Se lo voy a dar.* Or, *Voy a dárselo.*

Once we start attaching pronouns to the ends of verbs, there are rules that require written accent marks to be places on a certain syllable to maintain the stress in the correct place (i.e. where it naturally falls before the pronouns are attached). You will learn how to do this properly in Part 11.

For the purposes of this exercise, don't worry about the written accent mark rule. Instead, say the word out loud and place a written accent mark on the syllable that you think should carry the stress. This will let you know whether or not you are able to hear it. If you can't hear it, don't worry. You will learn the rule soon.

In the following sentences, find the direct and indirect objects, and decide which direct and indirect object pronouns could be used to replace them. Then, rewrite the sentence using both the direct and indirect object pronouns. Finally, translate the sentences into English.

Note: There may be sentences that do not have both a Direct and Indirect Object, so watch out!

Ejemplo: Voy a darle el jugo de manzana a la niña.

Translation: I am going to give the apple juice to the girl.

Indirect Object: la niña   Indirect Object Pronoun: le

Direct Object: el jugo de manzana   Direct Object Pronoun: lo

New sentence: Se lo voy a dar. / Voy a dárselo.

Translation: I am going to give her it. / I am going to give it to her.

1) *Quiero hacer un pastel para mi abuela.*

Translation:

Indirect Object: Indirect Object Pronoun:

Direct Object: Direct Object Pronoun:

New sentence:

Translation:

2) *La profesora va a hacer un examen difícil para los estudiantes.*

Translation:

Indirect Object: Indirect Object Pronoun:

Direct Object: Direct Object Pronoun:

New sentence:

Translation:

3) *Ricardo quiere visitar a su amigo en Sevilla.*

Translation:

Indirect Object: Indirect Object Pronoun:

Direct Object: Direct Object Pronoun:

New sentence:

Translation:

4) *Pedro y Sabrina escriben cartas a sus tíos en México.*

Translation:

Indirect Object: Indirect Object Pronoun:

Direct Object: Direct Object Pronoun:

New sentence:

Translation:

5) *Nosotros vamos a regalarle este suéter a nuestra mamá para su cumpleaños.*

Translation:

Indirect Object: Indirect Object Pronoun:

Direct Object: Direct Object Pronoun:

New sentence:

Translation:

6) *El camarero va a traer el postre para nosotros.*

Translation:

Indirect Object: Indirect Object Pronoun:

Direct Object: Direct Object Pronoun:

New sentence:

Translation:

7) *Luisa hace galletas para sus nietos.*

Translation:

Indirect Object: Indirect Object Pronoun:

Direct Object: Direct Object Pronoun:

New sentence:

Translation:

8) *Los monos lanzan plátanos a los turistas.*

Translation:

Indirect Object: Indirect Object Pronoun:

Direct Object: Direct Object Pronoun:

New sentence:

Translation:

9) *El perro comió el sándwich de la niña.*

Translation:

Indirect Object: Indirect Object Pronoun:

Direct Object: Direct Object Pronoun:

New sentence:

Translation:

10) *Tu hermano te pidió un favor.*

Translation:

Indirect Object: Indirect Object Pronoun:

Direct Object: Direct Object Pronoun:

New sentence:

Translation:

11) *Yo di las flores a ti.*

Translation:

Indirect Object: Indirect Object Pronoun:

Direct Object: Direct Object Pronoun:

New sentence:

Translation:

12) *¿Quién dio una barra de chocolate al bebé?*

Translation:

Indirect Object: Indirect Object Pronoun:

Direct Object: Direct Object Pronoun:

New sentence:

Translation:

Now, from English to Spanish!

1) I am going to give him a <u>balloon</u> (*globo*).

Indirect Object: Indirect Object Pronoun:

Direct Object: Direct Object Pronoun:

New sentence:

New Sentence Translation:

2) You want to write a letter to your friend.

Indirect Object: Indirect Object Pronoun:

Direct Object: Direct Object Pronoun:

New sentence:

New Sentence Translation:

3) Who is going to tell me the secret?

Indirect Object: Indirect Object Pronoun:

Direct Object: Direct Object Pronoun:

New sentence:

New Sentence Translation:

4) José gave his girlfriend a <u>ring</u> (*anillo*).

Indirect Object: Indirect Object Pronoun:

Direct Object: Direct Object Pronoun:

New sentence:

New Sentence Translation:

5) Who gave coffee to the <u>turtle</u> (*la tortuga*)?

Indirect Object: Indirect Object Pronoun:

Direct Object: Direct Object Pronoun:

New sentence:

New Sentence Translation:

6) Why did the cat steal your sock?

Indirect Object: Indirect Object Pronoun:

Direct Object: Direct Object Pronoun:

New sentence:

New Sentence Translation:

7) We gave María the cake for her birthday.

Indirect Object: Indirect Object Pronoun:

Direct Object: Direct Object Pronoun:

New sentence:

New Sentence Translation:

8) Create your own sentence with a Direct Object and Indirect Object. Use the sentences in the questions above as your guide.

Indirect Object: Indirect Object Pronoun:

Direct Object: Direct Object Pronoun:

New sentence:

New Sentence Translation:

Lesson 51: Practice with Direct/Indirect Object Pronouns

Translate the following questions into English, and the responses into Spanish.

1) *¿Puedes darme un dólar?*

1a) I'll give it to you, if you buy me an ice cream.

2) *Quiero escribirle una carta a mi amiga en España.*

2a) Why don't you email (*enviar por correo electrónico*) it to her?

3) *Vamos a regalarle las flores a nuestra mamá.*

3a) Why don't y'all gift them to me?

4) *¿Vas a comprar el libro para tu amigo?*

4a) No, I'm going to buy it for my girlfriend.

5) *¿Dónde va a poner los chocolates Sebastián?*

5a) He's going to hide them on the beach.

6) *¿Vas a traer pizza?*

6a) Yes, I am going to bring it.

7) *¿Vas a buscar el tocino?*

7a) Yes, I am going to look for it.

8) *¿La abuela nos va a cocinar un desayuno exquisito?*

8a) No, she is going to cook it for the dog! (Sarcasm intended!)

9) *¿Va a darte un abrigo Joaquín?*

9a) No, he is going to give it to his brother.

10) *¿Quién se va a comer todo el pastel?*

10a) I am going to eat it all!

Lesson 52: More Practice with Direct/Indirect Object Pronouns

Match the following words in English and Spanish. For detailed instructions on Active Vocabulary Learning, see page 9. Don't forget to copy new words over to your Glossary!

Delicious meat	Una canción de amor
A beautiful letter	Cada Navidad
The same card	La carne deliciosa
His sssay	Una comida exquisita
An exquisite meal	La misma tarjeta
Each Christmas	Su ensayo
A love song	Una carta linda

Direct & Indirect Object Pronouns

In the following English sentences:
1) Put a square around the subject (if the subject is implied, write it in).
2) Dotted underline the verb.
3) Underline the direct object.
4) Double underline the indirect object.

Then translate the sentences into Spanish, using the correct direct and indirect object pronouns and paying attention to word order.

***Ejemplo*:**

My mother gives me a present. – *Mi madre me da un regalo.*

She gives it to me. – *Me lo da.*

1) You send me the same card each Christmas.

1a) You send it to me each Christmas.

2) The man sings his wife a love song.

2a) He sings it to her.

3) The kids give the teacher an apple.

3a) They give it to him/her.

4) You pay the bill for us.

4a) You pay it for us.

5) I open the door for the old woman.

5a) I open it for her.

6) We cooked you guys an exquisite meal!

6a) We cooked it for you guys!

7) You two wrote me a beautiful letter.

7a) You wrote it for me.

8) The student <u>handed in</u> his essay to the teacher. (<u>to hand in</u> – *entregar*)

8a) He handed it in to her.

9) Your parents gave you a car as a birthday gift!

9a) They gave it to you as a birthday gift!

10) We gave the dog delicious meat.

10a) We gave it to him.

11) Make up your own sentence with a Direct Object and an Indirect Object. Use the sentences in the questions above as your guide.

11a) Replace the Direct Object and Indirect Object in your sentence above with pronouns.

Part 10 Quiz

Translate these sentences into Spanish.

Ejemplo:

Laura wrote a letter to her mother. *Laura le escribió una carta a su madre.*

Laura wrote it to her. *Laura se la escribió.*

1) Graciela sent a card to her sister.

1a) Graciela sent it to her.

2) Pilar gave a present to her grandmother.

2a) Pilar gave it to her.

3) The waiter brought a glass of wine to Sabrina.

3a) The waiter brought it to her.

4) Stefanie made coffee for me.

4a) Stefanie made it for me.

5) Emiliano saw a monkey on the bus.

5a) Emiliano saw it on the bus.

Part 10 Take-it-Apart Grammar
(for Reading Comprehension)

Take-It-Apart Grammar sections teach you to deconstruct sentences into their grammatical components, thereby improving comprehension and minimizing guessing.

Ejemplo: *Te quiere con todo el corazón.*

Step 1: Verbs
Instructions: Search for and write down any conjugated verbs in the conjugated verb box. Then fill out the remaining boxes for that verb.
Hint: If you see multiple verb columns, it means there is more than one congujaged verb!

Conjugated verb	quiere
Ending	-e
Infinitive	querer
Tense	Present
Subject	él/ella
English meaning	to love

Step 2: Direct Object/Indirect Object/Reflexive Pronouns
Instructions: Search for and write down any Direct Object, Indirect Object or Reflexive Pronouns. Use the Pronoun Possibilities Reference Chart on the next page to help you.
Hint: There may be more than one type of pronoun present.

Direct Object/Indirect Object/Reflexive Pronouns: te

Step 3: Translation
Instructions: Answer the following questions and use the information you've gathered to translate the sentence into English. Then, you may be asked to write the original Spanish sentence in a different tense in Spanish and translate the new meaning into English. Think of this as gramatical weight lifting. The more you do, the better you'll get.

Question or statement? Statement   Question word: N/A

Translation: He/she loves you with all his/her heart.

Rewrite in the Simple Future. Te va a querer con todo el corazón.

New Translation: He/she is going to love you with all his/her heart.

Pronoun Possibilities Reference Chart

Pronoun	Possible Translations		
	Direct Object Pronoun (Who or what?)	**Indirect Object Pronoun** (To whom or for whom?)	**Reflexive Pronoun** (Done to oneself)
me	me	to/for me	(refers to myself)
te	you	to/for you	(refers to yourself)
lo	it (masculine, singular)	----	----
la	it (feminine, singular)	----	----
le	----	to/for you formal, him, her	----
nos	us	to/for us	(refers to ourselves)
los	them (masculine, plural)	----	----
las	them (feminine, plural)	----	----
les	----	to/for you plural, them	----
se	----	if directly followed by a *lo/la*, *se* could mean the following: - to/for you formal/you plural - to/for him/her/them	(refers to himself/herself/ itself/themselves)

1) *¿Lo lavaraon bien?*

Conjugated verb	
Ending	
Infinitive	
Tense	
Subject	
English meaning	

Direct Object/Indirect Object/Reflexive Pronouns: _____

Question or statement? _____   Question word: _____

Translation: _____

Rewrite in the Simple Future. _____

New Translation: _____

2) *La voy a buscar.*

Conjugated verb	
Ending	
Infinitive	
Tense	
Subject	
English meaning	

Direct Object/Indirect Object/Reflexive Pronouns: _____

Question or statement? _____   Question word: _____

Translation: _____

Rewrite in the Preterite. _____

New Translation: _____

3) *Le dio un abrazo a su hijo.*

Conjugated verb	
Ending	
Infinitive	
Tense	
Subject	
English meaning	

Direct Object/Indirect Object/Reflexive Pronouns: _____

Question or statement? _____   Question word: _____

Translation: _____

Rewrite in the Simple Future. _____

New Translation: _____

4) ¿A quién le gusta viajar en avión?

Conjugated verb	
Ending	
Infinitive	
Tense	
Subject	
English meaning	

Direct Object/Indirect Object/Reflexive Pronouns: _____

Question or statement? _____   Question word: _____

Translation: _____

Rewrite in the Preterite. _____

New Translation: _____

5) ¿Lo escondió?

Conjugated verb	
Ending	
Infinitive	
Tense	
Subject	
English meaning	

Direct Object/Indirect Object/Reflexive Pronouns: _____

Question or statement? _____   Question word: _____

Translation: _____

Rewrite in the Simple Future. _____

New Translation: _____

6) *Te lo regalé.*

Conjugated verb	
Ending	
Infinitive	
Tense	
Subject	
English meaning	

Direct Object/Indirect Object/Reflexive Pronouns: _____

Question or statement? _____   Question word: _____

Translation: _____

Rewrite in the Simple Future. _____

New Translation: _____

7) *No me llamaste anoche, y por eso te llamo hoy.*

Conjugated verb		
Ending		
Infinitive		
Tense		
Subject		
English meaning		

Direct Object/Indirect Object/Reflexive Pronouns: _____

Question or statement? _____   Question word: _____

Translation: _____

Part 10 Writing Activities

My daily routine (reflexive verbs)

Record your routine for one day. Be sure to say **at what time** you do each activity, and **conjugate** each of the following verbs:

- *ponerse la ropa/ vestirse*
- *lavarse*
- *cepillarse el pelo/los dientes*
- *bañarse/ducharse*
- *despertarse*
- *levantarse*
- *acostarse*
- *dormirse*
- *divertirse*
- *desayunar*
- *almorzar*
- *cenar*
- *ir al trabajo/a la escuela/a la universidad*
- Anything else you do in your day

Por ejemplo: A las siete de la mañana me despierto.

What do you do to stay healthy?
(¿Qué haces para mantenerte saludable?)

Write a brief essay about what you do to stay healthy. You should have 3 paragraphs with the following topics:

Paragraph 1 (6-8 sentences):
- *¿Qué comida saludable comes?*
- *Yo como…*
- *Yo bebo…*
- *Yo debo comer _____ pero no me gusta(n).*
- *¿Por qué?*

Paragraph 2 (6-8 sentences):
- *¿Qué comida basura no comes?*
- *Yo no como mucho…*
- *Yo no bebo mucho…*
- *Yo no debo comer mucho _____ pero me encanta(n).*
- *¿Por qué?*

Paragraph 3 (6-8 sentences):
- *¿Qué tipo de ejercicio haces?*
- *¿Cuándo haces ejercicio?*
- *¿Cuántas veces a la semana haces ejercicio?*
- *¿Por qué?*

Remember to:
- Conjugate verbs correctly in the present tense *yo* form (except for "*me gusta(n)*" and "*me encanta(n)*".
- Use *mucho/a/os/as* for emphasis.
- Make sure adjectives (including "*mucho*") match nouns in gender and quantity.
- Try your best to compose an actual short essay. Don't just list a bunch of foods you eat and don't eat!
- Be descriptive and creative!

Part 11: Commands, Demonstratives & Comparatives/Superlatives

No Nonsense Glossary*

Apple	La manzana

*For instructions on building your No Nonsense Glossary, see pages 9-10.

Lesson 53: Affirmative *Tú* Commands (Imperative Mood)

An Affirmative Command (*una orden afirmativa*) is a way of telling someone to do something. There are different types of commands in Spanish, depending on your relationship to the person to whom you are speaking. If you are speaking to a friend, you would use an informal *tú* commnnd. If you are speaking to your boss or a person to whom you'd like to show respect, you would use a formal *usted* command. If you are speaking to a group of people, you would use an *ustedes* command (in Latin America), or a *vosotros* command (in Spain).

In this lesson, we will focus on affirmative *tú* commands. An affirmative command means you are telling someone to do something. A negative command would be telling someone not to do something.

***Ejemplos*: Pablo, set the table.** – *Pablo, pon la mesa.*
Emiliano, open the door. – *Emiliano, abre la puerta.*

How to form Regular Affirmative *Tú* Commands

Take the "*él/ella*" form of the verb in the present tense.

- ***Habla*** *con tu abuela.* – Talk to your grandmother.
- ***Come*** *más despacio.* – Eat more slowly.
- ***Comparte*** *con tu hermana.* – Share with your sister.

Translate the following commands into *Tú* commands in Spanish.

1) Eat your dinner.

2) Order a large pizza.

3) Help your brother.

4) Play with your cousin.

Common Irregular Affirmative *Tú* Commands

Can you guess which of the following Irregular *Tú* Commands go with which infinitives?

First, match the commands to the correct infinitives.

Then, fill in the English meaning. If you are unfamiliar with any of these verbs, be sure to consult the Most Common Spanish Verbs Reference Chart on pages 280-281, or a dictionary.

English Meaning	Irregular *Tú* Command	Infinitive
	Sé	*Decir*
	Ten	*Hacer*
	Ven	*Ir*
	Ve	*Irse*
	Vete	*Poner*
	Pon	*Salir*
	Haz	*Ser*
	Sal	*Tener*
	Di	*Venir*

Translate the following commands into *Tú* commands in Spanish. If you don't know a word, look it up and be sure to copy over any new words to your Glossary!

1) Go to school.

2) Go out with your friends.

3) Do your homework.

4) Tell the truth.

Lesson 53 Practice: Affirmative *Tú* Commands (Imperative Mood)

Write the following requests as commands, replacing any Direct and Indirect Objects with the appropriate Direct and Indirect Object Pronouns. Attach pronouns to affirmative commands!

As we mentioned with Direct and Indirect Object Pronouns, there are rules the require written accent marks to be places on a certain syllable to maintain the stress in the correct place (i.e. where it naturally falls before the pronouns are attached). You will learn how to do this properly in the next lesson.

For the purposes of this exercise, don't worry about the written accent mark rule. Instead, say the word out loud and place a written accent mark on the syllable that you think should carry the stress. This will let you know whether or not you are able to hear it. If you can't hear it, don't worry. You will learn the rule soon.

Ejemplo: Debes darme el bolígrafo (a mí). <u>Dámelo</u>.

1) Debes darle el coche a tu abuela. _____

2) Debes cocinar la cena para tu madre. _____

3) Debes regalarles las bufandas a los nietos. _____

4) Debes pedirme un taco para mí. _____

5) Debes decirle la verdad al juez. _____

6) Debes ponerte el abrigo. _____

7) Debes <u>tener cuidado (be careful)</u> en las montañas. _____

8) Debes salir con tus amigos esta noche. _____

9) Debes comprar muchos plátanos. _____

10) Debes leerle <u>el cuento de hadas (fairy tale)</u> a tu hija. _____

11) Debes comerte la hamburguesa. _____

12) Debes venir aquí. _____

13) Debes explicarme las noticias (a mí). _____

Lesson 54: When to Write Accents for Affirmative *Tú* Commands

Once we start attaching pronouns to the ends of verbs, there are rules the require written accent marks to be places on a certain syllable to maintain the stress in the correct place (i.e. where it naturally falls before the pronouns are attached).

We are going to practice this rule for with Affirmative *Tú* Commands, but keep in mind that this rule will also apply when attaching pronouns to infinitives, as well as to Affirmative *Usted* Commands.

This rule is only relevant to written Spanish. If you are more focused on speaking and understanding Spanish, then as long as you are able to place the stress on the proper syllable when speaking, you don't need to stress out (no pun intended!) about this rule.

(a) Write the Affirmative *Tú* Command for the following verbs. Don't forget irregulars and stem-changers!

(b) Underline the vowel of the second-to-last syllable in the command verb. Say it out loud to see if you can hear that this is where the stress naturally falls. In the event of a dipthong (two vowels combining to make one sound), underline the vowel with the strongest sound.

(c) Turn any direct/indirect objects into pronouns. Attach them to the command verb. Don't forget to attach reflexive pronouns first! Keep the vowel from step (b) underlined.

(d) Squiggle underline the vowel of the second-to-last syllable in this new command.

(e) If the straight line and the squiggle line are not both under the same vowel/syllable, then write an accent on the vowel with the straight line. Remember, this was where the accent originally fell in the first place! If both lines are under the same vowel/syllable, no accent is needed.

Ejemplo: *Buscar las llaves*
(a) Busca las llaves
(b) Busca las llaves
(c) Buscalas
(d) Buscalas
(e) Búscalas

1) *Dejar los libros*

(a)   (b)

(c)   (d)   (e)

2) *Esperar el autobús*
  (a)　　　　　　　　　　**(b)**
  (c)　　　　　　　　　　**(d)**　　　　　　　　　　**(e)**

3) *Jugar fútbol*
  (a)　　　　　　　　　　**(b)**
  (c)　　　　　　　　　　**(d)**　　　　　　　　　　**(e)**

4) *Olvidarse del problema*
  (a)　　　　　　　　　　**(b)**
  (c)　　　　　　　　　　**(d)**　　　　　　　　　　**(e)**

5) *Encontrar las flores*
  (a)　　　　　　　　　　**(b)**
  (c)　　　　　　　　　　**(d)**　　　　　　　　　　**(e)**

6) *Poner la mesa*
  (a)　　　　　　　　　　**(b)**
  (c)　　　　　　　　　　**(d)**　　　　　　　　　　**(e)**

7) *Conducir el coche*
  (a)　　　　　　　　　　**(b)**
  (c)　　　　　　　　　　**(d)**　　　　　　　　　　**(e)**

8) *Recordar los poemas*
  (a)　　　　　　　　　　**(b)**
  (c)　　　　　　　　　　**(d)**　　　　　　　　　　**(e)**

9) *Hacer la tarea*
  (a)   **(b)**
  (c)   **(d)**   **(e)**

10) *Ponerse el suéter*
  (a)   **(b)**
  (c)   **(d)**   **(e)**

11) *Ayudar al bebé*
  (a)   **(b)**
  (c)   **(d)**   **(e)**

Lesson 55: *Usted, Ustedes* & Negative Commands (Imperative Mood)

Singular *Usted* Commands

Take the *Yo* form of the verb in the present and add the "opposite" third person singular ending. The "opposite" ending means, if you are converting an –ar verb, you would attach the ending for –er/–ir verbs, and if you are converting an –er/–ir verb, you would attach the ending for –ar verbs in the Present Tense.

- *Señor, **hable** con el doctor.* – Sir, talk with the doctor.
- ***Coma** las verduras.* – Eat the vegetables.
- ***Comparta** el agua.* – Share the water.

Note: Pronouns attach to positive commands.

Common Irregular *Usted* Commands

Dar – **dé**   Saber – **sepa**
Estar – **esté**   Ser – **sea**
Ir – **vaya**   Ver – **vea**

Plural *ustedes* Commands

Take the "*yo*" form of the verb in the present and add the "opposite" third person plural ending.

- ***Hablen** con el jefe.* – Talk with the boss.
- ***Coman** todos los postres, por favor.* – Eat all of the desserts, please.
- *Estudiantes, **compartan** los libros.* – Students, share the books.

Negative Commands

Always make sure you have a **no** in front of the verb. This is what makes it negative.

Usted: Just add no!
Tú: If you already know your *Usted* commands, add an –s to the end of the negative formal command.

- *No **hables** en el cine.* – Don't talk in the movie theatre.
- *No **comas** el pastel.* – Don't eat the cake.
- *¡No **compartas** la pizza!* – Don't share the pizza!

Note: pronouns do NOT attach to negative commands. Instead, place them before the verb.

Examples of Regular Negative Commands

Infinitive	Formal Negative Command	Informal Negative Command	Uds. Negative Command
hablar	no habl**e**	no habl**es**	no habl**en**
comer	no com**a**	no com**as**	no com**an**
compartir	no compart**a**	no compart**as**	no compart**an**

Examples of Common Positive Commands (with attached pronouns)

When you are just starting out, commands can be difficult to compute in your head. It can be very helpful to memorize these commands as if they were vocabulary terms. That way, you won't have to think about them, and you will be ready when you need them!

Infinitive	*Tú*	*Usted*	*Ustedes*	Meaning
Callarse	Cállate	Cállese	Cállense	Be quiet
Dar	Dámelo	Démelo	Dénmelo	Give it to me
Decir	Dime	Dígame	Díganme	Tell me
Esperar	Espera	Espere	Esperen	Wait
Irse	Vete	Váyase	Váyanse	Go / Get out of here
Llamar	Llámame	Llámeme	Llámenme	Call me
Mandar	Mándame un mensaje	Mándeme un mensaje	Mándenme un mensaje	Send me a text
Pasar	Pasa	Pase	Pasen	Come in / Go ahead
Perdonar	Perdóname	Perdóneme	Perdónenme	Excuse me/ Sorry
Sentarse	Siéntate	Siéntese	Siéntense	Sit down / Be seated
Venir aquí	Ven aquí	Venga aquí	Vengan aquí	Come here

Examples of Common Negative Commands (pronouns before verb)

Infinitive	*Tú*	*Usted*	*Ustedes*	Meaning
Decir	No me digas	No me diga	No me digan	Don't tell me / You don't say
Olvidarse	No te olvides	No se olvide	No se olviden	Don't forget
Hacer	No lo hagas	No lo haga	No lo hagan	Don't do it!

Lesson 55 Practice: *Usted & Ustedes* Commands (Imperative Mood)

Practicar con las ordenes

A) Write the following requests as commands, replacing any Direct and Indirect Objects with the appropriate Direct and Indirect Object Pronouns. Remember to attach pronouns to affirmative commands!

B) Rewrite all commands as negative. Do not attach pronouns to negative commands!

C) Translate the sentences into English. If you don't know a word, look it up and be sure to copy over any new words to your Glossary.

Ejemplo: *Usted debe dar el bolígrafo a mí.* **(A)** Démelo. **(B)** No me lo dé.
(C) You should give me the pen./ Give me it./ Don't give me it.

Usted Commands

1) *Usted debe escribir el cuento para sus hijos.* **(A)** _____ **(B)** _____
(C)

2) *Usted debe cantar más.* **(A)** _____ **(B)** _____
(C)

3) *Usted debe comerse todo el flan.* **(A)** _____ **(B)** _____
(C)

4) *Usted debe ahorrar dinero.* **(A)** _____ **(B)** _____
(C)

5) *Usted debe esperar el autobús.* **(A)** _____ **(B)** _____
(C)

6) *Usted debe pagar la cuenta para nosotros.* **(A)** _____ **(B)** _____
(C)

7) *Usted debe comprar el suéter para su esposa.* **(A)** _____ **(B)** _____
(C)

8) *Usted debe ver el partido de fútbol americano de los Broncos de Denver.* **(A)** _____
(B) _____ **(C)**

Ustedes Commands

9) *Ustedes deben decírmelo (a mí).* **(A)** _____ **(B)** _____
(C)

10) *Ustedes deben salir de aquí.* **(A)** _____ **(B)** _____
(C)

11) *Ustedes deben tener cuidado.* **(A)** _____ **(B)** _____
(C)

12) *Ustedes deben ponerse las botas.* **(A)** _____ **(B)** _____
(C)

13) *Ustedes deben llevar un paraguas.* **(A)** _____ **(B)** _____
(C)

14) *Ustedes deben venir al congreso.* **(A)** _____ **(B)** _____
(C)

15) *Ustedes deben traer comida.* **(A)** _____ **(B)** _____
(C)

Lesson 56: Demonstratives

Adjectives (describe a noun):

This	**That**	**That over there**
Este	*Ese*	*Aquel*
Esta	*Esa*	*Aquella*
These	**Those**	**Those over there**
Estos	*Esos*	*Aquellos*
Estas	*Esas*	*Aquellas*

Pronouns (replace a noun)*:
*If there's no noun present, add an accent!

This	**That**	**That over there**
Éste	*Ése*	*Aquél*
Ésta	*Ésa*	*Aquélla*
These	**Those**	**Those over there**
Éstos	*Ésos*	*Aquéllos*
Éstas	*Ésas*	*Aquéllas*

Translate these sentences into Spanish.

1) These flowers are white, but those are blue.

2) Last year I went to this airport, but this year I'm going to that airport over there.

3) This painting is for that girl, but that painting is for this girl.

4) Those lakes over there are big, but these ones near this house are small.

5) This bacon is delicious, and that bacon is ok, but that one over there is disgusting!

6) Create your own. Use the sentences above as your guide.

Lesson 56 Practice: Demonstratives

Translate these sentences into Spanish. **Don't forget** to match adjectives to nouns (masculine/feminine and singular/plural)!

Ejemplos: I like this bicycle, but I don't like that bicycle.
　　　　　Me gusta esta bicicleta, pero no me gusta esa bicicleta.

　　　　　I like this bicycle, but I don't like that one.
　　　　　Me gusta esta bicicleta, pero no me gusta ésa.

1) I like this book, but I don't like that book.

2) I like this book, but I don't like that one.

3) I like this book, but I don't like that one over there.

4) This restaurant is good, but that restaurant is excellent.

5) This restaurant is good, but that one is excellent.

6) I eat this cheese, but I don't eat that cheese over there!

7) I eat this cheese, but I don't eat that one over there!

8) These pants are better than those pants.

9) These pants are better than those ones.

10) Those cakes are better than these cakes.

11) Those cakes are better than these ones.

12) That girl is older than these girls.

13) These beaches are more beautiful than those over there.

14) This apple juice is colder than that apple juice.

15) These sweaters are bigger than those ones.

16) This banana is more yellow than those ones over there.

17) This wine is older than those wines.

18) I like these shoes more than those ones.

19) I go to this mall a lot, but I never go to that one over there.

20) Which soup do you like better, this one or that one?

Lesson 57: Comparatives and Superlatives

A <u>**comparative**</u> is when there are two or more things that you are comparing.

Ejemplos:
- *El tocino es **mejor** que el jamón.* – Bacon is **better** than ham.
- *Colorado es **más grande** que Rhode Island.* – Colorado is **larger** than Rhode Island.

Mejor que – better than
Peor que – worse than
Mayor que – older than (for people)
Menor que – younger than (for people)
Más + [adjective] que – more _____ than (*más guapo que* – more handsome than)
Menos + [adjective] que – less _____ than (*menos caro que* – less expensive than)

A <u>**superlative**</u> is when something is the most extreme in a group.

Ejemplos:
- *Catalina es mi **mejor** amiga del mundo.* – Catalina in my **best** friend in the world.
- ***El gato más gordo** del mundo se llama Pepino.* – **The fattest cat** in the world is named Pepino.

Lo mejor – the best in general (**not** followed by a noun)
Lo peor – the worst in general (**not** followed by a noun)
El/la mejor – the best something (followed by a noun)
El/la peor – the worst something (followed by a noun)
El/la mayor – the oldest (for people)
El/la menor – the youngest (for people)
El/la [noun] más + [adjective] – the most _____ [noun]
El/la [noun] menos + [adjective] – the least _____ [noun]

Exercise

Fill in the blank with the appropriate word. For many questions, there may be more than one answer. Then translate these sentences into English.

1) *Juan tiene 27 años y José tiene 35 años. Juan es _____ que José. José es _____ que Juan.*

2) ¡Esta ensalada está deliciosa! Está _____ que la ensalada fea que comí ayer.

3) Mi novia es _____ bonita que todas las estrellas del cine.

4) Me encanta ganar el partido. ¡Es _____ (the best)!

5) La tortuga _____ (oldest) del mundo tiene 170 años.

6) Este queso es _____ (worse) que el queso de anoche.

7) ¿Quién es el actor más famoso del mundo? Brad Pitt es _____. Él es _____ que Tom Cruise.

8) Los perros son _____ que los gatos.

9) Las zanahorias son _____ que las papas fritas.

10) Mi hermano _____ tiene 5 años.

11) ¿Quién tiene el pelo _____ largo, Rosita o Melinda? Definitivamente, Rosita. El pelo de Melinda es _____ que el pelo de Rosita.

12) El Río de la Plata es el río _____ ancho del mundo. Es _____ que el Río de Colorado. (El Río de la Plata se ubica entre Uruguay y Argentina.)

13) En un restaurante: ¿Cuál es _____ (better), el pescado o el pollo? Camarero: El pescado, por supuesto. ¡El pescado es _____ (the best) platillo de todo el restaurante!

14) *No me gusta perder el celular. ¡Es _____ (the worst)!*

15) *En el verano, hace _____ que en el invierno.*

16) *El doctor gana _____ (more money) que la recepcionista.*

17) *El café tiene _____ cafeína que el té.*

18) *El _____ restaurante del mundo es _____.*

19) *La _____ película del mundo es _____.*

Part 11 Quiz

Translate the following sentences into Spanish.

1) These apples are green, but those apples are red.

1a) These apples are green, but those are red.

2) This evening, I'm going to this restaurant, but tomorrow I'm going to that restaurant over there.

2a) This evening, I am going to this restaurant, but tomorrow I'm going to that one over there.

3) This pizza is for that girl, but that pizza is for this girl.

3a) This pizza is for that girl, but that one is for this girl.

4) Those lakes are big, but these lakes near this house are small.

4a) Those lakes are big, but these ones near this house are small.

5) This bacon is delicious, and that bacon is ok, but that one over there is disgusting!

6) Give me the pen! Give me it! (Affirmative *tú* Command)

7) Write me a letter! Write me it! (Affirmative *tú* Command)

8) Sing her a song! Sing her it! (Affirmative *tú* Command)

Part 11 Take-it-Apart Grammar
(for Reading Comprehension)

Take-It-Apart Grammar sections teach you to deconstruct sentences into their grammatical components, thereby improving comprehension and minimizing guessing.

For detailed instructions, refer to page 176. Don't forget about the Pronoun Possibilities Reference Chart on page 177!

1) *Lo puse en mi mochila.*

Conjugated verb	
Ending	
Infinitive	
Tense	
Subject	
English meaning	

Direct Object/Indirect Object/Reflexive Pronouns: _____

Question or statement? _____   Question word: _____

Translation: _____

Rewrite in the Simple Future. _____

New Translation: _____

2) *Manuel no recuerda el nombre del restaurante. No lo recuerda.*

Conjugated verb		
Ending		
Infinitive		
Tense		
Subject		
English meaning		

Direct Object/Indirect Object/Reflexive Pronouns: _____

Question or statement? _____   Question word: _____

Translation: _____

Rewrite in the Preterite. _____

New Translation: _____

3) *Vinieron a la fiesta en un coche antiguo.*

Conjugated verb	
Ending	
Infinitive	
Tense	
Subject	
English meaning	

Direct Object/Indirect Object/Reflexive Pronouns: _____

Question or statement? _____   Question word: _____

Translation: _____

Rewrite in the Simple Future. _____

New Translation: _____

4) *¿Dónde puse el ensayo que escribí ayer?*

Conjugated verb		
Ending		
Infinitive		
Tense		
Subject		
English meaning		

Direct Object/Indirect Object/Reflexive Pronouns: _____

Question or statement? _____   Question word: _____

Translation: _____

Rewrite in the Simple Future. _____

New Translation: _____

5) *Buscaron la canoa en el río, pero no la encontraron.*

Conjugated verb		
Ending		
Infinitive		
Tense		
Subject		
English meaning		

Direct Object/Indirect Object/Reflexive Pronouns: _____

Question or statement? _____   Question word: _____

Translation: _____

Rewrite in the Present. _____

New Translation: _____

6) *¿Quién te encontró escondida detrás del árbol?*

Conjugated verb	
Ending	
Infinitive	
Tense	
Subject	
English meaning	

Direct Object/Indirect Object/Reflexive Pronouns: _____

Question or statement? _____   Question word: _____

Translation: _____

Rewrite in the Simple Future. _____

New Translation: _____

7) *Fueron a buscarlo en el centro comercial.*

Conjugated verb	
Ending	
Infinitive	
Tense	
Subject	
English meaning	

Direct Object/Indirect Object/Reflexive Pronouns: _____

Question or statement? _____   Question word: _____

Translation: _____

Rewrite in the Present. _____

New Translation: _____

8) ¿Quién le dio un dólar?

Conjugated verb	
Ending	
Infinitive	
Tense	
Subject	
English meaning	

Direct Object/Indirect Object/Reflexive Pronouns: _____

Question or statement? _____   Question word: _____

Translation: _____

Rewrite in the Simple Future. _____

New Translation: _____

Part 11 Writing Activities

Which one needs a written accent?

a) Write the missing singular or plural noun/adjective.
b) Underline the second-to-last syllable for each word.
c) Say the words out loud and decide where the accent falls.
d) If the accent falls on the syllable that is underlined, you do not need to write an accent mark.
e) If the accent falls on a different syllable, write an accent mark on that syllable.
f) Fill in the English meaning. If you're not sure, look it up.

	Singular	Plural	English meaning
1)	*frances*		
2)	*francesa*		
3)		*naciones*	
4)		*japoneses*	
5)		*irlandesas*	
6)	*estacion*		
7)	*ingles*		
8)		*tailandesas*	
9)	*holandesa*		

College Roommate Skit (reflexive verbs)

One of you will be head of a college dorm (*el dueño/la dueña de la residencia*). The other will be an incoming freshman. The dorm head is conducting interviews to match up roommates. The dorm head will ask questions about the student's daily schedule, lifestyle habits and hobbies, to find out which students would make good roommates.

You will conduct a total of **4 short interviews** and decide which pairs should go together.

Include the following:
- Reflexive verbs to talk about daily schedule
    - *¿A qué hora te levantas?*
    - *Yo me levanto a las 10:00 de la mañana.*
- *Te gusta/me gusta* to talk about preferences and hobbies

Be creative in writing different personalities for the students! Be sure to decide which students you will pair together.

Palabras útiles (useful words)

Temprano – early
Tarde – late
El ruido – noise
Estudiar – to study

Tener fiestas – to have parties
Tomar alcohol – to drink alcohol
Fumar – to smoke
Novio/novia – boyfriend/girlfriend

Part 12: Imperfect, Progressive, Perfect & Future Tenses

No Nonsense Glossary*

Apple	La manzana

*For instructions on building your No Nonsense Glossary, see pages 9-10.

Lesson 58: Imperfect Tense

Imperfect Tense Verb Endings for Regular Verbs

To conjugate a verb, take the infinitive (the form of the verb ending in –ar, –er or –ir). Remove the –ar, –er or –ir ending and add the appropriate ending listed below.

–ar verbs
(Shown with the verb *hablar* – to speak)

Yo	**habl*aba***	Nosotros	**habl*ábamos***
Tú	**habl*abas***	Vosotros	**habl*abais***
Usted	**habl*aba***	Ustedes	**habl*aban***
Él / Ella	**habl*aba***	Ellos / Ellas	**habl*aban***

–er/–ir verbs
(Shown with the verb *comer* – to eat)

Yo	**com*ía***	Nosotros	**com*íamos***
Tú	**com*ías***	Vosotros	**com*íais***
Usted	**com*ía***	Ustedes	**com*ían***
Él / Ella	**com*ía***	Ellos / Ellas	**com*ían***

Uses for the Imperfect (*el imperfecto*)

- **Actions that do not have a definite beginning or end, or are repeated habitually (generally translated as "used to" in English)**
  Comíamos juntos todos los días. – We used to eat together everyday.

- **To "set the stage" for another action that interrupts the first**
  Mientras dormía, sonó el teléfono. – While I was sleeping, the phone rang.
  Note: The interrupting verb (*sonó*) is in the Preterite because it had a definitive start and end.

- **Telling time in the past**
  Eran las ocho de la noche. – It was 8:00 p.m.

- **Talking about one's age in the past**
  ¿Cuántos años tenías en junio del año pasado? – How old were you in June of last year?

- **Talking about childhood or a past era in one's life**
  Cuando era niña vivía en España. – When I was a girl, I used to live in Spain.
  Cuando era joven jugaba en el parque todos los domingos. – When I was young, I used to play in the park every Sunday.

Common Irregular Verbs in the Imperfect Tense

Ser – to be (permanent)

Yo	**era**	Nosotros	**éramos**
Tú	**eras**	Vosotros	erais
Usted	**era**	Ustedes	**eran**
Él / Ella	**era**	Ellos / Ellas	**eran**

Ir – to go

Yo	**iba**	Nosotros	**íbamos**
Tú	**ibas**	Vosotros	ibais
Usted	**iba**	Ustedes	**iban**
Él / Ella	**iba**	Ellos / Ellas	**iban**

Ver – to see

Yo	**veía**	Nosotros	**veíamos**
Tú	**veías**	Vosotros	veíais
Usted	**veía**	Ustedes	**veían**
Él / Ella	**veía**	Ellos / Ellas	**veían**

Lesson 58 Practice: Imperfect Tense

Fill in the blank with the correct conjugation of the verbs in parentheses in the Imperfect Tense. Then, translate the sentences into English.

1) *Cuando Alicia era niña, _____ (comer) muchas verduras.*

2) *Mientras nosotros _____ (nadar) en el océano, ¡nos robaron el dinero!*

3) *Cuando finalmente me dormí, _____ (ser) las 2:00 de la mañana.*

4) *Antes de mudarte aquí, _____ (vivir) en México.*

5) *¿Cuántos años _____ (tener) ustedes cuando empezaron a leer?*

Translate these sentences into Spanish. Pay attention to which verbs should be in the Imperfect Tense and which should be in the Preterite Tense.

6) When I was a girl, I used to play with my friends after school.

7) It was 6:00 p.m. when we started watching the movie.

8) It was raining when Jimena left the mall.

9) When Paola was young, she used to eat a lot of chocolate.

10) Silvia was three years old when her younger brother was born.
    (to be born – *nacer*)

Lesson 59: Present Progressive Tense

Estar in the present   **+**   **Gerund (-ing)**

Yo	estoy	Nosotros	estamos
Tú	estás	Vosotros	estáis
Usted	está	Ustedes	están
Él / Ella	está	Ellos / Ellas	están

Yo estoy   **+**   *cocinando*
(I am)   (cooking)

Tú estás   **+**   *comiendo*
(You are)   (eating)

Él está   **+**   *escuchando*
(He is)   (listening)

Uses of the Present Progressive Tense (*el presente progresivo*)

To emphasize that something is in the process of happening.

- ¿Qué **estás haciendo**? – What **are you doing**?
- **Estoy cocinando**. – I am cooking.
- **Estás comiendo** una hamburguesa. – I **am eating** a hamburger.
- Él **está escuchando** música. – He **is listening** to music.

Lesson 59 Practice: Present Progressive

(A) Draw a square around the subject, and underline the object (if there is one) of the sentence.

(B) Then translate the sentence into Spanish. The Spanish infinitives have been provided for you, but don't forget to conjugate them correctly.

(C) *Star the sentences that do not use the Present Progressive.

Ejemplo: I am watching a movie. (*ver*)
　　　　　　Yo estoy viendo una película.

1) He is writing a letter. (*escribir*)

2) Y'all are eating bananas. (*comer*)

3) You are dancing salsa. (*bailar*)

4) The car is red. (*ser*)

5) The kids are sleeping. (*dormir*)

6) We are working. (*trabajar*)

7) He is stealing your backpack. (*robar*)

8) Are you happy today? (*estar*)

9) Why is he playing with his food? (*jugar*)

10) Where is the dictionary? (*estar*)

11) We are waiting for the bus. (*esperar*)

Lesson 60: Practice with Present Progressive

Las mamás y los hijos

Respond to the following questions a mother might ask her son/daughter, using a complete sentence in Spanish with the present progressive tense (*estar* + *-ando/-iendo*). You may use phrases from the word bank, or invent your own response.

Ejemplos: *¿Por qué no juegas con tu hermana?*
Why don't you play with your sister?

No quiero jugar con mi hermana, porque estoy mandando mensajes de texto con mi novio.
I don't want to play with my sister, because I'm texting with my boyfriend.

Word bank: *dormir una siesta, pintarse las uñas, masticar chicle, ver la tele, hablar por teléfono, leer un buen libro, escuchar música con audífonos, ver videos en YouTube, cantar en la ducha, comer una hamburguesa, bailar en el jardín, jugar videojuegos*

1) *¿Por qué no me hablas?*

2) *¿Por qué no me escuchas?*

3) *¿Por qué no te comes las verduras?*

4) *¿Qué haces en el sofá?*

5) *¿Por qué no haces la tarea?*

6) *¿Por qué no contestas al teléfono?*

7) *¿Por qué no sacas la basura?*

8) *¿Por qué no pones la mesa?*

9) *¿Por qué no le llamas a tu abuelita?*

10) *¿Por qué no estudias español?*

Lesson 60 Practice: Reflexive Verbs in Present Progressive

Translate these sentences into Spanish. Pay attention to which verbs are reflexive and will require a reflexive pronoun.

1) I am washing the car.

2) The boy is taking a bath.

3) María is going to bed.

4) The kids are waking up.

5) My younger sister is bathing the dog.

6) Y'all are brushing your teeth.

7) The dancers are getting dressed.

8) You are taking a shower.

9) We are sitting down.

10) The mother is dressing the baby.

Lesson 61: Past Progressive Tense

Estar in the imperfect + **Gerund (-ing)**

Yo	estaba	Nosotros	estábamos
Tú	estabas	Vosotros	estábais
Usted	estaba	Ustedes	estaban
Él / Ella	estaba	Ellos / Ellas	estaban

Yo estaba + **cocinando**
(I was) (cooking)

Tú estabas + **comiendo**
(You were) (eating)

Él estaba + **escuchando**
(He was (listening)

Uses of the Past Progressive Tense (*el pasado progresivo*)

To emphasize that something was in the process of happening.

- *¿Qué **estabas haciendo** ayer por la tarde?* – What **were you doing** yesterday afternoon?
- ***Estaba comiendo** tacos en casa.* – **I was eating** tacos at home.

To use with an interruptor.

- *¿Por qué no contestaste el teléfono cuando te llamé?* – Why didn't you answer the phone when I called you?
- *No contesté el teléfono porque **estaba viendo** la Copa Mundial cuando me llamaste.* – I didn't answer the phone, because **I was watching** the World Cup when you called me.

Note: It is also possible to use the Imperfect, instead of the Past Progressive, but the Past Progressive emphasizes that the action was in the process of taking place.

Lesson 61 Practice: Past Progressive & Preterite Tenses

Fill in the blank with the correct conjugation of the verbs in parentheses in the Past Progressive or Preterite Tenses. Then, translate the sentences into English.

1) **Fernando**: Te vi en la joyería ayer. ¿Qué _____? (estar + hacer)

   José: ¡(Yo) _____ (estar + comprar) un anillo para mi novia!

2) Mientras (while) (tú) _____ (estar + dormir) una siesta, esta carta _____ (llegar) por correo.

3) **María**: ¿Por qué (tú) no me _____ (estar + escuchar)?

   Nacho: Porque (yo) _____ (estar + ver) la tele.

4) Mientras el gato _____ (estar + buscar) ratones, el perro _____ (comer) todo el atún.

5) Mientras nosotros _____ (estar + charlar) en la bodega, el ladrón _____ (robar) tu coche.

6) **Mamá**: Si (tú) no _____ (estar + hacer) la tarea cuando la computadora _____ (descomponerse), entonces ¿qué _____ (estar + hacer)?

   Hijo: (Yo) _____ (estar + jugar) videojuegos.

7) **Enrique**: ¿Qué película _____ (estar + ver) ustedes cuando tu novia te _____ (besar).

   Miguel: (Nosotros) _____ (estar + ver) El Señor de los Anillos.

Lesson 62: Present Perfect Tense

The Present Perfect Tense (*el pretérito perfecto*) describes what a person **has** done, but notice that **tener** is not used, even though it means **to have**. It is formed by combining **haber** (conjugated in the Present) and the past participle.

Present Perfect Formula
[*haber* in present tense] + [past participle]

Yo	**he**	Nosotros	**hemos**
Tú	**has**	Vosotros	habéis
Usted	**ha**	Ustedes	**han**
Él Ella	**ha**	Ellos Ellas	**han**

Past Participles

-ar verbs: –ado
- *hablar: hablado* (talked/ spoken)

-er/-ir verbs: –ido
- *comer: comido* (eaten)
- *vivir: vivido* (lived)

Por ejemplos:
- <u>He</u> **visitado** *el Museo del Prado.* – I have visited the Prado Museum.
- <u>Has</u> **ido** *a Caracas, Venezuela.* – You have gone to Caracas, Venezuela.
- *Usted le* <u>ha</u> **escrito** *una carta a su madre.* – You have written a letter to your mother.
- *Él* <u>ha</u> **dormido** *7 horas.* – He has slept 7 hours.
- *¡Ustedes dos* <u>han</u> **causado** *un desastre en la cocina!* – You two have caused a disaster in the kitchen!

The auxilary verb (*haber*) and the past participle should not be separated. Object pronouns go immediately before *haber*.

- *¿Las* <u>has</u> **visto**? – <u>Have</u> you **seen** them?
- *Se lo* <u>he</u> **regalado**. – I <u>have</u> **gifted** it to her.

Irregular past participles for common Spanish verbs

Can you guess which of the following Irregular past participles go with which infinitives?

First, match the past participles to the correct infinitives.

Then, fill in the English meaning. If you are unfamiliar with any of these verbs, be sure to consult the Most Common Spanish Verbs Reference Chart on pages 280-281, or a dictionary.

English Meaning of Past Participle	Irregular *Tú* Command	Infinitive
	escrito	*Abrir*
	frito	*Cubrir*
	resuelto	*Decir*
	abierto	*Escribir*
	roto	*Freír*
	cubierto	*Hacer*
	vuelto	*Morir*
	muerto	*Poner*
	visto	*Resvolver*
	puesto	*Romper*
	dicho	*Ver*
	hecho	*Volver*

Lesson 62 Practice: Present Perfect

Respond to the following questions using complete sentences in Spanish.

1) ¿Has leído los libros de Harry Potter?

2) ¿Has cenado en un restaurant italiano?

3) ¿Has ido a París?

4) ¿Has visto las películas el Señor de los Anillos?

Translate these sentences into Spanish.

5) Stefanie has studied English for 15 years.

6) Y'all have read many books, but you haven't seen many movies.

7) The kids have already set the table.

8) We haven't arrived at the Costa del Sol yet.

9) Who has tried this delicious chocolate cake?

10) Why haven't you written your essay?

Lesson 63: Past Perfect Tense

The Past Perfect Tense, also called the Pluperfect (*el pluscuamperfecto*) describes what a person **had** done before something else that occurred in the past. It is formed by combining **haber** (conjugated in the Imperfect) and the past participle.

Past Perfect Formula
[*haber* in imperfect tense] + [past participle]

Yo	**había**	*Nosotros*	**habíamos**
Tú	**habías**	*Vosotros*	*habíais*
Usted	**había**	*Ustedes*	**habían**
Él *Ella*	**había**	*Ellos* *Ellas*	**habían**

Past Participles

-ar verbs: -ado
- *hablar: hablado* (talked/spoken)

-er/-ir verbs: -ido
- *comer: comido* (eaten)
- *vivir: vivido* (lived)

Por ejemplos:
- *Los niños habían desayunado antes de llegar a la escuela.* – The kids <u>had</u> **eaten** breakfast before arriving at school.
    - **Note:** Use the infinitive directly after *antes de* (before) or *después de* (after)
- *Ya habías vuelto a casa cuando empezó a llover.* – You had already gone home when it started to rain.
    - **Note:** The word *ya* (already) is often used with the Past Perfect Tense.

Just as with the Present Perfect Tense, the auxilary verb (*haber*) and the past participle should not be separated. Object pronouns go immediately before *haber*.

- *Se lo había regalado.* – I <u>had</u> **gifted** it to her.

Lesson 63 Practice: Present Perfect & Past Perfect

Translate these sentences into Spanish. If you don't know a word, look it up and be sure to copy over any new words to your Glossary!

Present Perfect

1) You have won many prizes at this event.

2) She has traveled to Barcelona many times.

3) They have already set the tables for the wedding.

4) Have you already called the hotel to make a reservation?

5) Have you seen the movie "Los Piratas del Caribe?"

Past Perfect

6) I had eaten six tacos before dinner.

7) You had gone swimming before the storm.

8) They had studied a lot before the exam.

9) We had already seen 14 dogs at the show when the horses arrived.

10) You guys had traveled through 11 countries before staying in Italy.

Lesson 64: Future Tense

The Future Tense (*el futuro*) describes things that **will** happen in the future. Using the Future Tense in Spanish sounds more formal than the Simple Future (*ir + a* + infinitive).

Future Tense Endings for Regular Verbs

For all regular verbs, take the infinitive and add the following endings.
Shown with the verb *hablar* (to speak).

Yo	hablar**é**	Nosotros	hablar**emos**
Tú	hablar**ás**	Vosotros	hablar**éis**
Usted	hablar**á**	Ustedes	hablar**án**
Él / Ella	hablar**á**	Ellos / Ellas	hablar**án**

Common Future Tense Verbs with Irregular Stems

For all irregular verbs, take the irregular stem and add the following endings.
Shown with the verb *decir* (to say/tell).

Yo	dir**é**	Nosotros	dir**emos**
Tú	dir**ás**	Vosotros	dir**éis**
Usted	dir**á**	Ustedes	dir**án**
Él / Ella	dir**á**	Ellos / Ellas	dir**án**

Decir – <u>dir</u> (to say/tell)
Haber – <u>habr</u> (to have, auxiliary verb)
Hacer – <u>har</u> (to do/make)
Ir – <u>ir</u> (to go)
Poder – <u>pod</u> (to be able to)
Poner – <u>pond</u> (to put/set)
Querer – <u>querr</u> (to want/love)
Saber – <u>sabr</u> (to know)
Salir – <u>saldr</u> (to go out)
Tener – <u>tendr</u> (to have)
Valer – <u>valdr</u> (to be worth)
Venir – <u>vendr</u> (to come)

Ejemplos

- *Yo haré la cena esta noche.* – I will make dinner tonight.
- *Tú irás al aeropuerto a las 4:30 de la mañana.* – You will go to the airport at 4:30 a.m.

Lesson 64 Practice: Future Tense

Translate these sentences into Spanish.

1) The plane will leave at 7:45 p.m.

2) The boys will spend (*pasar*) the summer with their grandmother on the island.

3) You will tell the truth at trial.

4) Silvina will be able to help you.

5) We will have to make plans to visit y'all next Christmas.

6) The students will read a lot before the exam.

7) My boyfriend will come visit me at college.

8) We will eat all of the ice cream!

9) I will go out to eat tomorrow night.

10) The blizzard will start at midnight.

Part 12 Quiz

Translate these sentences into Spanish. Be careful to choose the correct verb tense.

1) When I was a boy, I used to eat ham and cheese sandwiches for lunch.

2) It will snow in the mountains tomorrow.

3) Y'all are eating fried chicken.

4) It was 7:15 a.m. when Amelia woke up.

5) Jack has studied Spanish for four years.

6) Laura had danced salsa before, but she had never danced tango.

7) While Luisa was sleeping, her phone rang.

8) Reinaldo has never gone to Egypt.

9) Micaela will write a letter to her friend Sara in London.

10) While we were hiking, it started raining.

Part 12 Take-it-Apart Grammar
(for Reading Comprehension)

Take-It-Apart Grammar sections teach you to deconstruct sentences into their grammatical components, thereby improving comprehension and minimizing guessing. **For detailed instructions, refer to page 176. Don't forget about the Pronoun Possibilities Reference Chart on page 177!**

Note for Compound Verbs: Write the *haber* + participle in the box. Write the ending for *haber*, since the auxiliary verb *haber* is the one that is conjugated. Write the infinitive and English meaning of the participle, since *haber* will be the same for every verb in a perfect tense.

Ejemplo: *He bebido tanto café que ahora no puedo dormir.*

Conjugated verb	he bebido	puedo
Ending	-e	-o
Infinitive	beber	poder
Tense	present perfect	poder
Subject	yo	yo
English meaning	to drink	to be able to

Direct Object/Indirect Object/Reflexive Pronouns: None

Question or statement? statement   Question word: N/A

Translation: I've drunk so much coffee that now I can't sleep.

1) *He buscado la blusa en el armario, pero no la he encontrado.*

Conjugated verb		
Ending		
Infinitive		
Tense		
Subject		
English meaning		

Direct Object/Indirect Object/Reflexive Pronouns: _____

Question or statement? _____   Question word: _____

Translation: _____

Rewrite in the Present. _____

New Translation: _____

2) ¿Cuándo te lo van a pagar?

Conjugated verb	
Ending	
Infinitive	
Tense	
Subject	
English meaning	

Direct Object/Indirect Object/Reflexive Pronouns: _____

Question or statement? _____ Question word: _____

Translation: _____

Rewrite in the Preterite. _____

New Translation: _____

3) Si no la escribiste, entonces ¿quién la escribió?

Conjugated verb		
Ending		
Infinitive		
Tense		
Subject		
English meaning		

Direct Object/Indirect Object/Reflexive Pronouns: _____

Question or statement? _____ Question word: _____

Translation: _____

Rewrite in the Imperfect. _____

New Translation: _____

4) *Vi que trajiste mucha comida para el almuerzo. ¿Ya te la comiste?*

Conjugated verb			
Ending			
Infinitive			
Tense			
Subject			
English meaning			

Direct Object/Indirect Object/Reflexive Pronouns: _____

Question or statement? _____ Question word: _____

Translation: _____

Rewrite in the Present/Simple Future. _____

New Translation: _____

5) *¿Cómo son tus hábitos alimenticios hoy en día? Me dijiste que comías mucha comida basura cuando eras niño.*

Conjugated verb				
Ending				
Infinitive				
Tense				
Subject				
English meaning				

Direct Object/Indirect Object/Reflexive Pronouns: _____

Question or statement? _____ Question word: _____

Translation: _____

6) *¿Viste el espectáculo anoche? Recibió unas reseñas fabulosas en el periódico.*

Conjugated verb		
Ending		
Infinitive		
Tense		
Subject		
English meaning		

Direct Object/Indirect Object/Reflexive Pronouns: _____

Question or statement? _____   Question word: _____

Translation: _____

Rewrite in the Present Perfect. _____

New Translation: _____

7) *La profesora me dio un 100% en mi examen de español. ¡Mis padres no me lo van a creer!*

Conjugated verb		
Ending		
Infinitive		
Tense		
Subject		
English meaning		

Direct Object/Indirect Object/Reflexive Pronouns: _____

Question or statement? _____   Question word: _____

Translation: _____

Rewrite in the Simple Future. _____

New Translation: _____

Part 12 Writing Activities

My childhood (*Mi infancia*)

Escribe un ensayo sobre tu niñez. Escribe 15-20 oraciones. Usa el imperfecto para hablar sobre tu vida cuando eras pequeño(a).

Frases útiles:
Cuando era niño/a...
Cuando era joven...
Cuando tenía ___ años...

Algunas ideas:
¿Dónde vivías?
¿A qué escuela asistías?
¿Quién era tu mejor amigo?
¿A dónde ibas para divertirte?
¿Qué jugabas?
¿Qué hacía tu familia?
¿Qué te gustaba hacer? **Remember**: *gustaba* matches the object, not the subject!
¿Cómo eras? (alto, bajo, gordo, flaco, amigable, sociable, estudioso, travieso...)

Going out to Eat Skit

Part I

Work together to create a menu for your very own restaurant. Be sure to include names and descriptions of menu items, as well as prices.

Include the following topics:

- *Los Aperitivos*
- *Los Platos Principales*
- *Las Bebidas*
- *Los Postres*
- Don't forget to name your restaurant!

Part II

One of you will be the waiter, and the other will be the guest. Create a skit in which the waiter greets the guest and asks what they would like to order.

The guest will ask various questions before ordering, inquiring about menu items and cost.

Skit should be at least 5 minutes long.

Include a discussion of the following topics:

- What they should order if they are very hungry, not very hungry or thirsty
- How much the dishes cost
- Order a meal and drink
- Ask for silverware
- Report how the food is once it arrives
- Ask for the check
- Waiter tells the guest the amount verbally, and they discuss payment options

Part 13: Why Am I So Confused? – Confusing Little Words

No Nonsense Glossary*

Apple	La manzana

*For instructions on building your No Nonsense Glossary, see pages 9-10.

Lesson 65: *Por & Para*

These two Spanish prepositions have many uses and can be confusing for speakers of English. Since there are more uses for *por* overall, we suggest starting out by memorizing the main uses of *para* and using using *por* for everything else. The more you expose yourself to Spanish, the more more natural the distinction between the two will become. Here are some of the main uses of both, to get you started. There are more, but use this as a springboard.

Main Uses of *Por*	Main Uses of *Para*
1) To say "thank you" or "I'm sorry": *Gracias por escucharme.* – Thanks for listening to me. *Lo siento/perdón por gritar.* – I'm sorry for shouting.	**1) Purpose or use of something:** *Esta bolsita es para el sándwich.* – This baggie is for the sandwich.
2) Speed/ frequency: *Mi abuelo va al cine 2 veces por semana.* – My grandfather goes to the movies 2 times per/twice a week. *80 kilómetros por hora.* – 80 km per hour	**2) In order to/for the purpose of:** *Para aprender español hay que estudiar mucho.* – In order to learn Spanish, it is necessary to study a lot. *Voy al supermercado para comprar leche.* – I'm going to the supermarket to buy milk.
3) Passive construction: *El poema fue escrito por Shel Silverstein.* – The poem was written by Shel Silverstein.	**3) Recipient:** *Estas flores son para ti.* – These flowers are for you.
4) By/ through/ along: *Blanca Nieves caminaba por el bosque.* – Snow White was walking through the woods.	**4) Destination:** *La familia sale para Uruguay.* – The family is leaving for Uruguay.
5) Exchange: *Pagué $100 por la bicicleta.* – I paid $100 for the bike.	
6) Modes of communication/ transportation: *Yo viajo por avión.* – I travel by plane. *Mi amiga me escribe por correo electrónico.* – My friend writes to me by email.	
7) Length of time: *Roberto corrió por 2 horas.* – Roberto ran for 2 hours.	

Important Phrases with *Por*	Important Phrases with *Para*
Por ahora – for now	*¿Para qué?* – For what purpose?
Por allí – around there, that way	*Para + [infinitive]* – In order to + [verb]
Por aquí – around here, this way	*Para mí...* – In my opinion...
Por ejemplo – for example	
Por eso – therefore	
Por favor – please	
Por fin – finally	
Por lo menos – at least	
Por primera vez – for the first time	
¿Por qué? – Why?	
Porque – because	
Por supuesto – of course	
Por todas partes – everywhere	

Lesson 66: Confusing Words that start with "LL"

¿llevar, llegar, llaves, lavar, llenar, lleno, lavarse, llamar, llover?

Fill in the blank with the correct word from above. Don't forget to conjugate verbs, and make sure adjectives agree with nouns. There may be more than one correct option. Then, translate the sentences into English.

1) *Hace mucho frío. ¿_____ un suéter?*

2) *¡Nos comimos todo el pavo! Estoy tan _____ .*

3) *¿A qué hora _____ el avión?*

4) *Vamos a llegar tarde, porque no puedo encontrar las _____ del coche.*

5) Hay que _____ *las manos antes de comer.* (hay que – it is necessary to)

6) *El camarero _____ mi copa de vino.*

7) *¡Mira el vestido tan lindo que _____ esa mujer!*

8) *¿Cómo vas a llegar al concierto? ¿Tu papá te _____ en su auto?*

9) *¿Ya empezó la película? ¿Nosotros _____ tarde?*

10) *Si tú _____ la bolsa de basura, va a estar _____ .*

11) *¿Cuándo vas a _____ los platos? Están muy sucios.*

12) *¿Cómo vamos a entrar a la casa si perdiste la _____ ?*

13) *Pedro no viene a comer. Cuando lo _____ por teléfono me dijo que ya estaba _____ .*

14) *¿Puedes _____ la _____ a Manuel para que pueda abrir la puerta?*

15) *¿Te _____ el pelo con Herbal Essences?*

16) *Está nublado hoy. ¿Crees que va a _____ ?*

Lesson 67: Confusing words that start with "P"

¿poder, pedir, probar, probarse, perder, portarse?

Fill in the blank with the correct word from above. Don't forget to conjugate verbs! There may be more than one correct option. Then, translate the sentences into English. If you don't know a word, look it up and be sure to copy over any new words to your Glossary!

1) Los niños _____ bien durante la reunión.

2) ¿(Tú) _____ darle de comer al perro?

3) ¿(Tú) _____ el helado de Benjamín y Geraldo?

4) El abuelo siempre _____ las llaves.

5) ¿(Tú) _____ la camisa verde para ver si te queda bien?

6) ¿Qué _____ tu papá anoche en el restaurante?

7) ¿Cómo _____ tu hermano menor en la fiesta el sábado pasado?

8) ¡Tu mamá _____ cocinar muy bien!

9) Nuestro equipo _____ el partido ayer.

10) ¿Por qué no _____ las galletas de chocolate en la nueva pastelería? Son muy ricas.

11) Los chicos _____ los jeans en el almacén.

12) Ella no _____ volver a casa, porque se _____ en la ciudad y no sabe dónde está.

13) ¿Siempre _____ bien cuando eras niño?

14) ¿No quieres _____ algo de comer?

Lesson 68: Confusing Words that start with "D"

¿durante, detrás de, después de, dentro de, debajo de, delante de?

Fill in the blank with the correct word from above. There may be more than one correct option. Then, translate the sentences into English. If you don't know a word, look it up and be sure to copy over any new words to your Glossary!

1) *El gato se esconde _____ el árbol.*

2) *_____ la cena, vamos a comer el postre.*

3) *Sonó el celular _____ la película.*

4) *Hay que tomar agua _____ correr. (hay que – it is necessary to)*

5) *¿No tienes las llaves _____ la bolsa?*

6) *¡No pongas la basura _____ el sofá!*

7) *Los regalos de Navidad están _____ el árbol.*

8) *La farmacia está _____ el Super Target.*

9) *La chica linda está _____ el espejo, mirándose la cara.*

10) *No puedes hablar _____ el examen.*

11) *¿Quieres desayunar juntos después de _____ Prom/el baile?*

12) *El sótano está _____ la casa.*

13) *La cocina está _____ la casa.*

14) *Tienes que cortar el césped _____ la casa.*

Lesson 69: The word *que*

To Express Passage of Time

Hace **[time period]** *que* **[Present Tense].** – Something has been happening for [time period].
- *Hace 10 años que vivo en Colorado.* – I've lived in Colorado for 10 years.
- *Hace 5 años que estamos casados.* – We've been married for 5 years.
- *Hace mucho tiempo que no veo una buena película.* – I haven't seen a good movie for a long time.

Hace **[time period]** *que* **[Preterite Tense].** – Something happened [time period] ago.
- *Hace 10 años que me mudé a Colorado.* – I moved to Colorado 10 years ago.
- *Hace 5 años que nos casamos.* – We got married 5 years ago.

Another way to say the same thing is: **[Preterite Tense]** *hace* **[time period].**
- *Me mudé a Colorado hace 10 años.* – I moved to Colorado 10 years ago.
- *Nos casamos hace 5 años.* – We got married 5 years ago.

Hacía **[time period]** *que* **[Imperfect Tense].** – Something had happened for [time period].
- *Hacía mucho tiempo que no veía una buena película.* – I hadn't seen a good movie for a long time.

To Express Obligation or Necessity

Hay que – it is necessary to
- *Hay que lavarse las manos antes de comer.* – It is necessary to wash one's hands before eating.
- *Hay que estudiar mucho para el examen.* – It is necessary to study a lot for the test.

Tener que – to have to
- *Tengo que hacer más ejercicio.* – I have to do more exercise.
- *Tienes que comer menos grasas.* – You have to eat less fat.

To Compare

Más que/ menos que – More tan/ less tan
- *Rita tiene más dinero que Luisa.* – Rita has more money than Luisa.
- *Ricardo es más alto que Julián.* – Ricardo is taller than Julián.
- *Julia Alvarez es menos famosa que Jennifer Lopez.* – Julia Alvarez is less famous than Jennifer Lopez.

What/ Why?

Qué – *Qué* with an accent means "what."
- *¿Qué te gusta hacer?* – What do you like to do?

Por qué – why
- *¿Por qué comes tanto helado?* – Why do you eat so much ice cream?

Lesson 69 Practice: The word *que*

Translate the following sentences into Spanish.

1) I have to arrive at school at 8:00 A.M.

2) Catalina and Diego have been married for 8 years.

3) Josefina hadn't seen her mother for years.

4) It is necessary to pay the bill.

5) Flor left the party 20 minutes ago.

6) What time is it?

7) Why did we sell the house?

8) Elisa is taller than Marisol.

9) We have known each other for 3 years.

10) We met 3 years ago.

Part 13 Quiz

Translate these sentences into Spanish.

1) We arrived at the hotel at 4:30 p.m.

2) Have you tried this bacon?

3) Where did you put the car keys?

4) The chair is under the desk.

5) Juanito lost his socks at school.

6) Why did y'all put sugar on these strawberries?

7) After school, I am going to call my dad.

8) First we washed the dishes, and after that we washed our hands.

9) Did it start raining before or after you arrived?

10) What are you going to order at the restaurant?

Part 13 Take-it-Apart Grammar
(for Reading Comprehension)

Take-It-Apart Grammar sections teach you to deconstruct sentences into their grammatical components, thereby improving comprehension and minimizing guessing.

For detailed instructions, refer to page 176. Don't forget about the Pronoun Possibilities Reference Chart on page 177!

1) *¿Hace cuántos años que se conocen?*

Hint: Do not count *hace* as a conjugated verb in this sentence.

Conjugated verb	
Ending	
Infinitive	
Tense	
Subject	
English meaning	

Direct Object/Indirect Object/Reflexive Pronouns: _____

Question or statement? _____   Question word: _____

Translation: _____

Rewrite in the Preterite. _____

New Translation: _____

2) *Tenían que ir a una reunión en la casa de Alicia.*

Conjugated verb		
Ending		
Infinitive		
Tense		
Subject		
English meaning		

Direct Object/Indirect Object/Reflexive Pronouns: _____

Question or statement? _____   Question word: _____

Translation: _____

Rewrite in the Future. _____

New Translation: _____

3) *¿Hace cuántos años que están casados?*

Hint: Do not count *hace* as a conjugated verb in this sentence.

Conjugated verb	
Ending	
Infinitive	
Tense	
Subject	
English meaning	

Direct Object/Indirect Object/Reflexive Pronouns: _____

Question or statement? _____   Question word: _____

Translation: _____

Rewrite in the Preterite. _____

New Translation: _____

4) *Tienes que hacer la tarea antes de jugar tenis.*

Conjugated verb	
Ending	
Infinitive	
Tense	
Subject	
English meaning	

Direct Object/Indirect Object/Reflexive Pronouns: _____

Question or statement? _____   Question word: _____

Translation: _____

Rewrite in the Future. _____

New Translation: _____

5) *¿Hace cuántos días que la compraron?*

Hint: Do not count *hace* as a conjugated verb in this sentence.

Conjugated verb	
Ending	
Infinitive	
Tense	
Subject	
English meaning	

Direct Object/Indirect Object/Reflexive Pronouns: _____

Question or statement? _____   Question word: _____

Translation: _____

6) *Si tienes que comer más proteína, ¿por qué no tomas un batido de energía?*

Conjugated verb		
Ending		
Infinitive		
Tense		
Subject		
English meaning		

Direct Object/Indirect Object/Reflexive Pronouns: _____

Question or statement? _____   Question word: _____

Translation: _____

Rewrite in the Imperfect. _____

New Translation: _____

7) *A través del uso de colores brillantes, el artista expresa un sentimiento de juventud.*

Conjugated verb	
Ending	
Infinitive	
Tense	
Subject	
English meaning	

Direct Object/Indirect Object/Reflexive Pronouns: _____

Question or statement? _____   Question word: _____

Translation: _____

Rewrite in the Imperfect. _____

New Translation: _____

Part 13 Writing Activities

¡Estás de vacaciones!

One of you is on vacation, and the other is the concierge (*el conserje*). Create a scene in which the traveler is just arriving at the hotel, and the concierge is helping you book a tour. Write out your script, and be prepared to act it out!

- Decide where you are traveling, and make this clear in your dialogue.

- Book any kind of tour you want, but be sure to describe what it is. The tour should include at least 3 types of transportation (car, bus, boat, plane, walking, bike, horse, etc.).

- The concierge should offer the traveler at least 3 different options for departure/arrival times, allowing the traveler to choose.

- The concierge should tell the traveler how to dress appropriately for this tour.

- The concierge should provide at least 2 lunch options, allowing the guest to choose.

- The concierge and guest should discuss pricing.

- The concierge should give the traveler directions to arrive at the place where the tour leaves from.

- Your goal is 10 minutes of dialogue!

Asking for Directions #1: Downtown Boulder, Colorado

Answer the following questions in Spanish. Use the map of downtown Boulder, Colorado to help you. You can also practice giving directions in your own city.

[Map Credit: Downtown Boulder Partnership (www.BoulderDowntown.com) *¡Gracias!*]

***Palabras útiles*:**
Cerca de – close to
Lejos de – far from
Cuadras – blocks

1) *La estación del autobús está en la esquina de la Calle Catorce y Walnut. ¿Sí o no?*

2) *Estoy buscando la Casa de Té. ¿Está cerca del Parque Central? ¿Sí o no?*

3) *¿El Teatro de Boulder está muy lejos del juzgado? ¿Sí o no?*

4) *Estoy en el Hotel Boulderado. ¿Puedo ir en bicicleta al Parque Central? ¿Sí o no?*

5) *Quiero comer en un restaurante en la Calle Pearl y la Broadway. ¿Puedo caminar desde el Hotel St. Julien? ¿Sí o no?*

6) *Estoy en el Hotel Boulderado. Para llegar a la biblioteca, camino a la izquierda en Broadway. Después giro a la derecha en Canyon, y está a la derecha. ¿Sí o no?*

7) *Estoy en la Calle Pearl y la Quince. ¿Cómo llego al Hotel St. Julien?*

8) *Estoy en la Casa de Té. ¿Cómo llego a la Oficina de Correos?*

9) *Estoy en el Teatro de Boulder. ¿Cómo llego a la biblioteca?*

Section IV: The Subjunctive Mood

Part 14: The Subjunctive Mood – Long Live the King & Queen!

No Nonsense Glossary*

Apple	La manzana

*For instructions on building your No Nonsense Glossary, see pages 9-10.

Lesson 70: Present Tense in the Subjunctive Mood

What is the Subjunctive Mood?

The Subjunctive (*el subjuntivo*) is considered a **mood**, which is different from **tense**. A tense expresses a verb's relationship to time, while a mood expresses something about the speaker's relationship to what he/she is saying.

If you change a tense of a verb, you could make the verb occur in the past as opposed to the future. For example, "I went" (Past Tense) vs. "I will go." (Future Tense).

If you change the mood of a verb, you could express your degree of certainty that something will occur, your opinion about something occurring or or your desire for something to occur or not occur. For example, "I am going" (Indicative Mood) vs. "I wish I were going." (Subjunctive Mood).

With the exception of Commands, which are considered the Imperative Mood, all of the tenses you have learned up to this point have been in what is known as the Indicative Mood. Every tense you have learned can also exist in the Subjunctive Mood.

Main Uses of the Subjunctive Mood

To express doubt
- *Dudo que Elena vaya a ir a la fiesta esta noche.* – I doubt Elena will go to the party tonight.
- *Es dudoso que gane tu equipo.* – It's doubtful that your team will win.

To express a judgement

Wishing something on someone
- *Que tengas un buen fin de semana.* – Have a good weekend.
- *¡Que vivan los novios!* – Long live the bride and groom!
    - **Note:** Beginning a sentence with *Que* (this is different from *qué*, which means "what") in Spanish is like saying "I hope that".

Requests
- *Que me esperes.* – Wait for me.
- *Que prestes atención.* – Pay attention.
    - **Note:** This is similar to a Command, but feels slightly less strong.

Wishes/ wants/ desires
- *Espero que pases el examen.* – I hope you pass the test.
- *Quiero que estudies.* – I want you to study.
- *Ojalá que no llueva mañana.* – Hopefully it won't rain tomorrow.
  - **Note:** The Spanish word *ojalá* comes from the Arabic word *insh'allah*, meaning "God willing". It does not have religious connotations in modern Spanish, and is often translated as "hopefully".

How to form the Present Subjunctive

1) Begin with the verb in the 1st person singular of the present tense: (*yo*) **canto**

2) Remove the –o: **cant**

3) Add the following endings:

–ar verbs
(Shown with the verb *cantar* – to sing)

Yo	cant**e**	Nosotros	cant**emos**
Tú	cant**es**	Vosotros	cant**éis**
Usted	cant**e**	Ustedes	cant**en**
Él / Ella	cant**e**	Ellos / Ellas	cant**en**

–er/–ir verbs
(Shown with the verb *comer* – to eat)

Yo	com**a**	Nosotros	com**amos**
Tú	com**as**	Vosotros	com**áis**
Usted	com**a**	Ustedes	com**an**
Él / Ella	com**a**	Ellos / Ellas	com**an**

Common Verbs with Irregular *Yo* forms

Conocer: *conozco* – to know people/places
Hacer: *hago* – to do/ to make

Poner: *pongo* – to put/ set
Salir: *salgo* – to go out
Tener: *tengo* – to have

Common Irregular Verbs in the Present Subjunctive Mood

Ir – to go

Yo	**vaya**	Nosotros	**vayamos**
Tú	**vayas**	Vosotros	vayáis
Usted	**vaya**	Ustedes	**vayan**
Él / Ella	**vaya**	Ellos / Ellas	**vayan**

Ser – to be (default)

Yo	**sea**	Nosotros	**seamos**
Tú	**seas**	Vosotros	seáis
Usted	**sea**	Ustedes	**sean**
Él / Ella	**sea**	Ellos / Ellas	**sean**

Estar – to be (temporary)

Yo	**esté**	Nosotros	**estemos**
Tú	**estés**	Vosotros	estéis
Usted	**esté**	Ustedes	**estén**
Él / Ella	**esté**	Ellos / Ellas	**estén**

Saber – to know

Yo	**sepa**	Nosotros	**sepamos**
Tú	**sepas**	Vosotros	sepáis
Usted	**sepa**	Ustedes	**sepan**
Él / Ella	**sepa**	Ellos / Ellas	**sepan**

Haber – there is/there are
(auxiliary verb for Perfect Tenses)

Yo	**haya**	Nosotros	**hayamos**
Tú	**hayas**	Vosotros	hayáis
Usted	**haya**	Ustedes	**hayan**
Él / Ella	**haya**	Ellos / Ellas	**hayan**

Verbs Ending in –car/–gar/–zar in the Present Subjunctive

As you've seen with the Preterite Tense, there are some verbs that undergo a spelling change that does not affect their pronunciation.

–car verbs (c → qu)
(Shown with the verb *sacar* – to take/ to take out)

Yo	sa**que**	Nosotros	sa**que**mos
Tú	sa**que**s	Vosotros	sa**qué**is
Usted	sa**que**	Ustedes	sa**que**n
Él / Ella	sa**que**	Ellos / Ellas	sa**que**n

–gar verbs (g → gu)
(Shown with the verb *entregar* – to hand in)

Yo	entre**gue**	Nosotros	entre**gue**mos
Tú	entre**gue**s	Vosotros	entre**gué**is
Usted	entre**gue**	Ustedes	entre**gue**n
Él / Ella	entre**gue**	Ellos / Ellas	entre**gue**n

–zar verbs (z → c)
(Shown with the verb *almorzar** – to eat lunch)

Yo	almuer**c**e	Nosotros	almor**c**emos
Tú	almuer**c**es	Vosotros	almor**c**éis
Usted	almuer**c**e	Ustedes	almuer**c**en
Él / Ella	almuer**c**e	Ellos / Ellas	almuer**c**en

*Almorzar is also a stem-changing (o → ue) verb.

Lesson 70 Practice: Subjunctive v. Indicative v. Infinitive (Present)

In the following sentences, decide whether to conjugate the verb in parentheses in the Present Indicative, Present Subjunctive or to leave it in the Infinitive. Then, translate the sentences into English.

Ejemplo

Infinitive: *Me gusta tomar agua.*
    I like to drink water.

    (Always use the Infinitive directly after another conjugated verb, such as *gusta*)

Present Subjunctive: *Me gusta que tomes agua.*
    I like that you drink water.

    (Use the Subjunctive when telling someone else what you want them to do)

Present Indicative: *Yo tomo agua fría.*
    I drink cold water.

    (Use the Indiciative when simply stating what someone is does or is doing)

1) *Me gusta _____ (comer) frutas.*

2) *Me gusta que (tú) _____ (comer) frutas.*

3) *Yo _____ (comer) muchas frutas.*

4) *Catalina _____ (viajar) a Toronto cada verano.*

5) *Catalina quiere _____ (viajar) a Ginebra el verano que viene.*

6) *Es dudoso que Catalina _____ (viajar) a Miami este verano.*

7) *Vamos a _____ (venir) temprano a la fiesta.*

8) *No me gusta que (nosotros) _____ (llegar) tarde a la fiesta.*

9) *Nosotros _____ (venir) a la fiesta de Marcos.*

10) *No sé a dónde _____ (ir) ellos mañana.*

11) *Me encanta _____ (dibujar) flores.*

12) *Él _____ (estudiar) en la biblioteca.*

13) *¿Usted _____ (querer) _____ (comer) en un restaurante?*

14) *¿Por qué no _____ (ir) (nosotros) a la feria el domingo?*

15) *Es mejor que ella _____ (pedir) ayuda.*

16) *Mamá _____ (preferir) que el perro _____ (estar) limpio.*

Lesson 71: Practice with Subjunctive v. Indicative (Present)

Fill in the blank with the correct conjugation of the verb in parentheses. Be sure to decide whether to conjugate it in the present indicative or present subjunctive. Then, translate the sentences into English.

1) *Ojalá que _____ (llover) en el campo.*

2) *Recomendamos que ella _____ (ir) a un concierto de Juan Luis Guerra.*

3) *Espero que Uds. _____ (oír) a los niños que cantan en la fiesta.*

4) *Es probable que (tú) _____ (ver) un video de No Te Va Gustar (un grupo musical Uruguayo) en la red.*

5) *Yo dudo que tú _____ (practicar) salsa todos los días.*

6) *Yo sé que Venezuela _____ (estar) al oeste de Brasil.*

7) *Es improbable que nosotros _____ (divertirse) en la cárcel.*

8) *Yo creo que te _____ (gustar) cantar en la ducha.*

9) *Es triste que _____ (haber) tanta destrucción en la isla después de un huracán.*

10) *Es cierto que yo _____ (tener) el CD nuevo de Shakira para ti.*

11) *Dudo que ellos _____ (conocer) a mi madre.*

12) *Sé que el café _____ (ser) una cosecha importante en Colombia.*

13) *¡Te aconsejo que no _____ (salir) de la tienda sin comprar un regalo para tu esposa!*

14) *Me agrada que usted me _____ (mostrar) sus fotos de México.*

15) *No hay duda de que ahora ustedes _____ (entender) la canción en español.*

16) *Me gusta que ella _____ (preparar) mate (un té energizante que se toma en Argentina, Uruguay, Paraguay y Brasil) para todos.*

More Practice with Present Subjunctive

Complete the following sentences using the Present Subjunctive.

1) *Yo quiero que…*

2) *Yo quiero que tú me…*

3) *Yo espero que no…*

4) *Me alegro que…*

5) *Ojalá que la ciudad de Londres…*

6) *No puedo creer que…*

7) *Es imposible que…*

8) *¡Qué bendición que…!*

9) *La policía no quiere que…*

10) *Mi madre no puede creer que yo…*

Lesson 72: Imperfect Tense in the Subjunctive Mood

How to form the Imperfect Subjunctive (*el imperfecto del subjuntivo*)

1) Begin with the verb in the 3rd person plural of the preterite tense: **_cantaron_**

2) Remove the –ron: **_canta_**

3) Add the following endings: (endings are the same for –ar, -er and –ir verbs!)

<u>-ar verbs</u>
(Shown with the verb *cantar* – to sing)

Yo	canta**ra**	Nosotros	cantá**ramos***
Tú	canta**ras**	Vosotros	canta**rais**
Usted	canta**ra**	Ustedes	canta**ran**
Él Ella	canta**ra**	Ellos Ellas	canta**ran**

<u>-er/ -ir verbs</u>
(Shown with the verb *comer* – to eat)

Yo	comie**ra**	Nosotros	comié**ramos***
Tú	comie**ras**	Vosotros	comie**rais**
Usted	comie**ra**	Ustedes	comie**ran**
Él Ella	comie**ra**	Ellos Ellas	comie**ra**

For the *nosotros* form, also add an accent on the vowel before the ending.

When to use the Imperfect Subjunctive

- If the sentence (or clause) is in the preterite or imperfect
  No quería que te perdieras. – I didn't want you to get lost.

- If the sentence (or clause) is about a past experience or occurrence
  Espero que te divertieras ayer. – I hope you had fun yesterday.
  Espero que te hayas divertido ayer. – I hope you had fun yesterday. (More common)

- With *ojalá* to describe unlikely events
  Ojalá que ganara un millón de dólares. – If only I were to win a million dollars.

- [If] [Imperfect Subjunctive] + [conditional]
  Si pudiera viajar a cualquier lugar del mundo, iría a Portugal. –
  If I could travel anywhere in the world, I would go to Portugal.

- A formal way to make a request
  Quisiera pedir el flan. – I would like to order the flan.

Lesson 72 Practice: Imperfect Subjunctive

Fill in the blank with the correct conjugation of the verb in parentheses. Then, translate the sentences into English.

1) *Mi padre quería que yo _____ (ir) a la universidad.*

2) *No era probable que el hombre _____ (escribir) una carta.*

3) *El gato esperaba que los ratones _____ (aparecer).*

4) *El médico te aconsejó que no _____ (comer) tantas hamburguesas.*

5) *El abogado le aconsejó que _____ (decir) la verdad.*

6) *No era necesario que usted _____ (pagar) la cuenta.*

7) *¡Te pedí que no _____ (portarse) mal en la casa de tus abuelos!*

8) *El hijo le rogó al padre que le _____ (dar) dinero.*

9) *(A ustedes) los invité para que _____ (venir) a la fiesta.*

10) *La madre no quería que los niños _____ (saber) nada de los regalos de Navidad.*

11) ¡Te pedí que no _____ (tomar) esa foto tan horrible!

12) La muchacha celosa no quería que su ex-novio _____ (salir) con otra mujer.

13) El empleado se escondió para que el jefe no lo _____ (ver).

14) El profesor pidió que nosotros _____ (entregar) el examen.

15) Create your own sentence using the Imperfect Subjunctive. Use the questions above to guide you.

Lesson 73: Past Perfect Subjunctive

The Past Perfect Subjunctive, also called the Pluperfect Subjunctive (*el pretérito perfecto del subjuntivo*) is used to refer to an event that took place in the past, but when the beginning of the sentence is in the Present Tense. It is also used for events that will have taken place by a given time in the future.

Ejemplos:
    I hope you had fun at the party last night. –
    Espero que te hayas divertido en la fiesta anoche.
    Hopefully you'll have finished studying before the exam. –
    Ojalá que hayas terminado de estudiar antes del examen.

How to form the Past Perfect Subjunctive

Haber (in the Present Subjunctive) + [past participle]

Haber (in the Past Perfect Subjunctive)

Yo	**haya**	Nosotros	**hayamos**
Tú	**hayas**	Vosotros	**hayáis**
Usted	**haya**	Ustedes	**hayan**
Él / Ella	**haya**	Ellos / Ellas	**hayan**

Past Participle

-ar verbs
-ado
hablar: hablado

-er/-ir verbs
-ido
comer: comido

Lesson 73 Practice: The Subjunctive Mood in Present, Imperfect & Perfect Tenses

Translate these sentences into Spanish. If you don't know a word, look it up and be sure to copy over any new words to your Glossary!

1) I hope you like flan.

2) I hope you liked the flan my mother made for dessert last night.

3) Ernesto's father wants him to study medicine.

4) Last year, Pilar's mother wanted her to move to Spain.

5) I'm glad you enjoy playing tennis.

6) I'm glad you enjoyed playing tennis with me last week.

7) I can't believe you're not coming skiing with us this New Year's!

8) I can't believe you didn't go to the party at Nacho's house.

9) The doctor recommends that I do more exercise.

10) When I was a kid, the doctor recommended that I not eat sweets before bed.

11) I hope you enjoy your time with your family.

12) I hope you had a great Christmas.

13) Create your own pair of sentences, using the Present Subjunctive for the first sentence and the Past Perfect Subjunctive for the second sentence.

Lesson 74: Conditional Tense

The Conditional Tense (*el condicional*) describes things that **would** happen in the future. The other half of a sentence containing a conditional verb will often describe certain conditions that would need to be met. These conditions are are commonly described in the Imperfect Subjunctive.

Conditional Tense Endings for Regular Verbs

For all regular verbs, take the infinitive and add the following endings.
Shown with the verb *hablar* (to speak).

Yo	hablar**ía**	Nosotros	hablar**íamos**
Tú	hablar**ías**	Vosotros	hablar**íais**
Usted	hablar**ía**	Ustedes	hablar**ían**
Él / Ella	hablar**ía**	Ellos / Ellas	hablar**ían**

Common Conditional Tense Verbs with Irregular Stems

For all irregular verbs, take the irregular stem and add the following endings.
Shown with the verb decir (to say/tell).

Yo	dir**ía**	Nosotros	dir**íamos**
Tú	dir**ías**	Vosotros	dir**íais**
Usted	dir**ía**	Ustedes	dir**ían**
Él / Ella	dir**ía**	Ellos / Ellas	dir**ían**

Decir – <u>dir</u> (to say/tell)
Haber – <u>habr</u> (to have, auxiliary verb)
Hacer – <u>har</u> (to do/make)
Ir – <u>ir</u> (to go)
Poder – <u>pod</u> (to be able to)
Poner – <u>pond</u> (to put/set)

Querer – <u>querr</u> (to want/love)
Saber – <u>sabr</u> (to know)
Salir – <u>saldr</u> (to go out)
Tener – <u>tendr</u> (to have)
Valer – <u>valdr</u> (to be worth)
Venir – <u>vendr</u> (to come)

Ejemplo:
    ¡Yo tomaría el café si estuveria caliente! – I would drink the coffee if it were hot!

Lesson 74 Practice: Imperfect Subjunctive and Conditional

Complete the following sentences using the Imperfect Subjunctive and Conditional tenses.

Format: If [Imperfect Subjunctive], then [Conditional].

Ejemplo: *Si (yo) tuviera más dinero...* compraría un barco pirata.
   (If I had more money, I would buy a pirate ship.)

1) *Si (yo) pudiera viajar a cualquier parte del mundo...*

2) *Si (yo) fuera el rey del universo...*

3) *Si (yo) tuviera siete años...*

4) *Si viviéramos en otro planeta...*

5) *Si mi esposo/esposa/mamá/papá ganara la lotería...*

6) *Si tuviera 10 hijos...*

7) *...iría a Tierra del Fuego.*

8) *...lo llamaría Hugo.*

9) *...estaría eufórico.*

10) *...trabajaría/estudiaría menos horas.*

11) *...bailaría el waltz.*

12) *...se lo/la daría a mi hijo/hija/mamá/papá.*

Part 14 Quiz

Fill in the blank using the verb in parentheses in the Present Subjunctive.

1) *Ojalá que no _____ (nevar) mañana.*

2) *Recomendamos que tú _____ (ir) al hospital.*

3) *Espero que Uds. _____ (oír) al despertador.*

Fill in the blank using the verb in parentheses in the Imperfect Subjunctive.

4) *Mi madre quería que yo _____ (estudiar) francés.*

5) *La profesora pidió que nosotros _____ (entregar) la tarea.*

6) *El abogado le aconsejó que _____ (decir) la verdad.*

Fill in the blank using the verb in parentheses in the Past Perfect Subjunctive.

7) *Es dudoso que el muchacho _____ (beber) la leche anoche.*

8) *Es improbable que la niña _____ (portarse) bien ayer.*

9) *Me alegro que (tú) _____ (venir) a mi casa para mi cumpleaños.*

10) *¡Me agrada que (tú) _____ (hacer) la tarea!*

Translate these sentences into Spanish.

11) I hope you have fun skiing this weekend.

12) If you could meet one famous person, who would you meet?

13) Patricia's grandmother wants her to be a Spanish professor.

Part 14 Take-it-Apart Grammar
(for Reading Comprehension)

Take-It-Apart Grammar sections teach you to deconstruct sentences into their grammatical components, thereby improving comprehension and minimizing guessing. **For detailed instructions, refer to page 176. Don't forget about the Pronoun Possibilities Reference Chart on page 177!**

1) *¿Qué pidieron en el restaurante que no les gustó?*

Conjugated verb		
Ending		
Infinitive		
Tense		
Subject		
English meaning		

Direct Object/Indirect Object/Reflexive Pronouns: _____

Question or statement? _____   Question word: _____

Translation: _____

Rewrite in the Imperfect. _____

New Translation: _____

2) *¿Quieres que te haga la cena mañana por la noche?*

Conjugated verb		
Ending		
Infinitive		
Tense		
Subject		
English meaning		

Direct Object/Indirect Object/Reflexive Pronouns: _____

Question or statement? _____   Question word: _____

Translation: _____

Rewrite in the Imperfect. _____

New Translation: _____

3) *Ojalá que puedan encontrarlo.*

Conjugated verb	
Ending	
Infinitive	
Tense	
Subject	
English meaning	

Direct Object/Indirect Object/Reflexive Pronouns: _____

Question or statement? _____   Question word: _____

Translation: _____

Rewrite in the Past Perfect Subjunctive. _____

New Translation: _____

4) *Es dudoso que venga temprano el investigador.*

Conjugated verb		
Ending		
Infinitive		
Tense		
Subject		
English meaning		

Direct Object/Indirect Object/Reflexive Pronouns: _____

Question or statement? _____   Question word: _____

Translation: _____

Rewrite in the Imperfect. _____

New Translation: _____

5) *No creo que te pida ayuda tu hermana.*

Conjugated verb		
Ending		
Infinitive		
Tense		
Subject		
English meaning		

Direct Object/Indirect Object/Reflexive Pronouns: _____

Question or statement? _____   Question word: _____

Translation: _____

6) *Cuando encuentres a un buen hombre, hija mía, ¡cásate con él!*

Conjugated verb		
Ending		
Infinitive		
Tense		
Subject		
English meaning		

Direct Object/Indirect Object/Reflexive Pronouns: _____

Question or statement? _____   Question word: _____

Translation: _____

7) *¿Me sugieres que no coma más dulces?*

Conjugated verb		
Ending		
Infinitive		
Tense		
Subject		
English meaning		

Direct Object/Indirect Object/Reflexive Pronouns: _____

Question or statement? _____   Question word: _____

Translation: _____

Rewrite in the Imperfect. _____

New Translation: _____

8) *Ya va a anochecer. Debemos buscar un refugio para pasar la noche.*

Conjugated verb		
Ending		
Infinitive		
Tense		
Subject		
English meaning		

Direct Object/Indirect Object/Reflexive Pronouns: _____

Question or statement? _____   Question word: _____

Translation: _____

Part 14 Writing Activities

Travel / Study Abroad Scenarios

Answer the following essay questions in Spanish.

1) You have to extend your visa because you decide to stay an extra month. Where do you go? What do you tell the person working there?

2) You meet a new friend in the library. You ask her about herself, where she is from and what she's doing. You tell her about yourself, and then you ask her if she wants to hang out with you this weekend.

3) You've just gone to see a movie with friends, and now everyone is leaving to go home. How would you ask the best way to get a bus or taxi home?

4) You need a new toothbrush. Where do you go? How do you ask for what you need?

5) You want to take a weekend trip to see the mountains and the countryside. How do you ask a local person where to go and what to see?

Asking for Directions #2: Downtown Boulder, Colorado

Answer the following questions in Spanish. Use the map of downtown Boulder, Colorado on page 247 to help you. You can also practice giving directions in your own city.

1) *Estoy en la biblioteca. ¿Cómo llego al Hotel Boulderado?*

2) *Estoy buscando la estación del autobús. ¿En qué esquina está?*

3) *Tengo que enviar una carta. ¿A dónde puedo ir? ¿Cómo llego?*

4) *¡Estoy perdida! Me estoy quedando en el Hotel Saint Julien, pero tomé demasiado té en La Casa de Té, y ahora no sé cómo volver a mi hotel. ¿Usted puede ayudarme?*

5) *Quiero ver una obra teatral. ¿A dónde puedo ir? ¿Cómo llego?*

6) *Perdón, ¿el Parque Central está cerca de la estación de autobús? ¿Puedo caminar?*

7) *Estoy en la Calle Pearl y la Quince. ¿Cómo llego al juzgado?*

8) *Estoy cansada y no quiero caminar más. ¿Puedo tomar un taxi desde la Casa de Té a la biblioteca? ¿A cuántas cuadras está?*

Section V: Bonus Holiday Activities & Most Common Spanish Verbs Chart

Halloween: Spooky Spanish!

Fill in the blank with the correct word from the Word Bank. Then, translate the sentences into English. Don't forget to copy new words over to your Glossary!

El Vocabulario del Halloween

El Fantasma – ghost
El Vampiro – vampire
El cementerio – cemetery
volar – to fly

las paredes – walls
chupar sangre – to suck blood
nadie – nobody

Word Bank: *bailar, soy, naranja, vivo, gusta, día, noche, tú, dónde, discoteca, semana, encanta*

1) **Fantasma:** *¿De _____ eres, Vampiro?*

2) **Vampiro**: *Yo _____ de Transylvania. ¿Y tú, Fantasma?*

3) **Fantasma**: *Yo _____ en el cementerio, pero a veces me _____ pasar tiempo en las casas viejas.*

4) **Vampiro**: *¿Qué te gusta hacer los fines de _____?*

5) **Fantasma**: *¡Me _____ volar por paredes! ¿Y _____?*

6) **Vampiro**: *Yo salgo de _____ para chupar sangre. Es mucho más divertido que _____ en la discoteca.*

7) **Fantasma**: *¡A mí me gusta bailar en la _____ porque nadie puede verme!*

Thanksgiving: *del Día de Acción de Dar Gracias*

Match the correct English and Spanish foods. Then, write your ideal menu for a Thanksgiving Day feast (or any feast from your culture)! Feel free to include any foods that are not from the list below. Don't forget to copy new words over to your Glossary!

El Vocabulary del Día de Acción de Dar Gracias

Turkey	*el vino*
Stuffing	*el nabo*
Gravy	*el relleno*
Mashed potatoes	*las galletas*
Bread	*el pavo*
Turnip	*la espinaca*
Spinach	*el puré de papas*
Pumpkin pie	*a crema batida*
Apple pie	*la salsa espesa*
Whipped cream	*la tarta de calabaza*
Cookies/crackers/biscuits	*la tarta de manzana*
Wine	*el pan*

Christmas: *Navidad*

¿Dónde están los regalos de la Navidad?
– Where are the Christmas gifts?

Color the picture on the following page according to clues you are given. Label the recipients of the gifts.

El Vocabulario de Navidad

El árbol – tree
La estrella – star
El regalo – gift
El lazo – bow

Debajo de – under
Detrás de – behind
Delante de – in front of
A la derecha de – to the right of
A la izquierda de – to the left of

1) *El árbol es verde.*

2) *La estrella es amarilla.*

3) *Los ornamentos son rojos y blancos.*

4) *El regalo en el centro, con el lazo grande, es verde y azul. El regalo es de Luis.*

5) *El regalo de Lisa está debajo del regalo del Luis.*

6) *El regalo de Chris está a la izquierda del regalo de Lisa.*

7) *El regalo de Lisa es morado y amarillo.*

8) *El regalo de Pepe está delante del regalo de Lisa.*

9) *El regalo de Chris es blanco y negro.*

10) *El regalo a la derecha del regalo de Pepe tiene un lazo anaranjado.*

11) *El regalo de Noah es el regalo grande detrás del regalo con el lazo anaranjado.*

12) *Los tres regalos de los gatos están a la izquierda del regalo de Chris. Son rojos y verdes.*

13) *¿Cuál es el regalo misterioso?*

World Cup: *la Copa Mundial*

1) Match the World Cup Vocabulary in English and Spanish. Don't forget to copy new words over to your Glossary!
2) Write 10 questions and answers about the World Cup using the vocabulary provided below. You can write about scores, schedules, who is playing who, who you think will win, etc.

El Vocabulario para la Copa Mundial

The World Cup	*el jugador/los jugadores*
Soccer	*el minuto*
Goal	*¿Dónde?*
The score	*La Copa Mundial*
The player/players	*el gol*
The game	*¿Quién?*
The ball	*la ronda*
Minute	*¿Cuándo?*
Round	*el grupo*
Group	*el marcador*
Who?	*el partido*
Where?	*el fútbol*
When?	*la pelota*

Los verbos

- ***Jugar* – to play**
  - *¿Contra quién juega Colombia?* – Who is Colombia playing?
  - *¿Quién jugó el sábado?* – Who played on Saturday?
- ***Meter un gol* – to score a goal**
  - *¿Quién metió un gol?* – Who scored a goal?
- ***Vencer a* – to defeat (another team)**
  - *Uruguay venció a Italia.* – Uruguay defeated Italy.
- ***Ganar* – to win**
  - *¿Quién ganó el partido?* – Who won the game?
- ***Perder* – to lose**
  - *Italia perdió el partido.* – Italy lost the game.

Most Common Spanish Verbs Quick Reference Chart

Spanish Infinitive	English meaning	Irregular Yo form (Present Tense)	Stem-changing (Present Tense)	Irregular in Preterite Tense	Irregular Past Participle	Other Notes
abrir	to open				abierto	
almorzar	to have lunch		o → ue			
andar	to walk/go			anduv-		
bailar	to dance					
beber	to drink					
buscar	to look for			c → qu		
caer	to fall	caigo		i → y (in 3rd person/Ud(s).	caído	Accent marks on í in Preterite
caminar	to walk					
celebrar	to celebrate					
cerrar	to close					
cocinar	to cook					
comer	to eat					
comprar	to buy					
conducir	to drive	conduzco		conduj-		
conocer	to know (a person/place)	conozco				
contar	to tell a story/count		o → ue			
contener	to contain	contengo	e → ie	contuv-		
dar	to give			d-		
deber	should/to owe					
decidir	to decide					
decir	to say/tell	digo		dij-	dicho	
descansar	to rest					
dibujar	to draw					
dormir	to sleep		o → ue			
enseñar	to teach/show					
entender	to understand		e → ie			
entregar	to hand in			g → gu		
enviar	to send					
esconder	to hide					
escribir	to write				escrito	
escuchar	to listen					
esperar	to wait/hope					
estar	to be (temporary)	estoy*		estuv-		Accent marks on á (except *estamos*) in Present
estudiar	to study					
haber	have (auxilary verb)			hub-		*Auxilary verb for Perfect Tenses, Irregular in Present
hablar	to speak					
hacer	to do/make	hago		hic-, hizo (él/ell/Ud/)	hecho	

Spanish Infinitive	English meaning	Irregular Yo form (Present Tense)	Stem-changing (Present Tense)	Irregular in Preterite Tense	Irregular Past Participle	Other Notes
ir	to go	voy...*		fui...*	ido	*Fully irregular in Present, Preterite & Imperfect
jugar	to play		u → ue	g → gu		
leer	to read			i → y (in 3rd person/Ud(s).	leído	Accent marks on í in Preterite
llamar	to call					
llegar	to arrive			g → gu		
llenar	to fill					
llevar	to take/wear					
llover	to rain		o → ue			
mandar	to send					
manejar	to drive					
mantener	to maintain	mantengo	e → ie	mantuv-		
montar	to ride					
morir	to die		o → ue		muerto	
mostrar	to show		o → ue			
nadar	to swim					
oír	to hear	oigo		i → y (in 3rd person/Ud(s).	oído	*Irregular in Present & Preterite, Accent marks on í in Preterite
pagar	to pay			g → gu		
pedir	to ask for/order		e → i	pido, pidieron		
perder	to lose					
poder	to be able to		o → ue	pud-		
poner	to put/place	pongo		pus-	puesto	
practicar	to practice			c → qu		
preparar	to prepare					
probar	to try		o → ue			
producir	to produce	produzco		produj-		
querer	to want/love		e → ie	quis-		
recordar	to remember		o → ue			
regalar	to give as a gift					
saber	to know (facts or skills)	sé		sup-		
sacar	to take			c → qu		
salir	to go out/leave	salgo				
ser	to be (permanent)	soy...*		fui...*		*Fully irregular in Present, Preterite & Imperfect
tener	to have	tengo	e -→ e	tuv-		
tomar	to take/drink					
traducir	to translate	traduzco		traduj-		
traer	to bring	traigo		traj-	traído	
venir	to come	vengo	e → ie	vin-		
ver	to see	veo		v-	visto	
viajar	to travel					
vivir	to live					

Section VI: Appendix

Tips for Successful Use of the No Nonsense Spanish Workbook

The most successful Spanish learners have many tools in their toolbox. This workbook will be a fantastic addition to your Spanish learning toolkit, as it gives students a solid foundation of grammar and the underlying structure of the Spanish language. Having this kind of foundation will allow students to incorporate new vocabulary and concepts more efficiently, and to handle curveballs that may be thrown at them in the classroom or in the Spanish-speaking world.

Learning a language is a complex and challenging process. Don't be fooled by products that promise to make you fluent. It simply doesn't work that way. But don't be discouraged. Millions of people in this world speak more than one language, and you can too. With this workbook, the proper accompanying tools and some hard work and dedication, you will be well on your way to becoming a Spanish speaker!

1) Study with a live person!

Bear in mind that the purpose of language is communication with others, so you need to do more than study alone with a book. This workbook will be a great addition to your Spanish learning repertoire, but you will get more out of it if you are also studying Spanish in a classroom, with a private tutor or in an immersive setting.

There are a number of tutoring agencies online that can help you find private tutors in your area. If you have friends who speak Spanish, ask them if they would be willing to tutor you, or if they know someone who gives classes.

2) Use supplementary media in order to increase your vocabulary.

There are so many words in the Spanish language that not an even a native speaker knows them all! My advice is to choose topics that interest you and to seek out vocabulary in that area. If you plan to travel, you may also choose to focus on a certain dialect from a specific country. Spanish from Spain, for example, differs greatly from Mexican, Puerto Rican or Argentine Spanish.

Visit us on Facebook for media in Spanish from many different sources!

Facebook: www.facebook.com/No-Nonsense-Spanish-Workbook-101569754839122

Sources for Spanish Vocabulary:
- **wordreference.com** is a great tool for looking up new words, either from English to Spanish, or Spanish to English. Look up individual words, rather than trying to plug in entire sentences or paragraphs. Avoid google translate, as it is often inaccurate.
- **Flashcards** – You can find many apps for your phone or other devices. Take advantage of the thousands of premade flashcards or make your own.
- **Newspaper and magazine articles** – available online or in print. If you are traveling to Colombia, look for a Colombian newspaper. If you want to be able to communicate with the Spanish-speaking community in your part of the United States, find out where the majority of immigrants in your area are from. Look for publications from those countries. If you live in Miami, for example, you are likely to find a great deal of Cuban Spanish, and if you live in Arizona, you will find more Mexican Spanish.
- **Facebook and Youtube** – Liking facebook pages in Spanish or watching youtube in Spanish will cause there to be more Spanish in your newsfeed and suggested videos.
- **Music** – Create Pandora, Spotify or youtube stations in Spanish. When you find a song or artist you like, look up the lyrics and see if you can translate them.
- **Movies** – There are many movies and shows in Spanish available on Netflix and elsewhere. You can also watch with subtitles in English or in Spanish, depending on your level.

3) Study with friends.

Languages are meant to be spoken, so the more people you talk with, the more you will learn! Studying in groups can also help you encourage each other and hold each other accountable.

4) Study daily.

Spend at least 15 minutes a day reviewing your vocabulary, practicing grammar or reading an article. 15 minutes a day keeps your brain fresh and active, and is much more effective than cramming for 3 hours the night before your next class.

5) Stick with it!

Learning a new language is hard. It just is. So are most things in life that are worthwhile. If you are determined and motivated, you will learn. And once you get the ball rolling, it does get easier. Remember, languages are complex beasts. There is no one way to learn, and there is really no way to fail, unless you completely give up.

Best of luck to you as you embark upon the next level of your Spanish learning adventure. Together we can make the world a more bilingual place!

Answer Key

Please keep in mind that while many questions in this book do have a specific, correct answer, other questions may have more than one possible answer. Examples are provided to help guide you. If you do not have the exact same answer that appears here, it does not necessarily mean you are wrong. Also, keep in mind that the subject pronouns (*yo, tú, usted, él, ella, nosotros, vosotros, ustedes, ellos and ellas*) are optional in Spanish, so they may sometimes be included in the answers and other times not. Pay attention to whether or not your verbs are conjugated correctly, but it is your choice whether or not to include the subject pronouns.

Page 15
January – enero; February – febrero; March – marzo; April – abril; May – mayo; June – junio; July – julio; August – Agosto; September- septiembre; October – octubre; November – noviembre; December – diciembre

Page 17
Christmas – La Navidad; What is the date today? - ¿Cuál es la fecha de hoy? The first day of school – El primer día de escuela; New Year's Day – El Día de Año Nuevo; Birthday – el cumpleaños; When – Cuándo; Mother/father – la madre/el padre; My/your – mi/tu; The Day of the Dead – El Día de los Muertos; Christmas Eve – La Nochebuena

Page 18
1) Example: Hoy es el diez de mayo. 2) Example: Mi cumpleaños es el siete de marzo. 3) Example: El cumpleaños de mi madre es el veinte de octubre. 4) Navidad es el veintcinco de diciembre. 5) El Día de Año Nuevo es el primero de enero. 6) El Día de los Muertos es el primero/dos de noviembre. 7) Example: El primer día de escuela es el quince de agosto. 8) Example: El cumpleaños de mi padre es el veinticuatro de julio.

Page 19
Monday – el lunes; Tuesday – el martes; Wednesday – el miércoles; Thursday – el jueves; Friday – el Viernes; Saturday – el sábado; Sunday – el domingo

Page 20
1) Example: Hoy es martes, cinco de mayo. 2) Example: Mañana es miércoles, seis de mayo. 3) Example: Ayer fue lunes, cuatro de mayo. 4) Example: Mi cumpleaños es el doce de junio de mil novecientos setenta y nueve. 5) Example: El cumpleaños de mi papa es el veinticuatro de juno del mil novecientos cincuenta y dos. 6) Example: El último día de escuela es el veinicuatro de mayo. 7) La Nochebuena es el veinticuatro de diciembre. 8) Halloween es el treinta y uno de octubre. 9) El Día de Año Nuevo es el primero de enero.

Page 21
1) el dieciocho de mayo 2) el seis de junio 3) jueves, diecisiete de abril 4) sábado, veintiocho de febrero 5) lunes, veinticuatro de noviembre 6) miércoles, ocho de agosto 7) jueves, primero de septiembre 8) domingo, quince de marzo 9) martes, doce de julio

Page 22: Part 1 Quiz
1) el cuatro de abril 2) el diecisiete de octubre 3) lunes, veintiocho de enero 4) sábado, primero de julio 5) miércoles, siete de marzo 6) Viernes, 30 de mayo del dos mil quince 7) Navidad es el veinticinco de diciembre. 8) Example: Mi cumpleaños es el trece de mayo de mil novecientos ochenta y seis. 9) Example: El primer día de escuela es el primero de septiembre. 10) Example: Hoy es el catorce de febrero.

Page 23
Example: ¿Cuánto cuesta la manzana? La manzana cuesta un dólar con veinticinco centavos.

Page 25
In the morning (a.m.) – de la mañana; Half past – media; At night (p.m.) – de la noche; In the afternoon (p.m.) – de la tarde; Quarter past – cuarto ; Noon – mediodía; Midnight – medianoche
1) Son las nueve de la noche. 2) Son las cuatro y cuarto/quince de la tarde.

Page 26
3) Es la una de la mañana. 4) Son las dos y media/treina de la tarde. 5) Son las siete y cuarenta y ocho/ocho menos doce de la mañana. 6) Son las seis y veinticuatro de la mañana. 7) Son las ocho y cuarto/quince de la noche. 8) Son las tres y ocho de la mañana. 9) Son las once y cincuenta y nueve de la noche. 10) Es la una y media de la tarde. 11) Es mediodía./Son las doce de la tarde.

Page 28
1) noun – masculine, singular (cat) 2) noun – masculine, feminine (butterfly) 3) verb (to talk) 4) noun – masculine, plural (kids) 5) verb (to be) 6) noun – masculine, singular (banana/plantain) 7) verb (to put/set) 8) verb (to feel) 9) noun – feminine, plural (fruits) 10) verb (to have) 11) verb (to know) 12) noun – feminine, singular (food) 13) noun – feminine, plural (houses)

14) noun – masculine, singular (dog) 15) noun – feminine, singular (woman) 16) noun – masculine, singular (man) 17) noun – feminine, plural (salads) 18) verb (to sing)

Page 29

1) el chico alto (the tall boy) 2) la fresa roja (the red strawberry) 3) las mesas pequeñas (the small tables) 4) una mariposa bonita (a pretty butterfly) 5) los libros caros (the expensive books) 6) una cama grande (a big bed) 7) el camino largo (the long path) 8) la camiseta blanca (the white t-shirt) 9) los perros perezosos (the lazy dogs) 10) una manzana verde (a green apple) 11) unas hamburguesas deliciosas (some delicious hamburgers) 12) un gato gordo (a fat cat) 13) la montaña famosa (the famous mountain) 14) una mujer vieja (an old woman) 15) una clase interesante (an interesting class) 16) el coche rosado (the pink car)

Page 30

1) Rojo – red; 2) Verde – green; 3) Azul – blue; 4) Blanco – white; 5) Negro – black; 6) Anaranjado – orange; 7) Amarillo – yellow; 8) Gris – gray/grey; 9) Marrón/café – brown; 10) Morado/purpura – purple; 11) Rosado – pink; 12) Dorado – gold

Page 31

1) El sol es amarillo/anaranjado. 2) Example: Mi perro/gato es negro. 3) Example: Mi casa es blanca. 4) Example: Me camiseta es azul. 5) El café es marron. 6) El broccoli es verde. 7) El limón es Amarillo. 8) El tomate es rojo. 9) El cielo es azul. 10) Example: Mi color favorito es el rosado.

Page 32: Part 2 Quiz

1) Son las cuatro y media de la tarde. 2) Son las ocho y cuarto/quince de la mañana. 3) Son las doce y veinte de la tarde. 4) Son las once y cuatro de la mañana. 5) Son las dos menos cuarto/Es la una y cuarenta y cinco de la tarde. 6) Example: Son las nueve menos cuarto/ocho y cuarenta y cinco de la mañana. 7) Example: Mi casa es amarilla. 8) La nieve es blanca. 9) Example: Mi color favorito es el verde. 10) El pingüino es blanco y negro.

Page 33

Example: El infinitivo – lavar, El significado – to wash

Page 36

1) Example: ¿Quién es tu profesor favorito? Mi profesora favorita es la Señora Gonzalez. 2) Example: ¿Qué te gusta más, el rojo o el azul? Me gusta más el azul. 3) Example: ¿Cuándo es tu cumpleaños? Mi cumpleaños es el 5 de junio. 4) Example: ¿Dónde te gusta estudiar? Me gusta estudiar en casa. 5) Example: ¿Por qué te gusta el mes de junio? Me gusta el mes de junio porque es el verano. 6) Example: ¿Cómo te gusta viajar? Me gusta viajar en avión. 7) Example: ¿Cuántos perros tienes? Tengo un perro. 8) Example: ¿Cuál es tu color favorito? Mi color favorito es el anaranjado.

Page 37

Husband/wife – el esposo/la esposa; Cousin – el primo/la prima; My – mi/mis; Your – tu/tus; Mother/mom – la madre/mamá; Uncle/aunt – el tío/la tía; Father/dad – el padre/papá; Grandfather/grandmother – el abuelo/la abuela; Son/daughter – el hijo/ la hija; Brother/sister – el hermano/la hermana

Page 38

1) abuela; 2) padre 3) hermana 4) esposa 5) casados/divorciados; 6) abuela 7) tío 8) primo; 9) tía 10) abuelos 11) Example: Tengo una hermana. 12) Example: Tengo dos abuelas. 13) Example: Tengo cuatro tíos. 14) Example: Mi primo favorito tiene veinte años. 15) Example: Mi famila es de Sevilla, España.

Page 39

It's _____ degrees. – La temperatura está a _____ grados. It's sunny. – Hay sol./Está soleado. It's raining. – Llueve. It's windy. – Hay viento./Está ventoso. It's hot. – Hace calor. It's snowing. – Nieva. It's cold. – Hace frío. It's cloudy. – Está nublado. There's a storm. – Hay una tormenta. Spring – la primavera; Summer – el verano; Fall – el otoño; Winter – el invierno

Page 40

Answers will vary.

1) Example: Es invierno en Denver. Hace frío, nieva y la temperatura está a 28 grados Fahrenheit/-2 centígrados.

Page 41

Weather answers will vary.

Bolivia – Sucre/La Paz; Brasil – Brasília; Chile – Santiago; Colombia – Bogotá; Costa Rica – San José; Cuba – La Habana; Ecuador – Quito; El Salvador – San Salvador; Guatemala – La Cuidad de Guatemala; Honduras – Distrito Central (Tegucigalpa/Comayagüela); México – La Cuidad de México (Distrito Federal); Nicaragua – Managua; Panamá – La Ciudad de Panamá; Paraguay – Asunción; Perú – Lima; Puerto Rico – San Juan
La República Dominicana – Santo Domingo; Uruguay – Montevideo; Venezuela – Caracas

Page 42: Part 3 Quiz

1) Example: En Almería, está soleado y hace calor. La temperatura está a noventa grados Fahrenheit/treinta y dos centígrados. 2) Example: En Dublin, llueve. La temperatura está a cuarenta y cinco grados Fahrenheit/siete centígrados. 3) En Beijing, está nublado. La temperatura está a sesenta grados Fahrenheit/quince centígrados. 4) Hace más calor en Moscú/Asunción. 5) Hace más frío en Sydney/Nairobo. 6) Sí, hay una tormenta/No, no hay una tormenta en Vancouver. 7) Example: En Berlín, está nublado y hay viento. La temperatura está a cincuenta grados Fahrenheit/diez centígrados. 8) Example: Sí, me gustaría ir a nadar en Valparaíso porque hace calor. 9) Example: No me gustaría ir a esquiar en Colonia porque es verano. 10) Example: En El Cairo, hace calor y hay viento. La temperatura está a ochenta grados Fahrenheit/veintisiete centígrados. 11) Example: Sí, me gustaría volar una cometa en Santo Domingo porque hay viento. 12) Example: No, no me gustaría montar en bicicleta en Lima porque llueve.

Page 43
Example: El desayuno – pan tostado con café; El almuerzo – un sándwich de jamón y queso; La cena – Un pollo con espinaca

Page 45
At home – en casa; After school – después de la escuela; To ride horses- montar a caballo; To drink – tomar/beber, To go for a run – salir a correr; To do homework – hacer la tarea; Your best friend – tu mejor amigo; Peanut butter – la crema de maní/la mantequilla de cacahuete, Chocolate – el chocolate; To take a nap – dormir una siesta; To eat – comer; Fruit – la fruta

Page 47
1) Example: Me gusta comer galletas en Navidad. 2) Example: Me gusta pasear con el perro los fines de semana. 3) Example: A mi mejor amigo/a le gusta comer tacos en su cumpleaños. 4) Example: Me gusta beber café. 5) Example: Me gusta cocinar los domingos. 6) Example: Me gusta hacer ejercicio los lunes por la mañana. 7) Example: Me gusta ver la tele en casa. 8) Example: Me gusta ir al parque los sábados por la tarde. 9) Example: Me gusta estudiar español en la escuela. 10) Me gusta dormir una siesta después de la escuela. 11) Me gusta más comer fruta/chocolate. 12) Me gusta más hacer la tarea/montar a caballo. 13) Me gusta más dormir una siesta/salir a correr.

Page 48
Answers will vary. See examples in exercise.

Page 50
1-14) Answers to questions will vary.
1) ¿Te gusta jugar fútbol? Example: Sí, me gusta jugar fútbol./No, no me gusta jugar fútbol. 2) ¿Cuándo te gusta jugar fútbol? Example: Me gusta jugar fútbol los domingos. 3) ¿Te gusta beber/tomar refrescos? Example: Sí, me gusta beber/tomar refrescos./No, no me gusta beber/tomar refrescos. 4) ¿Por qué te gusta beber/tomar refrescos? Example: Me gusta beber/tomar refrescos porque son deliciosos. 5) ¿Te gusta esquiar? Example: Sí, me gusta esquiar./No, no me gusta esquiar. 6) ¿Dónde te gusta esquiar? Example: Me gusta esquiar en Aspen. 7) ¿Te gusta correr? Example: Sí, me gusta correr./No, no me gusta correr. 8) ¿Por qué te gusta correr? Example: Me gusta correr, porque es divertido. 9) ¿Te gustan las películas? Example: Sí, me gustan las películas./No, no me gustan las películas. 10) ¿Cuál película te gusta más, _____ o _____? Example: Me gusta más _____. 11) ¿Te gusta comer la crema de maní/la mantequilla de cacahuete? Example: Sí, me gusta comer la crema de maní/la mantequilla de cacahuete. 12) ¿Qué te gusta comer con la crema de maní/mantequilla de cacahuete? Example: Me gusta comer manzanas con crema de maní/mantequilla de cacahuete. 13) ¿Te gusta dormir siestas? Example: Sí, me gusta dormir siestas./No, no me gusta dormir siestas. 14) ¿Cuándo te gusta dormir siestas? Example: Me gusta dormir siestas después de la escuela.

Page 51
To play tennis – jugar tenis; To swim – nadar; To go to the beach – ir a la playa; To play videogames- jugar videojuegos; To watch horror movies – ver películas de terror; to go to parties – ir de fiesta; to sleep – dormir; To eat breakfast – Desayunar; To eat lunch – almorzar; To eat dinner – cenar; To have (drink) hot soup – tomar sopa caliente; To eat Chinese food – comer comida china; To drink green tea – tomar/beber té verde; Babies – los bebés; Kids – los niños; Dog – el perro; Cat – el gato; Chocolate covered strawberries – fresas con chocolate

Page 52
1) ¿A Miguel le gusta nadar? Sí, a Miguel le gusta nadar/No, a Miguel no le gusta nadar. 2) Example: A Miguel le gusta nadar en el océano. 3) ¿A tu mejor amigo/a le gusta jugar tenis? Example: Sí, a mi mejor amigo/a le gusta jugar tenis. 4) A mi mejor amigo/a le gusta jugar tenis porque es deportista. 5) ¿A Marcos y Susana les gusta comer comida china? Example: No, a Marcos y Susana no les gusta comer comida china. 6) A Marcos y Susana no les gusta comer comida china en niguna parte. 7) ¿A quién le gusta tomar sopa caliente después de esquiar? Example: A mí me gusta tomar sopa caliente después de esquiar.

Page 53
8) ¿A quién le gusta ir a la escuela los sábados? Example: ¡A nadie le gusta ir a la escuela los sábados! 9) ¿A quién le gusta jugar videojuegos por la tarde? Example: A los niños les gusta jugar videojuegos por la tarde. 10) ¿Por qué no le gusta tomar té verde a tu padre? Example: A mi padre no le gusta tomar té verde porque no le gusta el sabor. 11) ¿Qué les gusta hacer a los gatos los domingos por la mañana? Example: A los gatos les gusta dormir los domingos por la mañana. 12) ¿Cuándo les gusta comer helado a los niños? Example: A los niños les gusta comer helado los veranos por la tarde. 13) ¿Con quién le gusta almorzar a tu mejor amigo/a? Example: A mi mejor amigo/a le gusta almorzar conmigo. 14) ¿Dónde le gusta dormir al perro? Example: Al perro le gusta dormir en el sofá. 15) ¿Qué les gusta desayunar a tus abuelos? Example: A mis abuelos les gusta desayunar huevos revueltos con tocino. 16) ¿A qué hora le gusta cenar a tu hijo? Example: A mi hijo le gusta cenar a las seis de la tarde. 17) ¿A qué hora les gusta dormir a los bebés? Example: ¡A los bebés no les gusta dormir nunca! 18) ¿A quién le gusta ir de fiesta los viernes por la noche? Example: A los jóvenes les gusta ir de fiesta los viernes por la noche. 19) ¿Por qué no le gusta ver películas de terror a tu primo? Example: A mi primo no le gusta ver películas de terror porque no le gusta tener miedo. 20) ¿A quién le gusta ir a la playa en el invierno? Example: A mi esposo le gusta ir a la playa en el inverno.

Page 54
1) Example: Me gusta salir a cenar los sábados por la noche oche. 2) Example: Me gusta leer el periódico los domingos por la mañana. 3) Example: Me gusta ir a la playa cuando hace mucho calor. 4) Example: A mi madre le gusta esquiar cuando hace frío. 5) Example: A mi padre le gusta montar a caballo en el verano. 6) Example: A los perros les gusta correr. 7) Example: A mi mejor amigo/a le gusta descansar después de la escuela. 8) Example: Me gusta bailar en mi cumpleaños. 9) Example: Me gusta comer cereales en el desayuno. 10) Example: Me gusta ir a Barcelona de vacaciones. 11) Me gusta más el invierno/verano. 12) Example: A mis abuelos les gusta tomar té en el otoño.

Page 55: Part 4 Quiz
1) ¿Cuándo te gusta jugar fútbol? Example: Me gusta jugar fútbol después de la escuela. 2) Te gusta tomar/beber refrescos? Example: No, no me gusta tomar/beber refrescos. 3) Te gusta esquiar en el invierno? Example: Sí, me gusta esquiar en el invierno. 4) ¿A quién le gusta comer en un restaurante los viernes por la noche? Example: A mí me gusta comer en un restaurante los viernes por la noche. 5) ¿A quién no le gusta comer fresas con chocolate de postre? A mi abuela no le gusta comer freseas con chocolate de postre. 6) ¿Dónde te gusta salir a correr, en el parque o el gimnasio? Example: (A mí) me gusta salir a correr en el parque. 7) ¿Cuándo le gusta tomar café a tu mamá, por la mañana o por la noche? A mí mamá le gusta tomar café por la mañana. 8) ¿Por qué no te gusta ver películas por la mañana? Example: (A mí) no me gusta ver películas por la mañana porque estoy ocupado/a.

Page 56
9) ¿A quién le gusta hacer senderismo los fines de semana? Example: (A nosotros) nos gusta hacer senderismo los fines de semana. 10) ¿Cuándo te gusta hacer la tarea, los lunes por la mañana o los domingos por la noche? (A mí) me gusta hacer la tarea los lunes por la mañana/los domingos por la noche. 11) ¿Dónde les gusta jugar a los niños, en la escuela o en casa? A los niños les gusta jugar en la escuela/en casa. 12) ¿Por qué no le gusta ir de compras a Pepe en el centro comercial? Example: A Pepe no le gusta ir de compras en el centro comercial porque es tímido. 13) ¿Qué les gusta hacer a tus gatos los martes por la noche/tarde? Example: A mis gatos les gusta comer atún los martes por la noche/tarde. 14) ¿A tu papá le gusta leer revistas o ver la tele? Example: A mi papá le gusta ver la tele. 15) ¿A quién le gusta comer helado cuando llueve? Example: A los niños les gusta comer helado cuando llueve. 16) ¿(A ti) te gusta cocinar el desayuno? Example: Sí, (a mí) me gusta cocinar el desayuno. 17) ¿Por qué no te gusta compartir tu pizza conmigo? Example: No me gusta compartir mi pizza contigo porque tengo mucha hambre. 18) ¿Cuántas horas te gusta dormir? Example: Me gusta dormir ocho horas.

Page 57
Answers will vary. See examples in exercise.

Page 60
1-10) Answers will vary.
1) Example: Voy a hablar por teléfono con mi mejor amiga hoy por la noche.

Page 62
Students – los estudiantes; To eat cake – comer pastel; To drink wine – tomar/beber vino; To go to work – Ir al trabajo; To go to the gym – ir al gimnasio; To go to the library – ir a la biblioteca; To study for the test – estudiar para el examen; To go to the pool – ir a la piscina; To eat out at a restaurant – comer en un restaurante

Page 63
1) Mi hermano va a la escuela todos los días a las ocho de la mañana. 2) Voy a ir a la fiesta de mi mejor amigo el viernes a las siete y media de la noche. 3) Juanito va a hacer la tarea el lunes por la mañana. 4) Los estudiantes van a estudiar para el examen el lunes por la mañana. 5) Tomás va a la piscina los jueves a las cinco y cuarto de la tarde. 6-14) Answers will vary. 6) Example: Voy al gimnasio los lunes, miércoles y viernes a las cinco de la tarde.

Page 64
1) ¿A dónde vas esta noche/hoy por la noche? 2) ¿Cuándo vas a montar en monopatín? 3) ¿Por qué vas a comer chocolate en la cena? 4) ¿Con quién vas al cine? 5) ¿Dónde vas a comer esta noche/hoy por la noche? 6) ¿Qué vas a escribir? 7) ¿Cómo vas a bailar en la fiesta? 8) ¿Dónde vas a cantar? 9) ¿Quién va a ir de compras? 10) ¿Cuándo vas a viajar al Salvador?

Page 66
1) Mi gato es gris. 2) La camisa de Marisol es roja. 3) Nuestra casa es verde. 4) Su tío/el tío es Julio. 5) Su comida favorita es _____. 6) Su día favorito es el domingo. 7) Nuestros limones son amarillos. 8) Sus abuelos son de México. 9) Sus padres tienen ochenta y siete años. 10) Su esposa tiene cincuenta y cuatro años. 11) El hermano de Joaquina es mi amigo. 12) Nuestra hermana es de Chile. 13) Su (vuestro) coche/auto es azul. 14) Mis perros son negros. 15) El abuelo de Isabel se llama Diego.

Page 68
1) Mi calcetín 2) Tu casa 3) Su camisa 4) Nuestra pizza 5) Sus manzanas 6) Su coche/auto es azul. 7) Su pelo es negro. 8) Nuestro jardín es pequeño. 9) Sus plátanos son amarillos/bananas son amarillas. 10) ¿De quién es esta ensalada? Es suya. 11) ¿De quién es ese perro? Es nuestro. 12) ¿De quién son estas papas? Son tuyas. 13) ¿De quién es este helado? ¡Es mío!

Page 69: Part 5 Quiz
1-14) Answers will vary.
1) Mañana voy a... 2) Hoy estoy... 3) Sí, me gusta hacer la tarea./No, no me gusta hacer la tarea. 4) Mi número de teléfono es... 5) Mañana mi madre va a... 6) Mi profesor/a favorito/a es... 7) Tengo ____ años. 8) Mi abuela es de ____. 9) Este fin de semana mi familia va a... 10) Mi tío favorito se llama ____. 11) El cumpleaños de mi hermano/a es el ____ de ____. 12) Hoy por la noche mis padres van a... 13) Me gustan más las frutas/los chocolates. 14) Mi mejor amigo/a tiene ____ años.

Page 70
Answers will vary. See examples in exercise.

Page 74
1) es; She is my sister. 2) somos; We are sisters. 3) eres; You are from Colorado. 4) soy; I am nice. 5) eres; Where are you from? 6) es; Where is your father from? 7) es; My father is from Spain. 8) es; He is my grandfather. 9) somos; We are friends. 10) son; Y'all are from Mexico. 11) es; You (formal) are my teacher/professor. 12) eres; Are you Canadian?

Page 76
1) estás; How are you? 2) estoy; I am very well, thanks. 3) estamos; We are tired. 4) estoy; I am happy. 5) están; Are they happy? 6) está; Where is the dictionary? 7) están; My sisters are sad. 8) estamos; We are in Spanish class. 9) está; You (formal) are at home. 10) están; Y'all are at the park. 11) estoy; I am excited. 12) está; The ice cream is in the freezer.

Page 77
Backpack – la mochila; Computer – la computadora; Trash can – El bote de basura; Poster – el cartel; Computer screen – la pantalla de la computadora; Pencil sharpener – el sacapuntas; Flag – la bandera; Desk – el escritorio; Window – la ventana; Clock – el reloj; Chair – la silla; Keyboard – el teclado; Door – la puerta

Page 78
1) La computadora está encima del escritorio/pupitre. 2) La silla está debajo de la mesa. 3) ¿Dónde está mi mochila? 4) Tu mochila está aquí. 5) El teclado está delante de la pantalla de la computadora. 6) El reloj está debajo de la ventana. 7) ¿Dónde está el bote de basura? 8) El cartel de Pilar está detrás de la puerta. 9) El sacapuntas de Fernando está encima de la mesa. 10) La bandera americana está al lado del reloj. 11) Mi pupitre está delante de tu pupitre. 12) La silla de Emiliano está allí.

Page 79
Disorganized – Desordenado; Creative – creativo; Patient – paciente; Silly – gracioso; Serious – serio; Sociable – sociable; Organized – ordenado; Impatient – impaciente; Athletic – deportista; Lazy – perezoso; Hardworking – trabajador; Studious – estudioso; Talented – talentoso; Shy – tímido

Page 80
1) (Yo) soy ordenado/a/desordenado/a. 2) (Yo) soy sociable/tímido/a. 3) (Yo) soy serio/a/gracioso/a. 4) Mi madre es paciente/impaciente. 5) Mi padre es... 6) Mi perro es deportista/perezoso. 7) Los Broncos de Denver son talentosos/perezosos. 8) Example: A María le gusta correr. 9) Example: A Tomás le gusta leer. 10) Example: A ellas les gusta trabajar. 11) Example: La abuela es perezosa. 12) Example: Nacho es tímido. 13) Example: Tú eres creativo/a.

Page 82
To walk – caminar; To sing – cantar; To swim – nadar; To ride – montar; To draw – dibujar; To dance – bailar; To listen – escuchar; To practice – practicar; To rest – descansar; To speak – hablar; To teach – enseñar; To ski – esquiar; To dance – bailar

Page 83
1) nado; I swim in the ocean. 2) cantas; You sing very well. 3) camina; He walks home. 4) descansa; Mariana is resting this weekend. 5) escuchamos; We listen to music at night. 6) hablan; Y'all talk/are talking with the Spanish teacher/professor. 7) bailan; They dance on Sundays. 8) toma; Elena drinks coffee with milk. 9) saca; You (formal) take good photos. 10) toca; Samuel plays the piano.

Page 84
1) (Yo) escucho música. 2) Mi madre canta. 3) Tu hermana nada. 4) (Yo) bailo en casa. 5) (Yo) hablo con mis amigos. 6) Stefanie descansa los domingos. 7) (Nosotros) hablamos por teléfono. 8) Ellos caminan a la escuela. 9) Los niños nadan en la piscina. 10) (Yo) no bailo con mi mochila.

Page 85
1-9) Answers will vary.
1) Example: (Yo) estudio en la escuela. 2) Example: Josefina nada en el océano. 3) Example: (Yo) descanso en el sofá. 4) Example: Los niños cantan en el coro. 5) Example: (Nosotros) caminamos en el parque. 6) Example: Los amigos hablan por teléfono. 7) Example: (Tú) bailas en la fiesta. 8) Example: La profesora enseña la clase de español en la escuela. 9) Example: Los Broncos de Denver practican antes de un partido importante.

Page 86
1-11) Answers will vary.
1) Example: Juan estudia. 2) Example: María esquía. 3) Example: Carlos enseña en la universidad. 4) Example: Ellas bailan. 5) Example: (Nosotros) cantamos. 6) Example: Victoria habla por teléfono. 7) Example: (Nosotros) dibujamos. 8) Example: Manuela juega deportes. 9) Example: Ellas nadan. 10) Example: Mario monta en bicicleta. Example: Soy escritora. ¿Qué hago (yo)? (Tú) escribes.

Page 87: Part 6 Quiz
1) La silla está debajo de la mesa. 2) La manzana está encima del escritorio/pupitre. 3) Yo escucho música. 4) Mi madre canta. 5) Tu hermana nada. 6-10) Answers will vary. 6) Example: Yo tengo una fiesta para mi cumpleaños. 7) Example: Nosotros esquiamos en las montañas en el invierno. 8) Example: Los artistas dibujan en París. 9) Yo soy ordenado/a/desordenado/a. 10) Yo soy sociable/tímido/a.

Page 92
Ice tea – el té helado; French fries – las papas fritas; Orange juice – el jugo de naranja; Scrambled eggs – los huevos revueltos; Sausage – la salchicha; Bacon – el tocino; Cookie/cracker/biscuit – la galleta; Coffee – el café; With you/with me – contigo/conmigo; Milk – la leche; Ham and cheese sandwich – el sándwich de jamón y queso; Lemonade – la limonada; Soda/pop – el refresco; Hot dog – el perro caliente; apple – la manzana; Banana – la banana/el plátano

Page 93
1-15) Answers will vary.
1) Example: Generalmente, (yo) como huevos revueltos con tocino en el desayuno. 2) Example: Mi padre come un sándwich de jamón y queso en el almuerzo. 3) Example: Sí, en mi familia (nosotros) comemos salchichas y tocino. 4) Example: No, mi mamá no come perros calientes. 5) Example: No, (yo) no como galletas en el desayuno. 6) Example: No, los bebés no beben té

helado. 7) Example: Sí, (yo) comparto mi pizza con mi hermano. 8) Example: No, mi hermano no comparte sus papas fritas conmigo. 10) toman/beben 11) como 12) comes 13) tomamos/bebemos 14) come 15) toman/beben

Page 94
1) soy 2) comparte 3) comen 4) bebemos 5) están 6) somos 7) creo 8) comes 9) debe 10) compartes 11) es 12) están 13) hablan 14) baila 15) tengo 16) Tú compartes un perro caliente con tu amigo/a. 17) Los niños comen bananas/plátanos en el almuerzo./Los niños almuerzan bananas/plátanos. 18) El profesor/la profesora come un sándwich de jamón y queso.

Page 95
1) comes 2) están 3) habla 4) canta 5) bailamos 6) es 7) comen 8) hablamos 9) tengo 10) comes 11) hablas 12) gusta

Page 96
1) (Yo) nado en el agua azul. 2) (Nosotros) escuchamos música en el parque. 3) ¡(Tú) comes mucho! 4) Yo viajo a Santiago, Chile cada verano. 5) ¡A él no le gusta correr nada! 6) ¿A dónde vas para jugar tenis? 7) ¿A qué hora vas a ir a la fiesta? 8) (A nosotros) nos gusta descansar los domingos por la tarde. 9) ¿(A ti) qué te gusta más, vivir con familia o con amigos? 10) ¿Qué vas a hacer hoy?

Page 97
1) soy 2) va 3) comen 4) montamos 5) están 6) somos 7) voy 8) viajas 9) debe 10) vives 11) es 12) van 13) caminan 14) baila 15) tengo 16) (Tú) vas a esquiar en las montañas con tus amigos el sábado. 17) Usted debe ir de compras con su mamá este fin de semana.

Page 98
18) (Yo) voy a viajar al campo mañana. 19) Ustedes van a ver una película en casa. 20) Ellos van a comer en un restaurante el viernes. 21) Luisa baila los martes por la tarde. 22) Ustedes comen mucho tocino. 23) (Yo) tengo tarea todas las noches. 24) (Tú) vives con tu familia. 25) (Nosotros) vamos a montar en bicicleta mañana por la tarde. 26) Carolina es inteligente, y Roberto es simpático. 27) ¿(Tú) viajas a Lima, Perú todos los años? 28) Ustedes van a caminar en el parque esta tarde. 29) Los niños están felices, porque hoy es el cumpleaños de José. 30) (Yo) voy a correr con mi perro hoy. 31) ¿A qué hora van a cenar tú y tu familia? 32) ¿Cuándo vas a viajar tú a Bogotá, Colombia? 33) ¿Qué vas a hacer (tú) este fin de semana?

Page 99
1) voy 2) va 3) vamos 4) vas 5) beben 6) come 7) ven 8) canta 9) corre 10) gustan 11) (Yo) voy a un restaurante para comer pan. 12) (Tú) vas al cine para ver una película.

Page 100
13) (Tú) vas a Sevilla la semana que viene. 14) ¿A dónde va Sergio mañana? 15) ¿Quién va a tomar/beber el café encima de la mesa? 16) Ana come verduras todos los días. 17) Mi padres toman/beben refrescos todos los días. 18) Los niños corren en el parque después de la escuela. 19) (A mí) me gusta el fútbol. 20) Francisco canta en el club/la discoteca los jueves por la noche. 21) Mis abuelos siempre ven la tele por la mañana. 22) Por qué vas a montar en bicicleta en la playa? 23) ¿Con quién vas tú al cine?

Page 102
Almorzar – yo almuerzo, tú almuerzas, ud. almuerza, él/ella almuerza, nosotros almorzamos, (vosotros almorzáis), uds. almuerzan, ellos/ellas almuerzan; Poder – yo puedo, tú puedes, ud. puede, él/ella puede, nosotros podemos, (vosotros podéis), uds. pueden, ellos/ellas pueden; Recordar – yo recuerdo, tú recuerdas, ud. recuerda, él/ella recuerda, nosotros recordamos, (vosotros recordáis), uds. recuerdan, ellos/ellas recuerdan; Querer – yo quiero, tú quieres, ud. quiere, él/ella quiere, nosotros queremos, (vosotros queréis), uds. quieren, ellos/ellas quieren; Empezar – yo empiezo, tú empiezas, ud. empieza, él/ella empieza, nosotros empezmos, (vosotros empezáis), uds. empiezan, ellos/ellas empiezan, Pedir – yo pido, tú pides, ud. pide, él/ella pide, nosotros pedimos, (vosotros pedís), uds. piden, ellos/ellas piden

Page 103
1) almuerzas; You eat lunch with your father. 2) quiero; I want to eat Italian food. 3) empieza; English class starts at 10:45. 4) quieren; The sisters want to drink coffee with milk. 5) recuerda; The grandfather doesn't remember many things. 6) empiezo; I start studying at 9:00 p.m. 7) almorzamos, comemos; When we eat lunch at the cafe, we eat a lot. 8) recuerdan; Y'all remember the important vocabulary. 9) tiene; Mi grandmother is 96 years old. 10) empieza; Spring starts on March 21st. 11) puedes; You can learn Spanish! 12) pido; When I go to a Mexican restaurant, I always order beef tacos.

Page 104
1-7) Answers will vary.
1) (Yo) tengo _____ años. 2) (Yo) puedo comer _____ hamburguesas. 3) Mi perro/gato tiene _____ años. 4) Mañana voy a _____. 5) (Yo) hago la tarea a las _____. 6) Example: No, mi mamá no va al trabajo los sábados. 7) Hoy voy a cenar _____. 8) (Yo) tengo dos perros. 9) ¡Yo puedo comer doce salchichas! 10) Mi amigo/a va a la escuela todos los días. 11) (Yo) soy estudioso/a. 12) (Yo) como tocino cuando hago la tarea.

Page 105: Part 7 Quiz
1) (Yo) escucho música. 2) Mi madre canta. 3) Mi abuelo no recuerda cosas. 4) Mi hermana puede nadar. 5) La clase de español empieza a las 10:15 de la mañana. 6) Mi padre quiere comer comida mexicana. 7) (Yo) quiero bailar en casa. 8) Me gusta estar con amigos. 9) Las hermanas almuerzan al mediodía. 10) Yo descanso los domingos. 11) (Nosotros) hablamos por teléfono. 12) Ellos caminan a la escuela. 13) (Nosotros) almorzamos en la cafetería. 14) Mi abuela tiene noventa y nueve años.

Page 108
Math class – la clase de matemáticas; Science class – la clase de ciencias naturales; Chemistry class – la clase de química; Social Studies class – las clase de ciencias sociales; Classroom – la aula/salón de clase; Gym class – la clase de educación física,

Boring – aburrido; History class – la clase de historia; Interesting – interesante; Music class – la clase de música; World War II – La Segunda Guerra Mundial; Fun -divertido; English class – la clase de inglés – easy/difficult – fácil/difícil

Page 109
1-14) Answers will vary.
1) Estudio álgebra en la clase de matemáticas. 2) Example: Uso la computadora en la clase de inglés. 3) Estudio biología en la clase de ciencias naturales. 4) Example: Estudio literatura en la clase de español. 5) Example: Estudio la Segunda Guerra Mundial en la clase de historia. 6) Estudio una lengua nueva en la clase de español. 7) Example: Almuerzo al mediodía. 8) Tengo la clase de _____ en la quinta hora. 9) Tengo la clase de _____ en la primera hora. 10) Tengo la clase de _____ en la segunda hora. 11) Me gusta más la clase de ciencias naturales/ciencias sociales. 12) Example: Mi clase favorita es la clase de música porque soy creativa. 13) Example: Si, (a mí) me gusta mucho la clase de español también porque es interesante. 14) Example: No, (a mí) no me gusta la clase de matemáticas tampoco porque es difícil.

Page 110
Elementary school – la primaria; Middle school – la secundaria; High school – el colegio/la preparatoria; Paper – el papel; Calculator – la calculadora; Pencil – el lápiz; Book – el libro; Eraser – la goma de borrar; Pen – el bolígrafo; Notebook – el cuaderno; Backpack – la mochila; Folder – la carpeta; Bookstore – la librería; Library – la biblioteca; Dictionary – el diccionario

Page 111
1) El libro está en la biblioteca. 2) La calculadora está en mi mochila. 3) El diccionario está en la librería. 4) El bolígrafo está en la carpeta. 5) El papel está en el cuaderno. 6) La goma de borrar está en el lápiz. 7) La biblioteca está en la preparatoria/el colegio. 8) Mi mochila está en casa.

Page 112
1-9) Answers will vary.
1) Example: Sí, necesito una regla en la clase de matemáticas. 2) Example: Sí, quiero un diccionario para mi cumpleaños. 3) Example: No, no tengo una calculadora. 4) Example: Sí, veo la televisión por la noche. 5) Example: No, mi madre no necesita una regla cuando come. 6) Example: Sí, necesitamos un cuaderno en la clase de inglés. 7) Example: Sí, mi hermana quiere una mochila para Navidad. 8) Example: No, mi padre no necesita una goma de borrar. 9) Me gustan más los bolígrafos/los lápices.

Page 113
Soccer game – el partido de fútbol; To play golf – jugar golf; To go to the concert – ir al concierto; To go to the dance – ir al baile; The mall – el centro comercial; To go to the beach – ir a la playa; Jewelry store – la joyería; Piano lesson – la lección de piano; To go to the movies – ir al cine; The kid/boy – el muchacho; To play sports – jugar deportes

Page 114
1) Voy a jugar fútbol a las cinco de la tarde. 2) Mi familia y yo vamos a la playa a las once de la mañana. 3) Mi hermana va a la lección de piano a las tres y media/treinta de la tarde. 4) Mis amigos van a jugar golf a las cuatro y cuarto/quince de la tarde. 5) Voy a comer en el restaurante a las seis y media/treinta de la tarde. 6) Voy al concierto con mis amigos el sábado a las ocho de la noche. 7) Julián va al trabajo los lunes a las nueve y cuarto/quince de la mañana. 8) Voy a ir a la fiesta de mi amiga el viernes a las siete y media/treinta. 9) Vamos al gimnasio los jueves a las cinco y media/treinta de la tarde. 10) Desayuno todos los días a las ocho de la mañana.

Page 115
11) Los muchachos van a ver el partidos de fútbol el domingo a la una y media/treinta. 12) Voy a ir al baile el sábado a las nueve y media de la noche. 13) Hago la tarea los domingos a las ocho de la noche. 14) Juego videojuegos todos los días a las cuatro y cuarto/quince de la tarde. 15) Juego deportes los fines de semana. 16) ¡Siempre estudio el español! 17) No voy a la biblioteca nunca. 18) Almuerzo todos los días al mediodía. 19) Nado en la piscina a veces por la tarde. 20) Voy a ir al cine esta tarde.

Page 116
T-shirt – la camiseta; Socks – los calcetines; Jeans – los jeans/vaqueros/pantalones de mezclilla; Blouse – la blusa; Skirt – la falda; Boots – las botas; Coat – el abrigo; Sweatshirt – la sudadera; Long/short – largo/corto; Dress – el vestido; Pants – los pantalones; Too – demasiado; Shoes – los zapatos; To wear/have on – llevar puesto; Large/small – grande/chico; Sweater – el suéter; Raincoat – el impermeable

Page 117
1) ¿Te gustan los pantalones rosados de la Señora Gomez? 2) La muchacha tiene puesta una falda corta. 3) Sus botas son negras. 4) Me gustan los vestidos rojos. 5) La Señora Gonzalez tiene puesto un suéter morado con jeans anaranjados. 6) A Carla le gusta ponerse sudaderas grandes. 7) ¿Cuál blusa te gusta más, la negra o la blanca? 8) ¡Tus botas blancas son lindas! 9) A Joaquín le gusta ponerse calcetines verdes. 10) Su camiseta amarilla es demasiado chica/pequeña.

Page 118
1-13) Answers will vary.
1) Example: Cuando hace calor, me pongo una falda corta con una camiseta. 2) Example: Cuando hace frío, me pongo jeans con un suéter. 3) Example: Cuando llueve, me pongo un impermeable. 4) Example: Cuando nieva, me pongo un abrigo y botas. 5) Example: Cuando hace mucho calor, bebo té helado. 6) Example: Cuando llueve, vamos al cine. 7) Example: Voy a dormir. 8) Example: Mi hermano almuerza en una cafetería. 9) Example: El profesor lee. 10) Example: Los gatos duermen en la sombra. 11) Example: Mi mamá come pavo y puré de papas. 12) Example: Voy a beber agua fría. 13) Example: Voy a ponerme un vestido corto.

Page 119
Bakery/pastry shop – la pastelería; Barbeque – el asado; Soup – la sopa; Cake – El pastel; To be hungry – Tener hambre; Meat – la carne; Fresh vegetables – verduras frescas; Fruit salad – la ensalada de frutas; Spaghetti – el espagueti; Vegetable stand – la verdulería; Fruit stand – la frutería; Steak – el bistec; Supermarket – el supermercado; Fork – el tenedor; Knife – el cuchillo; Spoon – la cuchara; butcher/butcher's shop – la carnicería

Page 120
1-10) Answers will vary.
1) Example: Puedes ir al supermercado. 2) Example: Puedes ir a la verdulería. 3) Example: Puedes ir a la carnicería. 4) Example: Puedes ir a la pastelería. 5) Example: Puedes ir a la frutería. 6) Necesitas un tenedor. 7) Necesitas un tenedor y un cuchillo. 8) Necesitas un tenedor. 9) Necesitas una cuchara. 10) Necesitas un tenedor.

Page 121
Ice cream – el helado; To be good/bad for your health – ser bueno/malo para la salud; Apple juice – el jugo de manzana; Delicious/disgusting – delcicioso/asqueroso; A glass of wine – una copa de vino; Cheese – el queso; Hot tea – el té caliente; Carrots – las zanahorias; To exercise – hacer ejercicio; Hamburger – la hamburguesa; Butter – la mantequilla; Fat (dietary) – la grasa

Page 122
1) Comparto fresas con mi amigo/a, porque son deliciosas. 2) No tomo mucho café, porque no es bueno para la salud. 3) Como helado en el verano, porque me gusta mucho. 4) Tomas/bebes jugo de naranja en el desayuno, porque es bueno para la salud. 5) Mi amigo/a no come mucha mantequilla, porque es malo para la salud. 6) Los niños comen tocino en el almuerzo, porque es delicioso. 7) No tomo/bebo jugo de manzana el la cena, porque es asqueroso. 8-14) Answers will vary. 8) Example: No, no como muchas grasas, porque es malo para la salud. 9) Example: Cuando tengo hambre, como 2 hamburguesas. 10) Example: Sí, yo hago ejercicio para mantenerme saludable, porque soy deportista. 11) Example: Como zanahorias en la cena porque son buenas para la salud. 12) Example: Como pastel en mi cumpleaños, porque me gusta celebrar. 13) Example: Bebo té caliente antes de dormir, porque es relajante. 14) Example: Mi mamá bebe café en la mañana, porque es delicioso.

Page 123
Window – la ventana; Rug – la alfombra; Curtains – las cortinas; Alarm clock – el despertador; Painting – el cuadro; Pillow – la almohada; Bed – la cama; Bedspread/comforter – la colcha; Mirror – el espejo; Bedroom – el dormitorio; Lamp – la lámpara; Closet – el clóset; Night table – la mesita; Wardrobe/armoire – el armario/guardarropa; Dresser/bureau – la cómoda

Page 124
1-10) Answers will vary.
1) Example: Sí, tengo un espejo grande y cuadrado en mi dormitorio. 2) Example: Tengo dos almohadas en mi cama. 3) Example: Mi colcha es gris. 4) Example: Sí, tengo una alfombra azul en mi dormitorio. 5) Example: Tengo una ventana en mi dormitorio. 6) Example: Las cortinas son blancas. 7) Example: Sí, tengo un despertador negro que suena a las seis y media de la mañana. 8) Example: Sí, tengo un cuadro morado y azul en mi dormitorio. Está encima de la cama. 9) Example: Tengo una lámpara rosada en la mesita, al lado de la cama. 10) Tengo un clóset grande/pequeño.

Page 125
11-20) Answers will vary.
11) Example: Yo pongo las camisetas en el armario. 12) Example: Yo pongo los calcetines en la cómoda. 13) Example: Yo pongo los zapatos en el clóset. 14) Example: Yo pongo los pantalones en el clóset. 15) Example: Mi cama está al lado de la ventana. 16) Example: La mesita está al lado de la cama. 17) Example: La cómoda está debajo del espejo. 18) Example: La puerta está al lado de la cómoda. 19-20) Answers will vary. Use previous questions in exercise as examples.

Page 126
Refrigerator – el refrigerador; Sofa – el sofá; Table – la mesa; Chair – la silla; Stove – la estufa; Basement – el sótano; Washing machine – la lavadora; Patio – el patio; Room – el cuarto; To watch t.v. - ver la tele; To wash the dishes – lavar los platos; Dining room – el comedor; Kitchen – la cocina; Living room – la sala; Yard/garden – el jardín; Fireplace/hearth – el hogar; Big/small – grande/pequeño; Television (the appliance itself) – el televisor

Page 127
1-11) Answers will vary.
1) Example: Hay tres dormitorios en mi casa. 2) Example: El refrigerador está en la cocina. 3) Example: El sofá está en la sala. Es blanco. 4) Example: Hay una ventana en mi dormitorio. 5) Example: La estufa está en la cocina, al lado de refrigerador. 6) Example: Sí, hay un sótano en mi casa. 7) Example: Sí, hay un patio en mi casa. Hay una mesa y cuatro sillas en el patio. 8) Example: La lavadora está en un clóset. Es gris. 9) Example: Mi jardín es pequeño. 10) Example: Sí, hay una chimenea en mi casa. Está en la sala. 11) Example: El televisor está en la sala, delante del sofá.

Page 128
12-24) Answers will vary.
12) Example: Yo descanso en la sala. 13) Example: Cocino en la cocina. 14) Example: Almuerzo en el patio. 15) Example: Mi familia come en el comedor. 16) Example: Lavo los platos en la cocina. 17) Example: Hago la tarea en mi dormitorio. 18) Example: Veo la tele en la sala. 19) Example: Uso la computadora en mi dormitorio. 20) Example: Desayuno en la cocina. 21) Example: Mi dormitorio es azul. 22) Example: El comedor es rojo. 23) Example: Hay seis sillas en el comedor. 24) Mi cuarto favorito es mi dormitorio.

Page 129: Part 8 Quiz
1-13) Answers will vary.
1) Example: Almuerzo al mediodía cuando estoy en la escuela/el trabajo. 2) Example: Mi cumpleaños es el trece de mayo. 3) Example: Hoy está soleado y está a setenta grados Fahrenheit. 4) Example: Sí, necesito un cuaderno en la clase de ciencias sociales. 5) Example: No, no necesito un bolígrafo en la clase de educación física. 6) Example: Hoy es el seis de abril. 7) Example: Son las tres y media/treinta. 8) Example: Me gusta ir al parque con el perro durante el fin de semana. 9) (A mí) me gusta más trabajar/jugar deportes. 10) Example: (A mí) no me gusta correr tampoco. 11) Example: (A mí) también me gusta jugar videojuegos. 12) Soy tímido/a/sociable. 13) Mi madre es ordenada/desordenada.

Page 130
14-18) Answers will vary.
14) Example: tímido/a/reservado/a. 15) Example: En la cuarta hora tengo la clase de inglés. 16) Example: En la segunda hora tengo la clase de historia. 17) Example: difícil/aburrida 18) Example: interesante/fácil 19) La bandera está al lado del reloj. 20) La silla está detrás del escritorio/pupitre. 21) ¿Dónde está el bote de basura en esta sala de clase? 22) El jugo de manzana está encima de la mesa. 23) Desayuno huevos y salchichas./Como huevos y salchichas en el desayuno. 24) Comparto una pizza con mi amigo/a. 25) Yo soy creativo/a. 26) Tú eres perezoso/a. 27) (A mí) me gusta escuchar música y comer un sándwich de jamón y queso.

Page 139
1) comiste; What did you eat last night? 2) habló; Lisa talked with her son last Friday. 3) bailaron; You two danced at the club last night. 4) cantó; The grandmother sang in the choir/chorus last weekend. 5) dibujaste; Did you draw this wonderful drawing? 6) escribieron; The sisters wrote a letter to Santa Claus. 7) caminamos; Last week, we walked around/through the park. 8) descansó; The cat rested last night. 9) nadaste; Did you swim in the pool last week? 10) cocinó; What did Luz cook for breakfast? 11) fueron; Where did y'all go yesterday? 12) fuiste; What movie did you go see last Saturday? 13) quedé; I stayed home last night. 14) fue; My cousin went to the gym yesterday. 15) fui; I went to the mountains last Sunday. 16) hiciste; What did you do yesterday? 17) monté; I didn't ride my bike last night. 18) comió; Who ate at a restaurant last weekend?

Page 140
1) fui; 2) fue; fuimos; 4) fuiste; 5) bebieron; 6) comió; 7) vieron; 8) vio; 9) corrieron; 10) gustó

Page 141
1) Fuiste a la Ciudad de México el año pasado. 2) Fui a Costa Rica la semana pasada. 3) Fuimos a esquiar en las montañas el invierno pasado. 4) Luís fue al centro comercial para comprar una camiseta. 5) Sabrina y Patricia corrieron en el gimnasio anoche. 6) La mujer en el autobús vio a un niño/muchacho en una bicicleta. 7) Los estudiantes tomaron/bebieron mucho café antes del examen. 8) A Emiliano le gustó la comida china. 9) Los niños/muchachos vieron una película en el zoológico. 10) ¡Sebastián se comió toda la pizza en el desayuno esta mañana!

Page 142
To cook – cocinar; To swim – nadar; To exercise – hacer ejercicio; To work – trabajar; To sunbathe – tomar el sol; To celebrate – celebrar; To sleep – dormir; To travel – viajar; To buy – comprar; To dance – bailar; To rest – descansar; To kiss – besar; To eat – comer; To do/to make – hacer; To go hiking in the mountains – hacer senderismos en las montañas; To ski – esquiar

Page 143
1-13) Answers will vary.
1) Example: Hice ejercicio en el gimnasio ayer. 2) Example: Desayunamos pan tostado y café hoy./Comimos pan tostado y café en el desayuno hoy. 3) Example: Gabriela viajó a China el año pasado. 4) Example: Hice la tarea de español anoche. 5) Example: Rodrigo esquió en Vail/los Alpes el fin de semana pasado. 6) Example: Tomamos sol en la playa el verano pasado. 7) Example: La viejita compró pan y leche en el supermercado. 8) Example: Hiciste ejercicio en el gimnasio ayer por la tarde. 9) Example: Juan y María bailaron en la discoteca. 10) Example: Nos besamos en el Año Nuevo. 11) Example: Hice paella de cenar anoche. 12) Example: Los gatos descansaron en la alfombra. 13) Example: Silvia cocinó en el trabajo el viernes pasado.

Page 144: Part 9 Quiz
1) caminé; 2) vivieron; 3) hizo; 4) comimos; 5) comió; 6) habló; 7) fueron; 8-10) Answers will vary. 8) Example: Yo trabajé ayer. 9) Example: Yo desayuné cereales hoy./Yo comí cereales en el desayuno hoy. 10) Example: Yo viajé a Montevideo, Uruguay el año pasado.

Page 146
Note: When you are asked to rewrite the sentence in a different tense, you may have to change other parts of the sentence to make the time make sense. You will see examples of this in parentheses, but there may be multiple ways to do this.
1) Conjugated verb – vamos; Ending – amos; Infinitive – ir; Tense – present; Subject – nosotros; English meaning – to go; Q or S – statement; Question word – N/A; Translation – We're going/let's go to the park this weekend. Preterite – Fuimos al parque el fin de semana pasado. New Translation – We went to the park last weekend.
2) Conjugated verb – es; Ending – es; Infinitive – ser; Tense – present; Subject – él/ella; English meaning – to be; Q or S – statement; Question word – N/A; Translation – Today is the first day of Winter. Simple Future – (Mañana) va a ser el primer día de invierno. New Translation – (Tomorrow) is going to be the first day of Winter.

Page 147
3) Conjugated verb – fuiste; Ending – uiste; Infinitive – ir; Tense – preterite; Subject – tú; English meaning – to go; Q or S – question; Question word – A dónde; Translation – Where did you go last year? Simple Future – ¿A dónde vas (el año que viene)? New Translation – Where are you going (next year)?

4) Conjugated verb – hizo; Ending – o; Infinitive – hacer; Tense – preterite; Subject – él/ella/ud.; English meaning – to do; Q or S – statement; Question word – N/A; Translation – He/she/you formal did the homework. Simple Future – Va a hacer la tarea. New Translation – He/she/you formal is going to/are going to do the homework.

Page 148

5) Conjugated verb – llegas; Ending – as; Infinitive – llegar; Tense – present; Subject – tú; English meaning – to arrive; Q or S – question; Question word – qué; Translation –What time do you arrive at school, generally? Preterite – ¿A qué hora llegaste a la escuela? (Note: The word generalmente will need to be removed because the preterite tense denotes an action that is complete, not habitual.) New Translation – What time did you arrive at school?

6) Conjugated verb – quiere; Ending – e; Infinitive – querer; Tense – present; Subject – who; English meaning – to want; Q or S – question; Question word – quién; Translation – Who wants to go to the movies with me tonight? Simple future – ¿Quién va a querer ir al cine conmigo hoy por la noche? New Translation – Who is going to want to go to the movies with me tonight?

Page 149

7) Conjugated verb – gusta; Ending – a; Infinitive – gustar; Tense – present; Subject – él/ella; English meaning – to please; Q or S – question; Question word – quién; Translation – Who likes to wear beautiful dresses? Preterite – ¿A quién le gustó ponerse vestidos lindos? New Translation – Who liked wearing pretty dresses?

8) Conjugated verb – quiero (x2)/etsá; Ending – o/á; Infinitive – querer/estar; Tense – present/present; Subject – yo/él/ella; English meaning – to want/to be; Q or S – statement; Question word – N/A; Translation – I don't want to know if the glass is full or empty. I want a soda/pop! Simple Future – No voy a querer saber si el vaso está lleno o vacío. ¡Voy a querer un refresco! (Note: The sentence makes more sense if we put querer in the simple future but leave estar in the present.) New Translation – I'm not going to want to know if the glass is full or empty. I'm going to want a soda!

Page 154

1) lo; 2) la; 3) los; 4) las; 5) lo; 6) las; 7) los; 8) lo; 9) la; 10) los; 11) la

Page 155

1) Translation: I'm going to buy a new shirt. Direct Object: una camisa nueva; Direct Object Pronoun: la; New Sentence: La voy a comprar./Voy a comprarla. Translation: I'm going to buy it.

2) Translation: I want to eat some red apples. Direct Object: unas manzanas rojas; Direct Object Pronoun: las; New Sentence: Las quiero comer./Quiero comérlas. Translation: I want to eat them.

Page 156

3) Translation: Jorge needs to read the book. Direct Object: el libro; Direct Object Pronoun: lo; New Sentence: Jorge lo necesita leer/Jorge necesita leerlo. Translation: Jorge needs to read it.

4) Translation: Pepito lost some socks. Direct Object: unos calcetines; Direct Object Pronoun: los; New Sentence: Pepito los perdió. Translation: Pepito lost them.

5) Translation: Who is going to set the tables? Direct Object: las mesas; Direct Object Pronoun: las; New Sentence: ¿Quién las va a poner?/Quién va a ponerlas? Translation: Who is going to set them?

6) Translation: I'm looking for my younger brother. Direct Object: mi hermano menor; Direct Object Pronoun: lo; New Sentence: Lo busco. Translation: I'm looking for him.

7) Translation: Are you going to see the movie? Direct Object: la película; Direct Object Pronoun: la; New Sentence: ¿La vas a ver?/¿Vas a verla? Translation: Are you going to see it?

Page 157

1) les; 2) le; 3) le; 4) le; 5) le; 6) les; 7) le; 8) le; 9) le; 10) les; 11) les

Page 158

1) Translation: I want to make a cake for my grandmother. Indirect Object: mi abuela; Indirect Object Pronoun: le; New Sentence: Le quiero hacer un pastel./Quiero hacerle un pastel. Translation: I want to make her a cake.

2) Translation: The professor/teacher is going to make a difficult exam for the students. Indirect Object: los estudiantes; Indirect Object Pronoun: les; New Sentence: La profesora les va a hacer un examen difícil./La profesora va a hacerles un examen difícil. Translation: The professor/teacher is going to make them a difficult exam.

Page 159

3) Translation: Ricardo wants to visit his friend in Seville. Indirect Object: su amigo; Indirect Object Pronoun: le; New Sentence: Ricardo le quiere visitar en Sevilla./Ricardo quiere visitárle en Sevilla. Translation: Ricardo wants to visit him in Seville.

4) Translation: Pedro and Sabrina write letters to their aunt and uncle in Mexico. Indirect Object: sus tíos en México; Indirect Object Pronoun: les; New Sentence: Pedro y Sabrina les escriben cartas. Translation: Pedro and Sabrina write them letters.

5) Translation: We are going to give this sweater to our mom as a birthday gift. Indirect Object: nuestra mamá; Indirect Object Pronoun: le; New Sentence: Nosotros le vamos a regalar este suéter para su cumpleaños./Nosotros vamos a regalarle este suéter para su cumpleaños. Translation: We are going to give this sweater to her as a birthday gift.

6) Translation: Are you going to give the toy to your sister? Indirect Object: tu hermana; Indirect Object Pronoun: le; New Sentence: ¿Le vas a dar el jugete?/¿Vas a darle el juguete? Translation: Are you going to give her the toy?

7) Translation: My dad is going to make a reservation for my mom. Indirect Object: mi mamá; Indirect Object Pronoun: le; New Sentence: Mi papá le va a hacer una reservación./Mi papá va a hacerle una reservación. Translation: My dad is going to make her a reservation.

Page 162
1) divertirme; I like to have fun at parties. 2) me divierto; When I go to parties, I have a lot of fun. 3) acostarte; Do you want to go to bed late tonight? 4) te acuestas; What times do you go to bed, generally? 5) despertarte; What time are you going to wake up tomorrow? 6) te despiertas; What time do you wake up when you're on vacation? 7) bañarse, ducharse; Does the boy prefer to take baths or showers? 8) se baña; The boy takes a bath on Sundays. 9) lavarnos; We're going to wash our hands./Let's wash our hands. 10) nos lavamos; We wash our hands before eating. 11) me quedo, me levanto; When I stay at a hotel, I always get up early. 12) afeitarse; The boys/kids don't need to shave their faces (beards). 13) nos divertimos; We have fun at the beach. 14) se lavan; The cousins brush their teeth. 15) duchar (Note: the *te* is already there, before *vas*, so you don't need to add it again.) Are you going to shower before the wedding? 16) dormir (Note: the *me* is already there, before *quiero*, so you don't need to add it again.) I'm very tired. I want to go to sleep!

Page 165
1) Translation: I want to make a cake for my grandmother. Indirect Object: mi abuela; Indirect Object Pronoun: le; Direct Object: un pastel; Direct Object Pronoun: lo; New Sentence: Se lo quiero hacer./Quiero hacérselo. Translation: I want to make it for her.
2) Translation: The professor/teacher is going to make a difficult exam for the students. Indirect Object: los estudiantes; Indirect Object Pronoun: les; Direct Object: un examen difícil; Direct Object Pronoun: lo; New Sentence: La profesora se lo va a hacer./La profesora va a hacérselo. Translation: The professor/teacher is going to make it for them.
3) Translation: Ricardo wants to visit his friend in Seville. Indirect Object: su amigo; Indirect Object Pronoun: le; Direct Object: None; Direct Object Pronoun: N/A; New Sentence: Ricardo le quiere visitar en Sevilla./Ricardo quiere visitarle en Sevilla. Translation: Ricardo wants to visit him in Seville.
4) Translation: Pedro and Sabrina write letters to their aunt and uncle in Mexico. Indirect Object: sus tíos en México; Indirect Object Pronoun: les; Direct Object: cartas; Direct Object Pronoun: las; New Sentence: Pedro y Sabrina se las escriben. Translation: Pedro and Sabrina write them to them. (Note: Although this sounds a bit awkward in English, the Spanish use of both Direct and Indirect Object Pronouns here is not awkward.)

Page 166
5) Translation: We are going to give this sweater to our mom as a birthday gift. Indirect Object: nuestra mamá; Indirect Object Pronoun: le; Direct Object: este suéter; Direct Object Pronoun: lo; New Sentence: Se lo vamos a regalar para su cumpleaños./Vamos a regalárselo para su cumpleaños. Translation: We are going to give it to her as a birthday gift.
6) Translation: The waiter is going to bring us the dessert. Indirect Object: nosotros; Indirect Object Pronoun: nos; Direct Object: el postre; Direct Object Pronoun: lo; New Sentence: El camarero nos lo va a traer./El camarero va a traérnoslo. Translation: The waiter is going to bring it to us.
7) Translation: Luisa makes cookies/biscuits for her grandchildren. Indirect Object: sus nietos; Indirect Object Pronoun: les; Direct Object: galletas; Direct Object Pronoun: las; New Sentence: Luisa se las hace. Translation: Luisa makes them for them.
8) Translation: The monkeys throw bananas at the tourists. Indirect Object: los turistas; Indirect Object Pronoun: les; Direct Object: plátanos; Direct Object Pronoun: los; New Sentence: Los monos se los lanzan. Translation: The monkeys throw them at them.

Page 167
9) Translation: The dog ate the girl's sandwich. Indirect Object: la niña; Indirect Object Pronoun: le; Direct Object: el sándwich; Direct Object Pronoun: lo New Sentence: El perro se lo comió. Translation: The dog ate it (the thing that was hers).
10) Translation: Your brother asked you a favor. Indirect Object: tú; Indirect Object Pronoun: te; Direct Object: un favor; Direct Object Pronoun: lo; New Sentence: Tu hermanos te lo pidió. Translation: Your brother asked it of you.
11) Translation: I gave the flowers to you. Indirect Object: tú; Indirect Object Pronoun: ti; Direct Object: las flores; Direct Object Pronoun: las; New Sentence: Yo te las di. Translation: I gave them to you.
12) Translation: Who gave a chocolate bar to the baby? Indirect Object: el bebé; Indirect Object Pronoun: le; Direct Object: una barra de chocolate; Direct Object Pronoun: la; New Sentence: ¿Quién se la dio? Translation: Who gave it to him/her?

Page 168
1) Indirect Object: él; Indirect Object Pronoun: le; Direct Object: un globo; Direct Object Pronoun: lo; New Sentence: Yo se lo voy a dar./Yo voy a dárselo. Translation: I'm going to give it to him.
2) Indirect Object: tu amigo/a; Indirect Object Pronoun: le; Direct Object: una carta; Direct Object Pronoun: la; New Sentence: Tú se la quieres escribir./Tú quieres escribírsela. Translation: You want to write it to him/her.
3) Indirect Object: yo; Indirect Object Pronoun: me; Direct Object: el secreto; Direct Object Pronoun: lo; New Sentence: ¿Quién me lo va a decir?/Quién va a decírmelo? Translation: Who is going to tell me it?
4) Indirect Object: su novia; Indirect Object Pronoun: le; Direct Object: un anillo; Direct Object Pronoun: lo; New Sentence: José se lo dio/regaló. Translation: José gave it to her.

Page 169
5) Indirect Object: la tortuga; Indirect Object Pronoun: le; Direct Object: café; Direct Object Pronoun: lo; New Sentence: ¿Quién se lo dio? Translation: Who gave it to him/her/it?
6) Indirect Object: tú; Indirect Object Pronoun: te; Direct Object: el calcetín; Direct Object Pronoun: lo; New Sentence: ¿Por qué el gato te lo robó?/¿Por qué te lo robó el gato? Translation: Why did the cat steal it (the thing that belonged to you)?
7) Indirect Object: María; Indirect Object Pronoun: le; Direct Object: el pastel; Direct Object Pronoun: lo; New Sentence: Se lo dimos/regalamos para su cumpleaños. Translation: We gave it to her for her birthday.
8) Answers will vary.

Page 170
1) Can you give me a dollar? Te lo doy, si me compras un helado. 2) I want to write a letter to my friend in Spain. ¿Por qué no se la envías por correo electrónico? 3) We're going to give the flowers to our mom. ¿Por qué no me las regalan (a mí)? 4) Are you going to buy the book for your (male) friend? No, lo voy a comprar para mi novia./No, voy a comprarlo para mi novia./No, se lo voy a comprar a mi novia./No, voy a comprárselo a mi novia. 5) Where is Sebastián going to put the chocolates? Los va a esconder en la playa.

Page 171
6) Are you going to bring the pizza? Sí, la voy a traer./Sí, voy a traérla. 7) Are you going to look for the bacon? Sí, lo voy a buscar./Sí, voy a buscarlo. 8) Is grandma going to cook us an exquisite breakfast? No, ¡lo voy a concinar para el perro!/No, ¡voy a cocinarlo para el perro!/No, ¡se lo va a cocincar al perro!/No, ¡voy a cocinárselo al perro! 9) Is Joaquín going to give you a coat? No, se lo va a dar a su hermano. 10) Who is going to eat all the cake? ¡Me lo voy a comer todo!

Page 172
Delicious meat – La carne deliciosa; A beautiful letter – una carta linda; The same card – la misma tarjeta; His essay – su ensayo; An exquisite meal – una comida exquisita; Each Christmas – cada Navidad; A love song – una canción de amor

Page 173
1) You send me the same card each Christmas. – Me envías/mandas la misma tarjeta cada Navidad. You send it to me each Christmas. Me la envías/mandas cada Navidad. 2) The man sings his wife a love song. – El hombre le canta una canción de amor a su esposa. – He sings it to her. – Se la canta. 3) The kids give the teacher an apple. – Los niños/muchachos le dan una manzana a su profesor/profesora. They give it to him/her. – Se la dan. 4) You pay the bill for us. – Pagas la cuenta por nosotros. You pay it for us – Nos la pagas. 5) I open the door for the old woman. – Yo le abro la puerta para la viejita. I open it for her. – Se la abro. 6) We cooked you guys an exquisite meal! – ¡Les Cocinamos una comida exquisita para ustedes! We cooked it for you guys! – ¡Se la cocinamos!

Page 174
7) You wrote me a beautiful letter. – Escribiste una carta linda para mí. You wrote it for me. – Me la escribiste. 8) The student handed in his essay to the teacher. – El/la estudiante le entregó su ensayo al profesor/a la profesora. He handed it in to him/her. – Se lo entregó. 9) Your parents gave you a car as a birthday gift! – ¡Tus padres te regalaron un coche/auto para tu cumpleaños! They gave it to you as a gift! – ¡Te lo regalaron para tu cumpleaños! 10) We gave the dog delicious meat. – Le dimos carne deliciosa al perro. We gave it to him/her. – Se la dimos. 11-11a) Answers will vary.

Page 175: Part 10 Quiz
1) Graciela le envió/mandó una tarjeta a su hermana. 1a) Graciela se la envió/mandó. 2) Pilar le dio/regaló un regalo a su abuela. 2a) Se lo dio/regaló. 3) El camarero le trajo una copa de vino a Sabrina. 3a) Se la trajo. 4) Stefanie me hizo café. 4a) Stefanie me lo hizo. 5) Emiliano vio un mono en el autobús. 5a) Emiliano lo vio en el autobús.

Page 177
1) Conjugated verb – lavaron; Ending – aron; Infinitive – lavar; Tense – preterite; Subject – ellos/ellas/uds.; English meaning – to wash; DO/IO/R Pronouns – lo; Q or S – question; Question word – N/A; Translation – Did they/y'all wash it/him well? Simple Future – ¿Lo van a lavar bien? New Translation – Are they/y'all going to wash it/him well?

Page 178
2) Conjugated verb – voy; Ending – oy; Infinitive – ir; Tense – present; Subject – yo.; English meaning – to go; DO/IO/R Pronouns – la; Q or S – statement; Question word – N/A; Translation – I am going to look for it/her. Preterite – La fui a buscar. New Translation – I went to look for it/her.
3) Conjugated verb – dio; Ending – io; Infinitive – dar; Tense – preterite; Subject – él/ella; English meaning – to give; DO/IO/R Pronouns – le; Q or S – statement; Question word – N/A; Translation – He/she gave a hug to his/her son. Simple Future – La va a dar un abrazo a su hijo. New Translation – He/she is going to give a hug to his/her son.

Page 179
4) Conjugated verb – gusta; Ending – a; Infinitive – gustar; Tense – present; Subject – él/ella.; English meaning – to please; DO/IO/R Pronouns – le; Q or S – question; Question word – quién; Translation – Who likes to travel on a plane? Preterite– ¿A quién le gustó viajar en avión? New Translation – Who liked traveling on a plane?
5) Conjugated verb – escondió; Ending – ió; Infinitive – esconder; Tense – preterite; Subject – él/ella/ud.; English meaning – to hide; DO/IO/R Pronouns – lo; Q or S – question; Question word – N/A; Translation – Did he/she/your formal hide it? Simple Future – ¿Lo va a esconder? New Translation – Is he/she going to hide it?/Are you formal going to hide it?

Page 180
6) Conjugated verb – regalé; Ending – é; Infinitive – regalar; Tense – preterite; Subject – yo; English meaning – to give as a gift; DO/IO/R Pronouns – te, lo; Q or S – statement; Question word – N/A; Translation – I gave it to you as a gift. Simple Future – Te lo voy a regalar./Voy a regalártelo. New Translation – I'm going to give it to you as a gift.
7) Conjugated verb – llamaste/llamo; Ending – aste/o; Infinitive – llamar/llamar; Tense – preterite/present; Subject – tú/yo; English meaning – to call/to call; DO/IO/R Pronouns – me, te; Q or S – statement; Question word – N/A; Translation – You didn't call me last night, and that's why I'm calling you today.

Page 184
1) Come tu cena. 2) Pide una pizza grande. 3) Ayuda a tu hermano. 4) Juega con tu primo/a.

Page 185
Sé – ser (be); Ten – tener (have); Ven – venir (come); Ve – ir (go); Vete – irse (get out of here); Pon – poner (put/set); Haz – hacer (do/make); Sal – salir (go out); Di – decir (tell/say) 1) Ve a la escuela. 2) Sal con tus amigos/as. 3) Haz tu tarea. 4) Di la verdad.

Page 186
1) Dáselo. 2) Cocínasela. 3) Regálaselas. 4) Pídemelo. 5) Dísela. 6) Póntelo. 7) Ten cuidado en las montañas. (It would be strange to replace *cuidado* with a pronoun, because the phrase *tener cuidado* goes together to mean "be careful.") 8) Sal con tus amigos esta noche. (Note: tus amigos are not a direct object or indirect object because they come after the word *con*.) 9) Cómpralos. 10) Léeselo. 11) Cómetela. 12) Ven aquí. 13) Explícamelas.

Page 187
1) a) Deja los libros; b) Deja el libro; c) D<u>e</u>jalos; d) D<u>e</u>jalos; e) Déjalos

Page 188
2) a) Espera el autobús; b) Espera el autobús; c) Esp<u>e</u>ralo; d) Esp<u>e</u>ralo; e) Espéralo; 3) a) Juega fútbol; b) Juega fútbol; c) Ju<u>e</u>galo; d) Ju<u>e</u>galo; e) Juégalo; 4) a) Olvídate del problema; b) Olvídate del problema; c) Olv<u>i</u>datelo; d) Olv<u>i</u>datelo; e) Olivídatelo; 5) a) Encuentra las flores; b) Encuentra las flores; c) Encu<u>e</u>ntralas; d) Encu<u>e</u>ntralas; e) Encuéntralas; 6) a) Pon la mesa; b) Pon la mesa; c) P<u>o</u>nla; d) P<u>o</u>nla; e) Ponla; 7) a) Conduce el coche; b) Conduce el coche; c) Cond<u>u</u>celo; d) Cond<u>u</u>celo; e) Condúcelo; 8) a) Recuerda los poemas; b) Recuerda los poemas; c) Recu<u>e</u>rdalos; d) Recu<u>e</u>rdalos; e) Recuérdalos

Page 189
9) a) Haz la tarea; b) Haz la tarea; c) H<u>a</u>zla; d) H<u>a</u>zla; e) Hazla; 10) a) Ponte el suéter; b) Ponte el suéter; c) P<u>o</u>ntelo; d) P<u>o</u>ntelo; e) Póntelo; 11) a) Ayuda al bebé; b) Ayuda al bebé; c) Ay<u>u</u>dalo; d) Ay<u>u</u>dalo; e) Ayúdalo

Page 192
1) a) Escríbaselo. b) No se lo escriba. c) You should write the story for your children./Write it for them./Don't write it for them. 2) a) Cante más. b) No cante más. c) You should sing more./Sing more./Don't sing more. 3) a) Cómalo. b) No lo coma. c) You should eat all of the flan./Eat it./Don't eat it. 4) a) Ahórrelo. b) No lo ahorre. c) You should save money./Save it/Don't save it. 5) a) Espérelo. b) No lo espere. c) You should wait for the bus./Wait for it./Don't wait for it.

Page 193
6) a) Páguenosla. (Note: This one is a mouthful, so it might be less awkward in Spanish to simply say "páguenos la cuenta.") b) No la pague. c) You should pay the bill/check for us./Pay it for us./Don't pay it for us. 7) a) Cómpreselo. b) No se lo compre. c) You should buy the sweater for your wife./Buy it for her./Don't buy it for her. 8) a) Véalo. b) No lo vea. c) You should watch the Denver Broncos football game./Watch it./Don't watch it. 9) a) Díganmelo. b) No me lo digan. c) Y'all should tell me it./Tell me it./Don't tell me it. 10) a) Salgan de aquí. b) No salgan de aquí. c) Y'all should leave here./Leave here./Don't leave here. 1) a) Tengan cuidado. b) No tengan cuidado. c) Y'all should be careful./Be careful./Don't be careful. 12) a) Pónganselas. b) No se las pongan. c) Y'all should put your boots on./Put them on./Don't put them on. 13) a) Llévenlo. b) No lo lleven. c) Y'all should take an umbrella./Take it./Don't take it. 14) a) Vengan al congreso. b) No vengan al congreso. c) Y'all should come to the conference./Come to the conference./Don't come to the conference. 15) a) Tráiganla. b) No la traigan. c) Y'all should bring food./Bring it./Don't bring it.

Page 194
1) Estas flores son blancas, pero ésas son azules. 2) El año pasado fui a este aeropuerto, pero este año voy a aquel aeropuerto. 3) Este cuadro es para esa niña/muchacha, pero ese cuadro es para esta niña/muchacha. 4) Aquellos lagos son grandes, pero éstos cerca de esta casa son pequeños. 5) Este tocino está delcioso, y ese tocino está más o menos, ¡pero aquél está asqueroso! 6) Answers will vary.

Page 195
1) Me gusta este libro, pero no me gusta ese libro. 2) Me gusta este libro, pero no me gusta ése. 3) Me gusta este libro, pero no me gusta aquél. 4) Este restaurante es bueno, pero ese restaurante es excelente. 5) Este restaurante es bueno, pero ése es excelente. 6) Me como este queso, ¡pero no como aquel queso! 7) Yo Como este queso, ¡pero no como aquél! 8) Estos pantalones son mejores que esos pantalones.

Page 196
9) Estos pantalones son mejores que ésos. 10) Esos pasteles son mejores que estos pasteles. 11) Esos pasteles son mejores que éstos. 12) Esa niña/muchacha es mayor que estas niñas/muchachas. 13) Estas playas son más lindas que aquéllas. 14) Este jugo de manzana es más frío que ese jugo de manzana. 15) Estos suéteres son más grandes que ésos. 16) Este plátano es más amarillo que aquéllos./Esta banana es más amarilla que aquéllas. 17) Este vino es mayor que esos vinos. 18) Me gustan más estos zapatos que ésos. 19) Yo voy mucho a este centro comercial, pero nunca voy a aquél. 20) ¿Cuál sopa te gusta más (a ti), ésta o ésa?

Page 197
1) menor; mayor; Juan is 27 years old and José is 35 years old. Juan is younger than José. José is older than Juan.

Page 198
2) Example: mejor; This salad is delicious! It's better than the nasty salad that I ate yesterday. 3) Example: más; My girlfriend is prettier than all of the movie stars. 4) lo mejor; I love winning the game/match. It's the best! 5) más vieja/más grande; The oldest turtle in the world in 170 years old. 6) peor; This cheese is worse than the cheese last night. 7) Example: el más famoso; más famoso; Who is the most famous actor in the world? Brad Pitt is the most famous. He's more famous than Tom Cruise. 8) Example: más divertidos; Dogs are more fun than cats. 9) Example: más saludables; Carrots are healthier than potato chips. 10)

menor; My younger brother is 5 years old. 11) más; más corto/menos largo; Who has longer hair, Rosita or Melinda? Definitely, Rosita. Melinda's hair is shorter/less long than Rosita'a hair. 12) más; más ancho; The Río de la Plata (River Plate) is the widest river in the world. It's wider than the Colorado River. (The Río de la Plata is located between Uruguay and Argentina.) 13) mejor; el mejor; In a restaurant: Which is better, the fish or the chicken? Waiter: The fish, of course. The fish is the best dish in the whole restaurant!

Page 199
14) lo peor; I don't like to lose my cell phone. It's the worst! 15) Example: más calor; In the summer, it's hotter than in the winter. 16) más dinero; The doctor earns more money than the receptionist. 17) más; Coffee has more caffeine than tea. 18) Example: mejor/peor; _____; The best/worst restaurant in the world is _____. 19) Example: mejor/peor; _____; The best/worst movie in the world is _____.

Page 200: Part 11 Quiz
1) Estas manzanas son verdes, pero esas manzanas son rojas. 1a) Estas manzanas son verdes, pero ésas son rojas. 2) Esta tarde, voy a este restaurante, pero mañana voy a aquél restaurant. 3) Esta pizza es para esta niña/muchacha, pero ésa es para esta niña/muchacha. 4) Esos lagos son grandes, pero éstos cerca de esta casa son pequeños. 4a) Esos lagos son grandes, pero éstos cerca de esta casa son pequeños. 5) Este tocino está delicioso, y ese tocino está más o menos, ¡pero aquél está asqueroso! 6) ¡Dame el bolígrafo! ¡Dámelo! 7) ¡Escríbeme un a carta! ¡Escríbemela! 8) ¡Cántale una canción! ¡Cántasela!

Page 201
1) Conjugated verb – puse; Ending – e; Infinitive – poner; Tense – preterite; Subject – yo; English meaning – to put; DO/IO/R Pronouns – lo; Q or S – statement; Question word – N/A; Translation – I put it in my backpack. Simple Future – Lo voy a poner en mi mochila./Voy a ponerlo en mi mochila. New Translation – I'm going to put it in my backpack.

Page 202
2) Conjugated verb – recuerda (x2); Ending – a; Infinitive – recordar; Tense – present; Subject – él; English meaning – to remember; DO/IO/R Pronouns – lo; Q or S – statement; Question word – N/A; Translation – Manuel doesn't remember the name of the restaurant. He doesn't remember it. Preterite – Manuel no recordó el nombre del restaurante. No lo recordó. New Translation – Manuel didn't remember the name of the restaurant. He didn't remember it.

3) Conjugated verb – vinieron; Ending – ieron; Infinitive – venir; Tense – preterite; Subject – ellos/ellas/uds.; English meaning – to come; DO/IO/R Pronouns – None; Q or S – statement; Question word – N/A; Translation – They/y'all came to the party in an antique car. Simple Future – Van a venir a la fiesta en un coche antiguo. New Translation – They/y'all are going to come to the party in an antique car.

Page 203
4) Conjugated verb – puse/escribí; Ending – e/í; Infinitive – poner/escribir; Tense – preterite/preterite; Subject – yo/yo; English meaning – to put/to write; DO/IO/R Pronouns – None; Q or S – question; Question word – dónde; Translation – Where did I put the essay that I wrote yesterday? Simple Future – ¿Dónde voy a poner el ensayo que voy a escribir hoy? New Translation – Where am I going to put the essay that I'm going to write today?

5) Conjugated verb – buscaron/encontraron; Ending – aron/aron; Infinitive – buscar/encontrar; Tense – preterite/preterite; Subject – ellos/ellas/uds.; English meaning – to look for/to find; DO/IO/R Pronouns – la; Q or S – statement; Question word – N/A; Translation – They/y'all looked for the canoe in the river, but they/y'all didn't find it. Present – Buscan la canoa en el río, pero no la encuentran. New Translation – They/Y'all are looking for the canoe in the river, but they/y'all aren't finding it.

Page 204
6) Conjugated verb – encontró; Ending – ó; Infinitive – encontrar; Tense – preterite; Subject – él/ella; English meaning – to find; DO/IO/R Pronouns – te; Q or S – question; Question word – quién; Translation – Who found you hidden behind the tree? Simple Future – ¿Quién te va a encontrar escondida detrás del árbol? New Translation – Who is going to find you hidden behind the tree?

7) Conjugated verb – fueron; Ending – eron; Infinitive – ir; Tense – preterite; Subject – ellos/ellas/uds.; English meaning – to go; DO/IO/R Pronouns – lo; Q or S – statement; Question word – N/A; Translation – They/y'all went to look for it/him at the mall. Present– Lo van a buscar en el centro comercial./Van a buscarlo en el centro comercial. New Translation – They/y'all are going to look for it/him at the mall.

Page 205
8) Conjugated verb – dio; Ending – io; Infinitive – dar; Tense – preterite; Subject – él/ella; English meaning – to give; DO/IO/R Pronouns – le; Q or S – question; Question word – quién; Translation – Who gave him/her/you formal a dollar? Simple Future – ¿Quién le va a dar un dólar?/Quién va a darle un dólar? New Translation – Who is going to give him/her/you formal a dollar?

Page 206
1) francés; franceses; French; 2) francesa; francesas; French woman; 3) nación; naciones; nation; 4) japonés; japoneses; Japanese; 5) irlandesa; irlandesas; Irishwoman; 6) estación; estaciones; season/station; 7) inglés; ingleses; English; 8) tailandesa; tailandesas; Thai woman; 9) holandesa; holandesas; Dutchwoman

Page 211
1) comía; When Alicia was a girl, she used to eat lots of vegetables. 2) nadábamos; While we were swimming in the ocean, they stole our money! 3) eran; When I finally fell asleep, it was 2:00 a.m. 4) vivías; Before you moved here, you used to live in Mexico. 5) tenían; How old were y'all when you started reading? 6) Cuando yo era niña, jugaba con mis amigos/as después de la escuela. 7) Eran las seis de la tarde cuando empezamos a ver la película. 8) Llovía cuando Jimena salió/se fue del centro comercial. 9) Cuando Paola era niña, comía mucho chocolate. 10) Silvia tenía tres años cuando nació su hermano menor.

Page 213
1) He is writing a letter. – Él está escribiendo una carta. 2) Y'all are eating bananas. – Ustedes están comiendo bananas/plátanos. 3) You are dancing salsa. – Tú estás bailando salsa. 4) *The car is red. – El coche/auto es rojo. 5) The kids are sleeping. – Los niños/muchachos están durmiendo. 6) We are working. – Nosotros estamos trabajando. 7) He is stealing your backpack. – Él está robando tu mochila. 8) *Are you happy today? – ¿Estás feliz hoy? 9) Why is he playing with his food? – ¿Por qué está jugando con su comida? 10) *Where is the dictionary? – ¿Dónde está el diccionario? 11) We are waiting for the bus. – Nosotros estamos esperando el autobús.

Page 214
1-10) Answers will vary. 1) Example: No te quiero hablar, porque estoy leyendo un buen libro. 2) Example: No te quiero escuchar, porque estoy jugando videojuegos. 3) Example: No quiero comerme las verduras, porque me estoy comiendo una hambuerguesa. 4) Example: Estoy esuchando música con audífonos en el sofá. 5) Example: No quiero hacer la tarea, porque estoy durmiendo una siesta. 6) Example: No quiero contestar el teléfono, porque estoy viendo videos en YouTube. 7) Example: No quiero sacar la basura, porque estoy pintándome las uñas. 8) Example: No quiero poner la mesa, porque estoy bailando en el jardín. 9) Example: No quiero llamarle a mi abuelita, porque estoy cantando en la ducha. 10) No quiero estudiar español, porque estoy masticando chicle.

Page 215
1) Yo estoy lavando el coche/auto. 2) El niño/chico se está bañando/está bañándose. 3) María se está acostando/está acostándose. 4) Los niños/muchachos se están despertando/están despertándose. 5) Mi hermana menor está bañando al perro. 6) Ustedes se están lavando/cepillando los dientes/están lavándose/cepillándose los dientes. 7) Los bailarines se están vistiendo/están vistiéndose. 8) Tú te estás duchando/estás duchándote. 9) Nosotros nos estamos sentando/estamos sentándonos. 10) La madre está vistiendo al bebé.

Page 217
1) estabas haciendo; estaba comprando; Fernando: I saw you in the jewelry store yesterday. What were you doing? José: I was buying a ring for my girlfriend! 2) estabas durmiendo; llegó; While you were taking a nap, this letter arrived in the mail. 3) estabas escuchando; estaba viendo; María: Why weren't you listening to me? Nacho: Because I was watching TV. 4) estaba buscando; comió; While the cat was looking for mice, the dog ate all the tuna. 5) estábamos charlando; robó; While we were chatting, the thief stole your car. 6) estabas haciendo; se descumpuso; estabas haciendo; estaba jugando; Mamá: If you weren't doing your homework when the computer broke down, then what were you doing? Son: I was playing videogames. 7) estaban viendo; besó; estábamos viendo; Enrique: What movie were y'all watching when your girlfriend kissed you? We were watching Lord of the Rings.

Page 219
escrito – escribir (written); frito – freír (fried); resuelto – resolver (resolved); abierto – abrir (open/opened); roto – romper (broken); cubierto – cubrir (covered); vuelto – volver (returned); muerto – morir (dead); visto – ver (seen); puesto – poner (put/set); dicho – decir (said/told); hecho – hacer (done/made)

Page 220
1) Sí/No, no he leído los libros de Harry Potter. 2) Sí/No, no he cenado en un restaurante italiano. 3) Sí/No, no he ido a París. 4) Sí/No, no he visto la películas de el Señor de los Anillos. 5) Stefanie ha estudiado inglés for quince años. 6) Ustedes han leído muchos libros, pero no han visto muchas películas. 7) Los niños/muchachos ya han puesto la mesa. 8) Todavía no hemos llegado a la Costa del Sol. 9) ¿Quién ha probado/Quiénes han probado este pastel de chocolate delicioso? 10) ¿Por qué no has escrito tu ensayo?

Page 222
1) Tú has ganado muchos premios en este evento. 2) Ella ha viajado a Barcelona varias veces. 3) Ellos ya han puesto las mesas para la boda. 4) ¿Tú ya has llamado al hotel para hacer una reservación? 5) ¿Tú has visto la película <<Los Piratas del Caribe>>? 6) Ya me había comido seis tacos antes de la cena. 7) (Tú) habías ido a nadar antes de la tormenta. 8) Ellos habían estudiado mucho antes del examen. 9) (Nosotros) ya habíamos visto catorce perros en el concurso/la exhibición antes de que llegaran los caballos. 10) Ustedes habían viajado por once países antes de quedarse en Italia.

Page 224
1) El avión saldrá a las ocho menos cuarto (quince)/siete y cuarenta y cinco de la noche. 2) Los chicos/muchachos pasarán el verano con su abuela en la isla. 3) (Tú) dirás/Ud. dirá la verdad en el juicio. 4) Silvina podrá ayudarte/le./Silvina te/le podrá ayudar. 5) Tendremos que hacer planes para visitarles la próxima Navidad. 6) Los estudiantes leerán mucho antes del examen. 7) Mi novio me vendrá a visitar/vendrá a visitarme en la universidad. 8) ¡Nos comeremos todo el helado! 9) Saldré a comer mañana por la noche. 10) La nevada empezará a medianoche.

Page 225: Part 12 Quiz
1) Cuando era niño/chico, almorzaba sándwiches de jamón y queso/comía sándwiches de jamón y queso en el almuerzo. 2) Nevará en la montaña mañana. 3) Ustedes están comiendo pollo frito. 4) Eran las siete y cuarto/quince de la mañana cuando Amelia se despertó. 5) Jack ha estudiado español por cuatro años. 6) Laura había bailado salsa antes, pero nunca había bailado tango. 7) Mientras dormía Luisa, sonó su teléfono. 8) Reinaldo nunca ha ido a Egipto. 9) Micaela escribirá una carta a su amiga Sara en Londres. 10) Mientras hacíamos senderismo, empezó a llover.

Page 226
1) Conjugated verb – he buscado/ha encontrado; Ending – e/e; Infinitive – buscar/encontrar; Tense – present perfect (x2); Subject – yo (x2); English meaning – to look for/to find; DO/IO/R Pronouns – la; Q or S – statement; Question word – N/A;

Translation – I've looked for the blouse in the wardrobe, but I haven't found it. Present – Busco la blusa en el armario, pero no la encuentro. New Translation – I'm looking for the blouse in the wardrobe, but I'm not finding it.

Page 227

2) Conjugated verb – van; Ending – an; Infinitive – ir; Tense – present; Subject – ellos/ellas; English meaning – to go; DO/IO/R Pronouns – te, lo; Q or S – question; Question word – cuándo; Translation – When are they going to pay you it? Preterite– ¿Cuándo te lo pagaron? New Translation – When did they pay you it?

3) Conjugated verb – escribiste/escribió; Ending – iste/ió; Infinitive – escribir (x2); Tense – preterite (x2); Subject – tú, él/ella; English meaning – to write; DO/IO/R Pronouns – la (x2); Q or S – question; Question word – quién; Translation – If you didn't write it, then who wrote it? Imperfect – Si tú no la escribías, entonces ¿quién la escribía? New Translation – If you didn't used to write it, then who used to write it?

Page 228

4) Conjugated verb – vi/trajiste/comiste; Ending – i/iste/iste; Infinitive ver/traer/comer; Tense – preterite/preterite/preterite; Subject – yo/tú/tú; English meaning – to see/to bring/to eat; DO/IO/R Pronouns – te/la; Q or S – question; Question word – N/A; Translation – I saw that you brought a lot of food for lunch. Did you eat it all already? Present/Simple Future – Veo que traes mucha comida para almuerzo. ¿Ya te la vas a comer? New Translation – I see that you've brought a lot of food for lunch. Are you going to eat it already/now?

5) Conjugated verb – son/dijiste/comías/eras; Ending – on/iste/ías/as; Infinitive – ser/decir/comer/ser; Tense – present/preterite/imperfect/imperfect; Subject – ellos/tú/tú/tú; English meaning – to be/to tell/to eat/to be; DO/IO/R Pronouns – me; Q or S – question; Question word – cómo; Translation – How are your eating habits nowadays? Yo told me that you used to eat a lot of junk food when you were a boy.

Page 229

6) Conjugated verb – viste/recibió; Ending – iste/ió; Infinitive – ver/recibir; Tense – preterite (x2); Subject – tú/él; English meaning – to see/to receive; DO/IO/R Pronouns – None; Q or S – question; Question word – N/A; Translation – Did you see the show last night? It received some fabulous reviews in the newspaper. Present Perfect– ¿Has visto el espectáculo (remove anoche)? Ha recibido unas reseñas fabulosas en el periódico. New Translation – Have you seen the show? It has received some fabulous reviews in the newspaper.

7) Conjugated verb – dio/van; Ending – io/an; Infinitive – dar/ir; Tense – preterite/present; Subject – ella/ellos; English meaning – to give/to believe; DO/IO/R Pronouns – me/me/lo; Q or S – statement; Question word – N/A; Translation – The teacher/professor gave me a 100% on my Spanish exam/test . My parents aren't going to believe me/it. Simple Future – La profesora me va a dar un 100% en mi examen de español. ¡Mis padres no me lo van a creer! New Translation – The teacher/professor is going to give me a 100% on my Spanish exam/test. My parents aren't going to believe me/it!

Page 234

1-16) Answers may vary.

1) Example: llevas; It's very cold. Are you wearing a sweater? 2) Example: lleno/a; We ate all the turkey! I'm so full. 3) Example: llega; What time does the plane arrive? 4) llaves; We're going to arrive late, because I can't find the car keys. 5) Example: lavarse; It is necessary to wash one's hands before eating. 6) Example: llenó; The waiter filled my wine glass. 7) Example: lleva; Look at the beautiful dress that woman is wearing! 8) lleva; How are you going to get to the concert? Is your dad bringing you in his car? 9) llegamos; The movie already started. Did we arrive late? 10) llenas; llena; If you fill the bag with trash/garbage, it's going to be full. 11) lavar; When are you going to wash the dishes? They're very dirty. 12) llave; How are we going to get into the house if you lost the key? 13) Example: llamé; lleno; Pedro isn't coming to eat. When I called him on the phone, he told me that he was already full. 14) llevar; llave; Can you bring/take the key to Manuel so that he can open the door? 15) lavas; Do you wash your hair with Herbal Essences? 16) llover; It's cloudy today. Do you believe/think it's going to rain?

Page 235

1-14) Answers may vary.

1) Example: se portaron; The kids behaved well during to meeting. 2) Example: Puedes; Can you feed the dog? 3) Example: probaste; Did you try the Ben & Jerry's ice cream? 4) Example: pierde; The granfather always loses the keys. 5) Example: te probaste; Did you try on the green shirt to see if it fits you well? 6) Example: pidió; What did your dad order last night at the restaurant? 7) se portó; How did your younger brother behave at the party last Saturday? 8) puede; Your mom can cook very well! 9) perdió; Our team lost the game yesterday. 10) Example: pruebas; Why don't you try to chocolate cookies/biscuits at the new bakery? They're really delicious. 11) Example: se probaron; The boys tried on the jeans at the department store. 12) puede, perdió; She can't get back home, because she got lost in the city and doesn't know where she is. 13) te portabas; Did you always behave well when you were a boy? 14) pedir; Don't you want to order something to eat?

Page 236

1-14) Answers may vary.

1) Example: debajo del; The cat hides under the tree. 2) Después de; After dinner, we're going to eat dessert. 3) Example: durante; The cell phone rang during the movie. 4) después de; It's necessary to drink water after running. 5) Example: dentro de; Don't you have the keys inside of your purse/bag? 6) Example: debajo de; Don't put the trash/garbage under the sofa! 7) debajo de; The Christmas gifts are under the tree. 8) Example: dentro de; The pharmacy is inside of the Super Target. 9) delante de; The beautiful girl is in front of the mirror, looking at her face. 10) durante; You can't talk during the exam/test. 11) después de; Do you want to eat a big breakfast after the Prom/dance? 12) debajo de; The basement is underneath the house. 13) dentro de; The kitchen is inside of the house. 14) Example: delante de; You have to mow the lawn/cut the grass in front of the house.

Page 239
1) Tengo que llegar a la escuela a las ocho de la mañana. 2) Hace ocho años que están casados Catalina y Diego. 3) Hacía años que Josefina no veía a su madre. 4) Hay que pagar la cuenta/factura. 5) Flor se fue de la fiesta hace veinte minutos. 6) ¿Qué hora es? 7) ¿Por qué vendimos la casa? 8) Elisa es más alta que Marisol. 9) Hace tres años que nos conocemos. 10) Nos conocimos hace tres años.

Page 240: Part 13 Quiz
1) Llegamos al hotel a las cuatro y media/treinta de la tarde. 2) ¿Has probado este tocino? 3) Dónde pusiste las llaves de coche/auto? 4) La silla está debajo del escritorio/pupitre. 5) Juanito perdió sus calcetines en la escuela. 6) ¿Por qué pusieron ustedes azúcar en estas fresas/frutillas? 7) Después de la escuela, voy a llamar a mi papá. 8) Primero lavamos los platos, y después nos lavamos las manos. 9) Empezó a llover antes de o después de que llegaste? 10) ¿Qué vas a pedir en el restaurante?

Page 241
1) Conjugated verb – conocen; Ending – en; Infinitive – conocer; Tense – present; Subject – ellos/ellas/uds.; English meaning – to know (each other); DO/IO/R Pronouns – se; Q or S – question; Question word – cuántos; Translation – ¿How many years have you/they known each other (for)? Preterite– ¿Hace cuántos años que se conocieron? New Translation – How many years ago did you/they meet?

Page 242
2) Conjugated verb – tenían; Ending – ían; Infinitive – tener; Tense – imperfect; Subject – ellos/ellas/uds.; English meaning – to have to; DO/IO/R Pronouns – None; Q or S – statement; Question word – N/A; Translation – They/y'all had to go to a meeting at Alicia's house. Future – Tendrán que ir a una reunión en la casa de Alicia. New Translation – They/y'all will have to go to a meeting at Alicia's house.
3) Conjugated verb – están; Ending – án; Infinitive – estar; Tense – present; Subject – ellos/ellas/uds.; English meaning – to be; DO/IO/R Pronouns – None; Q or S – question; Question word – cuántos; Translation – How many years have they/y'all been married? Preterite – ¿Hace cuántos años que se casaron? New Translation – How many years ago did they/y'all get married?

Page 243
4) Conjugated verb – tienes; Ending – es; Infinitive – tener; Tense – present; Subject – tú; English meaning – to have to; DO/IO/R Pronouns – N/A; Q or S – statement; Question word – N/A; Translation – You have to do your homework before you play tennis. Future – Tendrás que hacer tu tarea antes de jugar tenis. New Translation – You'll have to do your homework before you play tennis.
5) Conjugated verb – compraron; Ending – aron; Infinitive – comprar; Tense – preterite; Subject – ellos/ellas/uds.; English meaning – to buy; DO/IO/R Pronouns – la; Q or S – statement; Question word – cuántos; Translation – How many days ago did they/y'all buy it?

Page 244
6) Conjugated verb – tienes/tomas; Ending – es/as; Infinitive – tener/tomar; Tense – present (x2); Subject – tú (x2); English meaning – to have to/to drink; DO/IO/R Pronouns – None; Q or S – question; Question word – por qué; Translation – If you have to eat more protein, why don't you drink an energy shake? Imperfect– Si tenías que comer más proteína, ¿por qué no tomabas batidos de energía? New Translation – If you had to eat more protein, why didn't you drink energy shakes?
7) Conjugated verb – expresa; Ending – a; Infinitive – exprear; Tense – present; Subject – él; English meaning – to express; DO/IO/R Pronouns – None; Q or S – statement; Question word – N/A; Translation – Through the use of bright colors, the artist expresses a feeling of youth. Imperfect– A través del uso de colores brillantes, el artista expresaba un sentimiento de juventud. New Translation – Through the use of bright colors, the artist expressed/used to express a feeling of youth.

Page 246
1) Sí, la estación del autobús está en la esquina de la Calle Catorce y Walnut. 2) Sí, la Casa de Té está cerca del Parque Central. 3) No, el Teatro de Boulder no está muy lejos del juzgado. 4) Si, puedes ir en bicicleta al Parque Central. 5) Sí, puedes caminar a un restaurante en la Calle Pearl y Broadway desde el Hotel St. Julien. 6-9) Answers will vary. 6) Example: No, la biblioteca está en Arapahoe, a la derecha. 7) Example: Camina a la izquierda en la Calle Quince y gira a la derecha en Walnut. El Hotel St. Julien está a cinco cuadras, a la izquierda. 8) Example: Camina por la Calle Trece hasta llegar a Walnut. Gira a la derecha en Walnut, y la Oficina de Correos está a la izquierda, en la esquina de la Calle Catorce y Walnut. 9) Camina por la Calle Catorce hasta llegar a Arapahoe. Gira a la derecha en Arapahoe, y la biblioteca está a tres cuadras, a la derecha.

Page 254
1) comer; I like to eat fruit. 2) comas; I like that you eat fruit. 3) como; I eat a lot of fruit. 4) viaja; Catalina travels to Toronto each summer. 5) viajar; Catalina wants to travel to Geneva this coming summer. 6) Es doubtful that Catalina will travel to Miami this summer.

Page 255
7) venir; We're going to come to the party early. 8) lleguemos; I don't like that we're going to be late to the party. 9) venimos; We're coming to Marcos's party. 10) vayan; I don't know where they're going tomorrow. 11) dibujar; I love to draw flowers. 12) estudia; He studies at the library. 13) quiere; comer; Do you (formal) want to eat at a restaurant? 14) vamos; Why don't we go to the fair on Sunday? 15) pida; It's better that she ask for help. 16) prefiere; esté; Mom prefers the dog to be clean.

Page 256
1) llueva; Hopefully it will rain the countryside. 2) vaya; We recommend that she go to a Juan Luis Guerra concert. 3) oigan; I hope that y'all hear the kids that are singing at the party. 4) ves; It's likely/probable that you will see a video of No Te Va Gustar online. 5) practiques; I doubt that you practice salsa everyday. 6) está; I know that Venezuela is next to Brazil. 7) nos

divertamos; It's unlikely/improbable that we will have fun in jail. 8) gusta; I believe/think that you like to sing in the shower. 9) haya; It's sad that there's so much destruction on the island after a hurricane.

Page 257
10) tengo; It's true/certain that I have Shakira's new CD for you. 11) conozcan; I doubt that they know my mother. 12) es; I know that coffee is an important crop in Colombia. 13) salgas; I'm advising you not to leave the strore without buying your wife a gift! 14) muestre; I'm pleased you're showing your photos from Mexico. 15) entienden; There is no doubt that now y'all will understand the song in Spanish. 16) prepare; I like that she prepares mate for everyone.

Page 258
1-10) Answers will vary. Use questions on pages 256-257 to guide you.

Page 260
1) fuera; My dad wanted me to go to college/university. 2) escribiera; It wasn't likely/probable that the man would write a letter. 3) aparecieran; The cat waited for the mice to appear. 4) comieras; The doctor advised you not to eat so many hamburgers. 5) dijeras; The attorney/lawyer advised you to tell the truth. 6) pagara; It wasn't necessary for you to pay the bill/check. 7) te portaras; I asked you not misbehave at your grandparents' house! 8) diera; The son begged his father to give him money. 9) vinieran; I invited y'all so you would come to party. 10) supieran; The mother didn't want the kids to know anything about the Christmas gifts.

Page 261
11) tomaras; I asked you not to take that horrible photo/picture! 12) saliera; The jealous girl didn't want her ex-boyfriend to go out with another woman. 13) viera; The employee hid so that the boss wouldn't see him. 14) entregáramos; The professor/teacher asked us to hand in the exam/test. 15) Answers will vary.

Page 263
1) Espero que te guste el flan. 2) Espero que te haya gustado el flan que hizo mi madre de postre anoche. 3) El padre de Ernesto quiere que él estudie medicina. 4) El año pasado, la madre de Pilar quería que ella se mudara a España. 5) Me alegro que te guste jugar tenis. 6) Me alegro que te haya gustado jugar tenis conmigo la semana pasada. 7) ¡No puedo creer que no vengas a esquiar con nosotros este Año Nuevo! 8) No puedo creer que no hayas ido a la fiesta a la casa de Nacho. 9) El doctor me recomienda que haga más ejercicio. 10) Cuando yo era niño/a, el doctor recomendaba que no comiera dulces antes de acostarme/dormir. 11) Espero que disfrutes el tiempo con tu familia. 12) Espero que hayas tenido una buena Navidad.

Page 265
1-12) Answers will vary.
1) Example: Si yo pudiera viajar a cualquier parte del mundo, iría a _____. – If I could travel anywhere in the world, I would go to _____. 2) Example: Si yo fuera el rey del universo, curaría todas las enfermedades. – If I were king of the universe, I would cure all disease. 3) Example: Si yo tuviera siete años, jugaría todo el día en el jardín. – If I were seven years old, I would play in the yard all day. 4) Example: Si viviéramos en otro planeta, extrañaría a la Tierra. – If we lived on another planet, I would miss the Earth. 5) Example: Si mi esposo ganara la lotería, pagaría todas las cuentas. 6) Example: Si tuviera 10 hijos, cocinaría mucho. 7) Example: Si tuviera un mes de vacaciones, iría a Tierra del Fuego. 8) Example: Si tuviera un hámster, lo llamaría Hugo. 9) Example: Si se curara el coronavirus, estaría eufórica. 10) Example: Si tuviera más dinero, trabajaría menos horas. 11) Example: Si fuera a una boda, bailaría el vals. 12) Si ganara una motocicleta, se la daría a mi papá.

Page 266: Part 14 Quiz
1) nieve; 2) vayas; 3) oigan; 4) estudiara; 5) entregáramos; 6) dijera; 7) haya bebido 8) se haya portado; 9) hayas venido; 10) hayas hecho; 11) Espero que te diviertas esquiando este fin de semana. 12) Si pudieras conocer a una persona famosa, ¿a quién conocerías? 13) La abuela de Patricia quiere que sea profesora de español.

Page 267
1) Conjugated verb – pidieron/gustó; Ending – ieron/ó; Infinitive – pedir/gustar; Tense – preterite (x2); Subject – ellos/ellas/uds.; English meaning – to order/to please; DO/IO/R Pronouns – les; Q or S – question; Question word – Qué; Translation – What did they/y'all order at the restaurant that they/y'all didn't like? Imperfect – ¿Qué pedían en el restaurante que no les gustaba? New Translation – What did they/y'all used to order at the restaurant that they/y'all didn't like?

Page 268
2) Conjugated verb – quieres/haga; Ending – es/a; Infinitive – querer/hacer; Tense – present/present subjunctive; Subject – tú/yo; English meaning – to want/to make; DO/IO/R Pronouns – te; Q or S – question; Question word – N/A; Translation – Do you want me to make you dinner tomorrow night? Imperfect – ¿Querías que te hiciera la cena mañana por la noche? New Translation – Did you want me to make you dinner tomorrow night?

3) Conjugated verb – puedan; Ending – an; Infinitive – poder; Tense – present subjunctive; Subject – ellos/ellas/uds.; English meaning – to be able to; DO/IO/R Pronouns – lo; Q or S – statement; Question word – N/A; Translation – Hopefully they/y'all can find it/him. Past Perfect Subjunctive – Ojalá que hayan podido encontrarlo. New Translation – Hopefully they/y'all were able to find it/him.

Page 269
4) Conjugated verb – es/venga; Ending – es/an; Infinitive – ser/venir; Tense – present/present subjunctive; Subject – él (x2); English meaning – to be/to come; DO/IO/R Pronouns – None; Q or S – statement; Question word – N/A; Translation – It's doubtful that the investigator will come early. Imperfect – Era dudoso que viniera temprano el investigador. New Translation – It was doubtfall that the investigator would come early.

5) Conjugated verb – creo/pida; Ending – o/a; Infinitive – creo/pedir; Tense – present/present subjunctive; Subject – yo/ella; English meaning – to believe/to ask for; DO/IO/R Pronouns – te; Q or S – statement; Question word – N/A; Translation – I don't believe your sister will ask you for help.

Page 270
6) Conjugated verb – encuentres/cásate; Ending – es/a; Infinitive – encontrar/casarse; Tense – present subjunctive/affirmative tú command; Subject – tú (x2); English meaning – to find/to marry; DO/IO/R Pronouns – se; Q or S – statement; Question word – N/A; Translation – When you find a good man, honey, marry him!
7) Conjugated verb – sugieres/coma; Ending – es/a; Infinitive – sugerir/comer; Tense – present/present subjunctive; Subject – tú/yo; English meaning – to suggest/to eat; DO/IO/R Pronouns – me; Q or S – question; Question word – N/A; Translation – Are you suggesting that I not eat any more sweets? Imperfect – ¿Me sugeriste que no comiera más dulces? New Translation – Were you suggesting that I not eat any more sweets?

Page 271
8) Conjugated verb – va/debemos; Ending – a/emos; Infinitive – ir/deber; Tense – present (x2); Subject – él/ella, nosotros; English meaning – to go/should; DO/IO/R Pronouns – None; Q or S – statement; Question word – N/A; Translation – The sun is going to set already/now. We should look for a shelter to spend the night.

Page 273
1-8) Answers will vary. 1) Example: Camina a la izquierda en Arapahoe hasta llegar a Broadway. Gira a la izquierda en Broadway, y el Hotel Boulderado está a cinco cuadras, a la derecha. 2) La estación de autobús está en la esquina de la Calle Catorce y Walnut. 3) Example: Puedes ir a la Oficina de Correos. Está en la esquina de la Calle Quince y Walnut, enfrente de la estacíon de autobús. 4) Example: ¡Claro que sí! El Hotel St. Julien no está muy lejos de la Casa de Té. Camina a la derecha a la Calle Trece hasta llegar a Walnut. Gira a la derecha en Walnut, y el Hotel St. Julien está a tres cuadras, a la izquierda. 5) Example: Puedes ir al Teatro de Boulder. Está en la esquina de la Calle Catorce y Spruce. 6) Example: Sí, el Parque Central está cerca de la estación del autobús. Está a sólo tres cuadras, puedes caminar. 7) Example: Camina por la calle peatonal (pedestrain mall) de la Calle Pearl, y el juzgado está a dos cuadras, a la derecha. 8) Example: No, la biblioteca está a sólo dos cuadras. ¡No vale la pena (it's not worth it) tomar un taxi!

Page 275: Halloween Bonus Activity
1) dónde; Ghost: Where are you from, Vampire? 2) soy; I'm from Transylvania. How about you, Ghost? 3) vivo, gusta/encanta; I live in the cemetery, but sometimes I like to/love to spend time in old houses. 4) semana; Vampire: What do you like to do on the weekends? 5) gusta/encanta, tú; I like to/love to fly through walls! How about you? 6) noche, bailar; Vampire: I go out at night to suck blood. It's much more fun than dancing at the club. 7) discoteca; Ghost: I like dancing at the club because nobody can see me!

Page 276: Thanksgiving Bonus Activity
Turkey – el pavo; Stuffing – el relleno; Gravy – la salsa espesa; Mashed potatoes – el puré de papas; Bread – el pan; Turnip – el nabo; Spinach; la espinaca; Pumpkin pie – la tarta de calabaza; Apple pie – la tarta de manzana; Whipped cream – la crema batida; Cookies/crackers/biscuits – las galletas; Wine – el vino

Page 277: Christmas Bonus Activity
1) The tree is green. 2) The star is yellow. 3) The ornaments are red and white. 4) The gift in the center, with the big bow, is green and blue. It's Luis's gift. 5) Lisa's gift is under Luis's gift. 6) Chris's gift is to the left of Lisa's gift. 7) Lisa's gift is purple and yellow. 8) Pepe's gift is in front of Lisa's gift. 9) Chris's gift is black and white. 10) The gift to the right of Pepe's gift has an orange bow. 11) Noah's gift is the big gift behind the gift with the orange bow. 12) The three gifts for the cats are to the left of Chris's gift. They are red and green. 13) Which is the mystery gift?

Page 279: World Cup Bonus Activity
The World Cup – La Copa Mundial; Soccer – el fútbol; Goal – el gol; The score – el marcador; The player/players – el jugador/los jugadores; The game – el partido; The ball – la pelota; Minute – el minuto; Round – la ronda; Group – el grupo; Who? – ¿quién?; Where? – ¿Dónde?; When? – ¿Cuándo?

Made in the USA
Las Vegas, NV
30 June 2021